THE LION AND THE FOX

THE
LION
AND THE
FOX

Two Rival Spies and the Secret Plot
to Build a Confederate Navy

ALEXANDER ROSE

MARINER BOOKS
New York   Boston

HarperCollins books may be purchased for educational, business, or sales promotional use. For information, please email the Special Markets Department at SPsales@harpercollins.com.

A hardcover edition of this book was published in 2022 by Mariner Books.

FIRST MARINER BOOKS PAPERBACK EDITION PUBLISHED 2023.

Designed by Chloe Foster

The Library of Congress has catalogued a previous edition as follows:

Names: Rose, Alexander, 1971- author.
Title: The lion and the fox : two rival spies and the secret plot to build a Confederate Navy / Alexander Rose.
Other titles: Two rival spies and the secret plot to build a Confederate Navy
Description: New York : Mariner Books, an imprint of HarperCollins, 2022. | Includes bibliographical references and index.
Identifiers: LCCN 2022026041 (print) | LCCN 2022026042 (ebook) | ISBN 9780358393252 (hardcover) | ISBN 9780063277892 (paperback) | ISBN 9780358394990 (ebook)
Subjects: LCSH: United States—History—Civil War, 1861-1865—Blockades. | Spies—Confederate States of America—Biography. | Bulloch, James Dunwody, 1823-1901. | Dudley, Thomas H. (Thomas Haines), 1819-1893. | Consuls—United States—Biography. | United States—History—Civil War, 1861-1865—Secret service. | Warships—Confederate States of America—History. | Confederate States of America. Navy—History. | United States—Foreign relations—Great Britain. | Great Britain—Foreign relations—United States.
Classification: LCC E600 .R67 2022 (print) | LCC E600 (ebook) | DDC 973.7/5—dc23/eng/20220701
LC record available at https://lccn.loc.gov/2022026041
LC ebook record available at https://lccn.loc.gov/2022026042

ISBN 978-0-06-327789-2

23 24 25 26 27 LBC 5 4 3 2 1

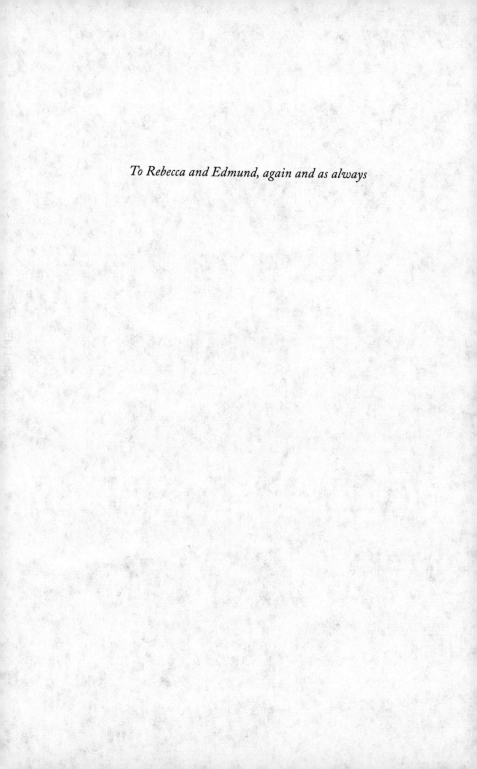

To Rebecca and Edmund, again and as always

Who hath taken this counsel against Tyre, the crowning city, whose merchants are princes, whose traffickers are the honorable of the earth?

—ISAIAH 23:8

Where the lion's skin will not reach, it must be patched out with the fox's.

—PLUTARCH

CONTENTS

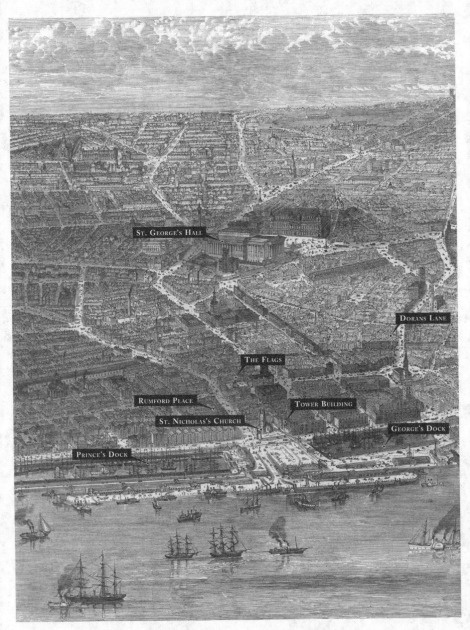

Liverpool around the time of the Civil War

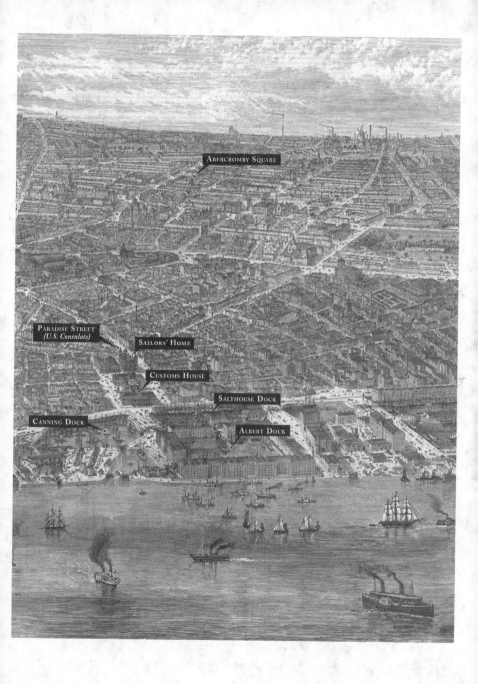

ABERCROMBY SQUARE

PARADISE STREET
(U.S. Consulate)

SAILORS' HOME

CUSTOMS HOUSE

SALTHOUSE DOCK

CANNING DOCK

ALBERT DOCK

THE LION AND THE FOX

The Bloody Spot

I

A s his ship plowed toward the Mersey, the Mississippi River of England, Thomas Dudley finally glimpsed his destination. Liverpool, coal dark and forbidding amid the murky fog, was rising ominously before him. It had been a long voyage to the "Bloody Spot," as the mighty port was known, and Dudley would soon find out why.

A doleful, dismal sound—a great bell repeatedly tolling, as if welcoming him to Hades—echoed across the cold, roiling water. It seemed to resonate from the very vault of the deep. But it was not in fact a call for the dead; no, it was merely the famous Bell-Buoy, a marker that pealed fast or slow depending on the agitation of the waves. In a calm, it was dumb. In a breeze, it rang gently. And amid turbulence, it served as an urgent tocsin alerting mariners to flee.

When Dudley and his family disembarked the passenger ship *Africa* at Prince's Dock that November 19, 1861, he might have wondered whether he ought to have heeded the Bell-Buoy's warning. As they gingerly made their way along the quay, the Dudleys were pestered by quacks selling liquor-laced snake oil, shiv-armed con men flogging painted "gold rings," and pubescent thieves who stalked the innocent like Sicilian assassins until, quick as a flash, a pocket was picked. Perhaps, instead of becoming the new American consul here, he should have taken that ambassadorship to Japan that President Lincoln had offered him.

Now heading toward the street, he could see the so-called body seekers roaming the docks for the corpses of those who had fallen overboard or been washed in from the river, the latter usually murder victims. The rubbish rakers, too, were at work: Tattered paupers picked through heaps of dunnage—broken cargo crates and other waste—hoping to find some overlooked treasure, like a length of rope or a few copper nails.

For newcomers like Dudley, setting foot in Liverpool was a harrowing experience. America could be rough but not like this. The first shock were the beggars, ragged and wretched. Here it was not the existence of the penniless that staggered, it was the scale of poverty, so much so that there were four official gradations: the almost poor, the poor, the very poor, and the permanently destitute.

They lined the external wall of the dock. Some were crippled sailors fallen on hard times and others former factory workers whose limbs had become entangled in a machine's spindles and cogs. But the majority were women, so parched and starved they resembled mummies; cadaverous teens with the gallows in their eyes; and shoeless children with pinched faces and scrawny bodies, whose mothers strove to scratch a living darning socks or selling pigs' feet while their fathers, if they knew them, were at sea. The sailor's life was a precarious one: A man would be away for months at a time and he was rarely advanced cash. For those left behind, the rent was always overdue and everything was in pawn.

All along the waterfront, businesses catered to the marine trade. Many were respectable. Some sewed flags; chandlers sold holystones for swabbing wooden decks and cotton rags for cleaning steam valves; other firms made paint. Tarpaulins, ropes, and sails were their own specialties. For a quick bite, one could pick up from numerous stalls chunks of sweaty cheese and cuts of greasy bacon, dubious-looking potted herrings, and only slightly rotten apples scrumped from some landowner's orchard. For life at sea, sailors bought Epsom salts and hair oil from the apothecary or stopped by secondhand shops for cracked crocks and discarded forks. For the wife and kids, there were tinsel ornaments, ancient furniture perhaps better employed as firewood, vermin-infested mattresses, and cheap toys.

Cheek by jowl with the better merchants were the hundreds of black market "marine store dealers," who dealt in goods stolen from the docks. A cartel of them called the "Forty Thieves" was run by one Bernard Connelly, known in the underworld as "Long Barney." The most notorious dealer in Liverpool when Dudley arrived, he stood at six foot five, terrified police constables, and boasted a lengthy criminal record of assaults, swindles, counterfeiting, and general mayhem. Thanks to the activities of Connelly and his like, the number of convictions for theft in Liverpool was seventeen times higher than that of the cities of Manchester, Salford, Bolton, and Preston *combined*.

Then there were the "lodging houses" where "crimps" like Paddy Dreadnought and Shanghai Davies bribed owners to allow them to kidnap drunk-into-a-stupor boarders and sell them off to a captain needing crew for runs to China or America. Occasionally, the tables were turned: The redoubtable Ma Smyrden, a landlady of Pitt Street, had recently become a legend for foisting a corpse onto the local crimp.

Even in the better lodging houses, proprietors packed in as many customers as they could. In one memorable instance, ninety-two people were squeezed into a house meant for nineteen. That may have been an outlier, but not by so much: Liverpool was by far the most densely populated city in the country. In 1844, a Dr. Duncan discovered that in one area 7,938 people were crammed into 811 houses, a figure he equated to a density of nearly 660,000 people per square mile. In comparison, the world's densest city today is Manila, at somewhat more than 100,000 people per square mile, with New York City—by far the highest in the United States—standing at a paltry 27,000.

Liverpool had until recently been a small seaside town, but immigration and industrialization had caused its population to explode from 138,000 in 1821 to 444,000 in the year Dudley stepped ashore. There was nowhere to put the new arrivals, many from rural Ireland and England. And so some

39,000 residents, described as "pale, yellow, ghastly, parchment-faced looking creatures," lived troglodytically in 7,800 smoke-fugged cellars, with tens of thousands more wedged into the nooks and crannies of every typhus-ridden tenement. Another 25,000 children lived on the streets and on their wits.

The housing shortage naturally pushed people onto the streets and into pubs in search of personal space. Gibraltar Row, which Dudley would have seen to his left as he left Prince's Dock, was one of the worst streets in Liverpool. It was crammed with grog shops, spirit vaults, penny-ale cellars, and gin palaces, where it was not unusual to see a three-year-old knocking back booze with his older siblings for company. Inevitably, there was a criminal element: illegal gambling, fencing of stolen goods, bare-knuckle boxing, and dogfighting, usually. And scams, it goes without saying. Victims ("flats") were mercilessly bamboozled, fleeced, plundered, and swindled by numberless sharpers, magsmans, duffers, smashers, and cross-my-palm-with-silver clairvoyants.

In Liverpool, for many there wasn't much else to do but drink. As there were no licensing laws—anyone could essentially open a tavern in his or her own house—the number of drinking establishments in Liverpool would, if all lined up, have extended some eleven and a half miles. Within a radius of 150 yards of the Sailors' Home in Canning Place, for instance, there were no fewer than forty-six pubs for the recuperating and the impoverished to frequent.

The Victorian equivalent of drug and opioid abuse—smuggled rum, rotgut gin, and a Liverpool specialty, "swipes," the mixed dregs of near-empty beer barrels—was the leading cause of crime. One judge observed that nine out of every ten cases that came before him were prompted by either drunkenness or a desire to acquire money to get (more) drunk.

Booze-fueled violence was everywhere. Dudley, walking around, would surely have noticed that old women greatly outnumbered old men. So many males died young that their average life expectancy was seventeen years. Fighting was so endemic that elsewhere in Britain, not exactly a teetotaler's paradise, "giving a bit of Liverpool" was shorthand for a form of combat known locally as "purring," whose practitioners smashed a broken bottle into someone's face, bit off his nose or ear, and then kicked his head in with iron-toed boots. A ribald jest or an accidental jostle often escalated quickly to an entertaining street melee involving dozens, occasionally hundreds, of men from rival factions: sailors versus policemen, carpenters versus sailmakers, Protestants versus Catholics, Irish versus everybody.

Women were almost as violent as men, with a third of assault prosecutions in Liverpool being against them. Elizabeth Kelly and her two delightful daughters, well-known to the police as the "terrors of Midghall Street," used whatever weapon came to hand to pick fights, while other members of the gentler sex preferred to blind with their fingernails, bite out chunks of flesh, stab with glass shards, or fling sulfuric acid to get their point across.

Given the environment, small wonder that Liverpool's homicide rate was extraordinarily high, even for the time. Firearms, perhaps surprisingly, were rarely employed—using a noisy gun meant the hangman—but a knife, axe, crowbar, or garotte allowed one to avoid attracting a copper's notice. In a typical year, 1858, for instance, there were nearly five hundred murders, around the same number as in modern-day Chicago, though the latter has more than six times the population and gun crime is common. And those were just the victims the authorities knew about.

The thousands of sailors wandering the streets added much to the local color. Not for nothing did Charles Dickens, who visited the city just before the Civil War, lament of the "poor mercantile Jacks" that their lot in Liverpool was to be "hocussed, entrapped, anticipated, cleaned out," for many boozers were connected to both a pawnshop and a knocking shop (to avoid any awkward confusion, gay brothels were generally signified by exotic names like Aladdin's Palace). After filling up at the pub and heading to the conveniently located bordello, customers would be drugged, mugged, and stripped, obliging them to go into debt to the adjoining pawnbroker, who had just bought their clothes. It was always a treat for a hooting crowd to see a sailor sheepishly wandering back to his ship clad only in his skivvies, if that.

There were more prostitutes in Liverpool per capita than anywhere else in Britain, perhaps the world. One dockside street alone boasted twenty-two brothels. Desperation, a lack of alternative employment, and drink were the usual avenues into the trade, and pimps and procuresses wandered the alleys and taverns looking for recruits. Some were married factory workers ("dolly-mops") looking to feed their families while their husbands were at sea, but most often they were runaways: lost, raped, abandoned. According to the Reverend Isaac Holmes, chaplain of the Liverpool workhouse, most of the latter would be dead—from disease, abuse, assault, suicide, failed abortions, or alcoholism—within three to five years.

With good reason, Liverpool was regarded as the most violent, vice-ridden, crime-soaked locale in Europe, and widely believed to be a low-lying place inhabited by low, lying people. As he shielded his children's eyes from its squalor and depravity, Dudley rued his decision to come to this modern Sodom-on-the-Sea, though at least he could console himself (and his alarmed wife) with the thought that he would be here for just a year before returning home. That was the usual stretch consuls served abroad, after all. Unfortunately for him, nothing would be usual about his new position, for Dudley had just unwittingly inherited the most important intelligence posting in the world.

II

Dudley's path to Liverpool had been a winding one. Descended from a long line of humble Quaker farmers, Dudley was born in 1819 in Burlington County in New Jersey. His father died shortly after his advent, and Dudley worked, like his three older siblings, on his mother's farm. Educated at a district school, he married a fellow Quaker, Emmaline Matlack (who bore him four children in rapid succession), and eventually became a lawyer in nearby Camden.

Now in his early forties, Dudley was tall for the day at six feet, with piercing eyes, a high forehead, dark brown wavy hair, and an admirable beard. His dress and habits were as austere and frugal as his simple faith

Thomas Dudley

demanded. A pious Quaker who believed that every man alone was responsible through his deeds to his Maker, Dudley had a remorseless fixation on the truth, come what may. To reveal it, "no difficulty daunted and no obstacle deterred him," said a fellow attorney. As his opponents would painfully learn, "he persevered with indomitable energy and unceasing assiduity until his object was attained."

When he was young, Dudley had been passing a graveyard at midnight and saw an eerie white specter in the moonlight. Dudley could have run away, but instead, trembling with fear and knees a-knocking, he told himself "there is no such thing as a ghost" and pressed forward to investigate. It turned out that the terrifying apparition was but a ram with its horns caught in the bushes, struggling to free itself. The beast was more scared of him than he of it. As Dudley said, the lesson was "that we must not be influenced by groundless fears in what reason tells us is untrue." It was a lesson that would stick with him in the years to come.

To a man of both faith and reason like Dudley, slavery was the ultimate untruth. Its proponents claimed the enslavement of some was a natural condition, that those who lived under the lash enjoyed a happiness denied to free laborers, and that they, the enslavers, were in fact the *truly* enslaved—by a government that sought to intervene in their affairs. All lies, thought Dudley.

In 1845, Dudley put principle into practice when he was visited by Benjamin Cooper, a fellow Quaker. Cooper had a singular request: Maria Johnson and her three young children, all free, had been kidnapped into slavery and were being driven on the fatal road south. The Society of Friends had taken up a collection to buy them back, but all were too fearful to pursue them. Dudley knew Maria. She had long ago worked on his mother's farm. He volunteered without a second's hesitation.

Disguised in what he imagined to be a slave-trader outfit (broad-brimmed hat, whip, and two pistols), Dudley followed their trail and found them near Head of Elk, Maryland. He introduced himself to the kidnapper, a creature named William Chance, and offered to buy the family so he could transport them to Alabama and Mississippi.

Chance was willing to sell Maria and sixteen-month-old Susan for $150, but it was too late for the older boy and girl. They had already been sent to Baltimore for sale. In order to keep up the ruse, Dudley later said, he had treated Maria quite roughly. It was only after Chance had left that he released her from her shackles and asked if she recognized him. Afraid to look at her new master, Maria said no, only for Dudley to wonder aloud whether she remembered the little boy "who used to play pranks on the cows you milked . . . and make them kick the pail over?" Then he told her she and Susan were going home. Later, Dudley ventured into Baltimore and managed to purchase Maria's son for $90, but the daughter was lost forever, having been bought by a local woman. If nothing else, the episode only sharpened Dudley's loathing for slavers and deepened his belief that the "peculiar institution" must be destroyed, but when and how remained opaque.

Eleven years later, in 1856, a life-changing disaster showed him the way. On the bitterly cold night of March 15, Dudley was aboard a paddle-wheeled ferry shuttling between Philadelphia and Camden. While crossing the Delaware, a fire broke out near the smokestack, and the hundred or so passengers crammed themselves into the bow as the fire roared toward them.

The flames licked their clothes, and many jumped overboard, including Dudley. A number were knocked out by the gnashing paddle wheels, but he managed to scramble onto an ice floe, where he watched dozens die. It was a scene, a friend would later write, "which naturally had an effect upon his nervous system . . . of which he rarely ever spoke."

An unconscious Dudley was eventually hauled to a nearby hotel to be tallied among the dead. That would have been the end of the story had not a colleague happened by and resuscitated him. By some miracle, Dudley was brought back to the land of the living.

His thaumaturgic survival cemented a personal faith that he had been spared to fulfill a divine mission. Had he not died and risen from the grave? His purpose on this earth, Dudley decided, was to eradicate slavery, and to that end he entered politics as chairman of New Jersey's Republican State Executive Committee.

Dedicating himself to putting an abolitionist in the White House, Dudley was, in May 1860, a New Jersey delegate to the Republican National Convention, then meeting in Chicago to nominate a candidate for the coming election. There, Dudley, through some deft backroom wire pulling, performed signal service for Abraham Lincoln by persuading most of his state's delegates to vote for him.

As reward, in mid-1861 the new president offered Dudley a reward: He could become minister to Japan or Liverpool consul. Dudley claimed the latter. A consulship in a noncapital city was a far lesser station than an ambassadorship, but for Dudley, whose health would never fully recover from the ferry disaster, it was important to be close to good doctors. He told his Camden law firm clients that he'd soon be back.

Little did Dudley know, the domestic struggle between two nations had followed him across the Atlantic to faraway Liverpool, where a Confederate spy had embarked on a mission to arm the South with a clandestine navy. The Bloody Spot would be Thomas Dudley's home for longer than he ever imagined.

ONE

On Secret Service

I

On April 23, 1861, a day after returning from a routine mail run to New Orleans on the steamer *Bienville*, Captain James Bulloch visited the offices of his employers, the New York and Alabama Steam Ship Company, at 68 Murray Street in Manhattan. There, he found a mysterious letter awaiting him. It was from the newly installed Confederate attorney general, Judah Benjamin, and would be one of the last letters delivered by the U.S. Mail across the North-South border for the next four years.

This was also the last time, as it happened, that Bulloch was to visit 68 Murray Street, for there was no more work for him—or at least, work that he was willing to do. Following the recent outbreak of war between the Union and the Confederacy, President Lincoln's imposition on April 19 of a naval blockade of the entire Southern coast meant that Bulloch was no longer permitted to steam farther than Washington. And then, after one of the managing directors assigned Bulloch to convey troops to the capital aboard the *Bienville*, the captain decided to tender his resignation instead. Hence the office visit—and, unexpectedly, Bulloch's introduction to the secret world.

In his letter, Benjamin got straight to the point. If Bulloch was interested in a special mission to Britain, he should "come to Montgomery

[Alabama] without delay" to meet the new Confederate secretary of the navy, Stephen Mallory. He should also reserve a berth on a steamship departing Montreal about a month hence for the Mother Country.

It was a strange request, one seemingly from out of the blue. But Bulloch soon traced its origin to an odd interaction he'd had in New Orleans on April 13, ten days earlier, when the *Bienville* had been preparing to depart for New York on what would turn out to be his final voyage as her captain. At 10:00 A.M., he'd heard vague reports that a new Confederate States Army had shelled the Union garrison at Fort Sumter, South Carolina.

War had finally come, and with it two officials on behalf of Louisiana governor Thomas Moore a few hours later. The governor wished to purchase the *Bienville*, they said, at whatever price Bulloch named. Bulloch refused, saying the ship was not his to sell. He had a duty to return her to her New York owners.

After vainly offering a bribe, the visitors threatened that they could forcibly seize the ship, but her captain remained as disconcertingly cool as ever. When Bulloch asked them to leave, they retreated with much ill grace and warned him not to depart for New York until they had checked with the governor.

Governor Moore, having been informed of this obstinate steamship captain, telegraphed Confederate president Jefferson Davis to confirm that his men could take the ship. Soon afterward, Davis ordered Moore not to "detain the *Bienville*" under any circumstances.

You are free to go, a very surprised Bulloch was told at 10:00 P.M. by the two equally bemused officials.

And now, about a week and a half later, there was this letter with its curious offer.

What Bulloch did not know was that Davis had been acting on the advice of Mallory and Benjamin. While it would have been easy to expropriate the *Bienville*, which would have made a valuable addition to the blue-water Confederate Navy, then precisely one ship strong, Secretary Mallory had urged the president to sacrifice her to keep Bulloch from attracting unwelcome Union attention. Had the *Bienville* been seized, her captain would naturally have been suspected as being complicit. Wiser, surely, to allow Bulloch to return her to New York to avoid trouble.

Why? Because Mallory urgently needed the right man for the Confederacy's most important mission. Bulloch, he could see from his files, was no ordinary sailor. Ordained into the Holy Order of the Sea in the Old Navy, Bulloch had learned how to navigate, to interpret charts, to perform trigonometrical calculations, to read the stars, and to plot a course from the masters of sail. He could splice a rope and clew up the topsails, clear the hawse, and cat the anchor with the best of them, yet he was also familiar with the newer technology of steam—to which the U.S. Navy had committed itself in 1853, when it had ordered six powered 50-gun frigates and five sloops. Indeed, one observer had earlier noticed Bulloch's proficiency with the wonder energy of the nineteenth century: During the voyage, the captain had overseen an engine almost as silent as "a bank or counting-room" and there had been none of the "tearing and rending escape of steam, deafening and distracting all" that plagued less experienced commanders.

Even better, Bulloch was rare in having hands-on experience of shipbuilding, an incredibly complex business. Frustrated at the glacial pace of promotion and the limited pay of a naval officer, Bulloch had reluctantly resigned from the navy to become a mail ship captain in the fall of 1854. Since business was good, his new employers had put him in charge of superintending the construction of two new steamers, one of which would become the *Bienville*—a vessel he essentially designed to his own specifications. For Mallory's very specific purposes, someone who understood the finer points of technical drawing, knew the ins and outs of contracts, had overseen work in a shipyard, *and* had grappled with the intricacies of ship financing was an extraordinarily valuable asset.

Best of all, perhaps, was that Bulloch was completely *clean*. He was a civilian with military experience who was neither compromised nor conflicted. As he said himself, "I was only a private individual engaged in the ordinary business of life. I had become completely identified with the shipping enterprises in New York. I had no property of any kind in the South," either of the human or territorial variety.

Optics aside, though, Bulloch was very much of the South. His people had been there, Georgia specifically, since the early eighteenth century, and they had always been affluent, if not rich, slaveowners. His father, for instance, accumulated enough money to build (or rather, have his slaves build) Bulloch Hall near Roswell. Brass candelabras, silverware, and delicate china were hauled, clattering and tinkering all the way, hundreds of miles over muddy roads to furnish his miniaturized copy of the Parthenon.

Young James had been born in 1823 and lost his mother, the daughter of a senator, to tuberculosis when he was seven. In a match that raised a few society eyebrows, two years later his father married the youthful widow of that selfsame senator. James joined her existing three children in a (happily, by all accounts) blended family.

For the boy, the curious family dynamics were nevertheless discomfiting. He had once been an only child, the doted-upon prince of the household, whose every wish had been granted. Now he was one of four, with four more soon to come. He turned inward and learned to use guile, or charm, to extract what he wanted in a competitive environment. Armed with what he called a bottomless capacity for "prudent reserve," Bulloch prized circumlocution, cunning, and artful ambiguity above all, seeing in them a worldliness that allowed him to sneak, crab-like, toward his goal. Later, Bulloch would sculpt a demeanor of amused, ironic detachment and unflappable effortlessness intended to match this sophisticated self-image.

Unlike the pious Quaker consul who would become his nemesis, Bulloch was not given to religious feeling and he distanced himself from politics, especially of the ideological sort. He particularly disdained Republicans, saying that the South wanted only to retain its rights and had no intention of "preserv[ing] that institution [slavery] in perpetuity." Bulloch was aware, of course, that there was *every* intention of preserving that institution in perpetuity under the guise of retaining states' rights, but to him slavery was just the way of the world—how life had always been. Blood, class, and nostalgia rooted him in the South and its practices, even though he himself had never owned slaves and had spent little time below the Mason-Dixon Line after joining the U.S. Navy at age sixteen, in 1839.

Indeed, Bulloch rarely gave much thought to the great issue of the day. In February 1859, for instance—the same month Oregon entered the Union as a free state; Arkansas forced its black residents to choose between exile and slavery; and 436 men, women, and children were being transported to Savannah to be sold off to pay a gambling debt in what would be the largest auction in American history—a writer friend of Herman Melville's named Richard Henry Dana voyaged to Havana aboard Captain Bulloch's ship. Dana was a fervent abolitionist, but despite many conversations with the "cool, quiet, gentlemanly" Bulloch, he could not recall his acquaintance ever mentioning slavery.

The captain, it seems, was accustomed to keeping his views to himself, especially around those he knew would disapprove. Only to his family, Bulloch said, did he admit that "my heart and my head were with the South." With his mariner's sense, Bulloch felt a storm brewing and he privately resolved to stand "ready to act in harmony with my convictions at the proper time." A little more than two years later, that "proper time" had arrived.

II

After destroying Benjamin's incriminating letter, Bulloch stopped by a telegraph office to book a ticket to Liverpool on the *North American,* departing Montreal on May 17. It was critical not to leave New York in a hurry. His return of the *Bienville* might have "removed any suspicion of my 'loyalty,'" but the city authorities could still arrest him if they believed he were up to no good. So Bulloch very quietly transferred his assets to his wife, Harriott, to avoid possible confiscation, and kissed his family, including two infants, goodbye.

On May 2, he packed a small suitcase and caught the train to Philadelphia, then switched trains for Pittsburgh before heading west to Cincinnati. From there, he could take a steamboat to cross the Kentucky border to Louisville. Kentucky was still in the Union, but Bulloch considered it friendly territory. There he "should be free from the danger of being asked at any moment to stop and give an account of myself."

Bulloch felt a flutter of worry when, at the Cincinnati dock, guards were questioning passengers. But another man—evidently trusted by the soldiers, yet a Confederate sympathizer Bulloch had recently met—claimed that Bulloch was a friend of his and that they were going to Louisville on business. Bulloch was allowed to board without any hassle.

After reaching Nashville, it was a pleasant train journey through Chattanooga and Atlanta to Montgomery. Just before midnight on May 7, an exhausted Bulloch arrived at the Exchange Hotel, the city's best, and went straight to bed.

He had an appointment the next morning.

III

Montgomery was perhaps not the most promising place to situate the capital of an invented country. William Howard Russell, the world's most famous war correspondent, was touring America for *The Times* of London and happened to be in Montgomery at the same time as Bulloch (they stayed in the same hotel, maybe greeted each other in the lobby). Even if the town's well-wooded environs were agreeable, he commented, "the streets here are very hot, unpleasant, and uninteresting."

With a population of around nine thousand "not very attractive" people (Russell's words) and numberless mosquitoes, Montgomery could serve as capital for only a short time. Just a couple of weeks after Bulloch's arrival, Richmond, Virginia, would become the seat of the Confederate government.

Until then, an influx of state legislators, congressional delegates, cabinet secretaries, and newly created generals were caffeinating the once sleepy town. Seeing them all up close, Russell, who had been romantically sympathetic to Southern independence, now counted them as fanatics committed to the "propriety, righteousness, and divinity of slavery," which he found repulsive, especially after watching a slave auction held just outside the hotel.

While President Jefferson Davis enjoyed his own leased "White House" and the provisional Congress set up shop in the grandly porticoed Alabama State Capitol, the executive branch of the government rented a building on Commerce Street partly occupied by an insurance company. There, every possible bit of space, even the broom cupboard, was quickly converted into an office for someone important.

And it was there, just around the corner from the Exchange Hotel, that Bulloch headed after breakfast on May 8. He arrived to find offices marked only by pieces of paper pasted on doors with their occupants' names, departments scattered around various floors, and no one knowing who was where, let alone who he was. Eventually, in a freshly whitewashed hallway, he bumped into short, stout Judah Benjamin, who helpfully escorted Bulloch to Mallory's digs.

IV

When it came to navies, Mallory knew his onions. The Florida senator had once chaired the Committee on Naval Affairs, and had long kept abreast of the newest technology, like rifled guns firing fuse-equipped shells and experimental ironclads.

After the usual pleasantries, Mallory and Bulloch had a long discussion, spread over two days, about the critical importance of the Confederate Navy to winning the war. Overshadowing their talk was President Lincoln's imposition of a naval blockade of the South a few weeks earlier, on April 19.

Mallory outlined the situation for Bulloch. Compared with the U.S. Navy, its Confederate counterpart was a pitiful thing. Lincoln had forty-two commissioned ships, and while many were either abroad, decrepit, small, or broken, that was still forty-one more than the South had.

Lincoln was sure to build more, and quickly. He had the industrial power already to hand, while the Confederacy was distinctly at a disadvantage. Of the 1,071 American merchant vessels built in 1860, for example, a mere eighty-four originated in the South. And of the ten navy yards in operation, just two (Norfolk and Pensacola) were below the Mason-Dixon Line. What's more, neither of those had the manufacturing capacity to outfit a navy. The South had hardly any iron foundries, marine-engine factories, or ordnance facilities, let alone the requisite stockpiles of raw materiel.

The only way to acquire an oceangoing Confederate Navy, then, was from abroad. It would be smaller than its Union opponent, of course, but it would be more advanced, more lethal, and better captained. That said, one could hardly walk in and buy a spare fleet off the shelf, so Mallory and Bulloch together drummed up a three-stage plan to secure victory for the South.

Stage One was to break the blockade. Bulloch would buy or underwrite a swarm of fast, civilian-crewed *blockade-runners* to smuggle in the arms and munitions that the South's under-equipped, hastily raised army needed to fight. Some of these could later be converted into coastal or riverine military vessels.

Still, getting the runners past the U.S. Navy's frigates and sloops standing guard at sea would be no easy matter. To draw them away, Mallory wanted *commerce-raider cruisers* to harass and sink Union merchant shipping. Once Yankee businessmen started complaining about their losses, Lincoln would have to divert his warships to their protection, thereby rending holes in his own blockade. That was Stage Two.

Stage Three would take the fight directly to the U.S. Navy. At least two powerful, highly advanced *ironclad* warships, each capable of sinking any ship they intercepted or of wreaking havoc in Northern harbors and dockyards, would be commissioned. "Such a vessel . . . could traverse the entire coast of the United States, prevent all blockades, and encounter . . . their entire Navy," Mallory believed. With just a few of these armored behemoths, the South's "inequality of numbers may be compensated by invulnerability."

The upshot, then, was that in the short-term, the runners would keep the South supplied and form the nucleus of a navy. In the medium, the raiders would demoralize the Union and weaken the blockade. And in the long, the ironclads would destroy the U.S. Navy with impunity.

Most important, Mallory and Bulloch were thinking in terms of grand strategy. The intention of their war on the waters was not merely to sink some ships or to create some financial headaches for Northern merchants. No, the overarching objective was to persuade the British, rulers of the world's mightiest empire and arbiters of the high seas, that the Confederate States of America was a force to be reckoned with. If all went as planned, Great Britain would ally with its friends in the South against the North.

And if that happened, Lincoln—staggering under the lightning strikes of the Confederate Army as the omnipotent Royal Navy blockaded *his* ports—was finished. To win the war, all the South had to do was not lose until an armistice was offered by a humbled North that recognized its independence and thus the right to maintain slavery. Bulloch, in that instance, would be the man who saved the South.

It was a tall order, but Bulloch was confident that he could pull it off. The free-trading British were already annoyed with Lincoln's blockade, which they interpreted as merely a cover to protect Northern industrialists from competition by restricting their commerce with the South. That meant there would be no problem, Bulloch believed, acquiring the necessary ships in friendly Britain.

In fact, the very friendliest place in Britain would be his home base: Liverpool. There, Bulloch assured Mallory, the shipyards would be falling over themselves to build the blockade-runners, commerce raiders, and modern ironclads the Confederacy needed to win.

The only outstanding issue, said Bulloch, was money. Ships were expensive. Mallory assured him on that score. The navy secretary had already arranged for a confidential contact at Fraser, Trenholm & Company in Liverpool to handle the financial details. That firm, a branch of a powerful and well-connected Charleston-based cotton-trading company, would serve as the Confederacy's, and Bulloch's, de facto banker. Bulloch would have all the cash and credit he'd need.

Last of all, Mallory asked Bulloch when he could start. "I have no impedimenta," the Georgian replied. He would leave immediately.

V

The next afternoon, May 9, Bulloch was on his way. He had an easy time of it crossing over to Windsor, Ontario, to take the Grand Trunk

Railway to Montreal, where he picked up his previously reserved ticket. Right on schedule, Bulloch boarded the steamship *North American* on May 17.

As Bulloch settled into his stateroom for the voyage to Liverpool, he considered himself very clever in having evaded Union detection. As far as the Northern authorities were concerned, he thought, James Bulloch had simply vanished into thin air when he'd left New York more than two weeks earlier.

Unfortunately for Bulloch, the Union, in fact, knew exactly what he was doing and where he was going, if not exactly where he was. That spring, the federal government had begun to monitor communications between North and South. By happenstance, a treasury agent named Hollis White had been tapping the telegraph line between New York and Niagara Falls when he had picked up details of Bulloch's message in late April booking passage to Liverpool. He duly informed his superiors in Washington that a suspected Confederate was due to depart via Montreal.

At the time, this vague warning didn't seem very urgent, and it was ignored. Not until May 15, when Bulloch was already in Canada, could Union officials put two and two together. It was on that day the *Richmond Dispatch* reported that one "J.D. Bullock," an "agent for the Government," was leaving for Liverpool carrying at least $400,000 to buy "ten steam gun-boats for coast defenses."

Some fool in the Confederate Congress or the navy department had obviously flapped his mouth off to the reporter, and the New York newspapers soon republished the piece. The article was filled with factual errors, but the most telling damage came from its confirming that "Bullock" was on a secret mission to Britain to acquire ships.

He was now a known enemy agent operating abroad—but the game had just begun.

TWO

The White Gold

I

Benjamin Moran, the assistant secretary of the United States Legation—the embassy—in London was rarely a happy man. Misanthropic and depressive, he derived a degree of mildly sadistic pleasure from denying passports to Confederate sympathizers wanting to get back to America.

But today, Thursday, May 16, 1861, was going to be a good day. After five years in harness as minister to London, the "bad mannered, illiterate, presumptuous, and offensive" George Dallas was finally leaving. Moran counted the minutes until 3:00 P.M., when his hated boss would take his leave of Queen Victoria.

Moran hoped his replacement would be better, but it wasn't looking promising. When Charles Francis Adams appeared at Buckingham Palace to present his diplomatic credentials, Moran sniffed that the new ambassador, in deference to Yankee down-home custom, was wearing a black dress coat rather than a frock coat. Moran thought it made him look like a butler, or an undertaker at best. (The queen, in a rare quip, murmured to a courtier, "I am thankful we shall have no more American funerals.")

Moran's apprehensions were soon relieved. Unlike Dallas, Adams was as wholeheartedly devoted to preserving the sacred Union as he.

Benjamin Moran,
casting his beady eye upon the world

Though he devoted his free time to studying rare coins, which Moran lamented was beneath his own noble hobby of stamp collecting, he decided that Adams had been a shrewd choice by Lincoln.

At the age of fifty-three, Adams, the son and grandson of presidents (John Quincy Adams and John Adams, respectively), held the same post in London as they once had. He was at once a reassuring, suitably aristocratic presence with his distinguished lineage and elegant mien, but also a physical reminder that his forebears had been resolute defenders of American interests.

Adams certainly had his work cut out for him. Three days earlier, the British had unexpectedly issued a Proclamation of Neutrality, bestowing upon the Legation a potentially explosive diplomatic crisis.

Neutrality was a fallback position for the British, prompted by the fact that they had no clear idea of what the war was about and (more cynically) wanted to wait-and-see how Lincoln's naval blockade panned out. Some thought the fighting was a banal struggle for land and pronounced a pox on both North and South. Many criticized a tyrannical Union for trying to prevent the plucky Southerners from going their own way, while others sneered at the Confederates as spoiled brats taking their toys home because they hadn't gotten what they wanted. What was absolutely clear to everyone was that slavery was a peripheral reason for the outbreak of war. Few in Britain favored its retention, but most assumed it was an embarrassing anachronism that would eventually wither on the vine.

To the British, in short, the Civil War came across as yet another of their rancorous colonial cousins' periodic fits of madness. For every argument in favor of backing the Union, there was as good a one in favor of the Confederacy. And an even better one to steer clear until the dust settled and an obvious winner emerged. "For God's sake," Foreign Secretary Lord John Russell warned, "let us if possible keep out of it."

The result, the Proclamation of Neutrality, fully satisfied neither Unionist nor Confederate, which was perhaps the intention. The North was annoyed at the British recognizing that an official state of war existed between "the Government of the United States of America" and "certain States styling themselves the Confederate States of America." In other words, that two distinct entities existed rather than, as Washington saw it, there being one legitimate government fighting a domestic police action against a gang of rebels. The good news was that Britain, at least for the time being, was hedging its bets by not defining the Confederacy as a fully legitimate *government*, which greatly aided the Union.

Southerners, on the other hand, were insulted that the proclamation assigned the Confederacy the legal status of "belligerent" rather than of sovereign state. They had expected more full-hearted British support, even an Anglo-Confederate alliance. Yet the belligerent halfway house was much better than nothing. First, it meant that the South was granted several key rights not extended to "rebels," such as being permitted to dock its warships in British ports for repairs or re-coaling. Second, it held out hope that Britain would eventually bet the house on the South.

Minister Adams's task, then, was to keep Britain out of the war. The Confederates in Britain, conversely, were just as intent on luring it in.

II

Success either way hinged on the outcome of Lincoln's blockade. On April 19, as Bulloch and Mallory discussed in Montgomery, the president had announced that no ship could enter or exit any Southern port. Most Confederates laughed off his diktat: This arrogant fool was declaring a mere "Paper Blockade"—and they had a point. A woefully underprepared U.S. Navy was expected to watch a coastline of 3,549 miles stretching from Virginia to the Rio Grande.

Not only that, but Lincoln was trying to do it with but a handful of ships. There was no possible way they could prevent every vessel, or even the great majority of them, from sneaking past their warders trying to guard hundreds of bays, rivers, inlets, and ports.

Most important, though, the South believed it had international law on its side. Five years earlier, in 1856, the Great Powers—though not the United States—had adopted the Declaration of Paris. According to this treaty, "blockades, in order to be binding, must be effective; that is to say, maintained by a force sufficient really to prevent access to the coast of the enemy."

With so few ships available, it was blazingly obvious that Lincoln's blockade could not be "effective," as the declaration had defined it, and so was not "binding" upon Britain or any other signatory. The British, the world's greatest importers and exporters, could respect it or ignore it as they wished.

Jefferson Davis may have scoffed at Lincoln's "monstrous pretension" that London would bend the knee to Washington's demands, but thoughtful strategists were more concerned. It would not take Union planners long to grasp that to strangle the South, legally or not, the blockaders did not have to cover the entire seaboard, just the seven deep-water ports of New Orleans, Charleston, Savannah, Mobile, Galveston, Wilmington, and Norfolk—through which virtually all the South's foreign trade passed.

Just as alarming was that the Union was frantically dragooning any passable merchant ship to beef up numbers. By the end of May, the navy had already bought twelve steamers and leased nine more from private owners. While the majority of these ships could be defined at best as being serviceable, quantity nevertheless has its own quality: They only had to be good enough to make the blockade *look* sufficiently effective to persuade Britain to respect the no-sail zone.

For that reason, it was critical for the Confederates to prove that the blockade was too porous to count as "effective" by running it on a massive scale. If it were shown to indeed be made of paper, easily ripped and holed, then British merchants would enthusiastically trade with the South,

James Bulloch, secret agent

keeping it flush with cash while pushing London into the Confederate embrace. Once the blockade fell, the end of British neutrality was nigh.

The Union knew this, too. Thus, their first priority was to find Bulloch, the agent dispatched to Britain to destroy the blockade. They'd missed catching him crossing the Canadian border and had not prevented his boarding the *North American* in Montreal, but at least he'd be easy to spot once he arrived in Liverpool. According to an urgent dispatch from Secretary of State William Seward to Legation officials, he was "a very dark, sallow man with black hair and eyes, whiskers down each cheek but shaved clean off his chin and below, dark mustache, about 5'8" high."

Observe his movements carefully, they were ordered.

III

For weeks, the old sea dog Bulloch had enjoyed broad horizons and brisk breezes aboard the *North American* as she plowed her solitary furrow through the Atlantic's white-capped waves. But today, June 4, they were approaching Liverpool, where the sea lanes turned into the maritime equivalent of a permanent rush hour.

Traffic on the Mersey

The *North American* negotiated the Mersey, a river the color and texture of a mud puddle, striving to avoid a collision. Jamming the waterway were swarms of red-sailed little droghers hauling salt and tobacco on local runs; giant, four-masted luxury steam liners for the well-heeled; battered immigrant ships taking poor Irish to Australia and America to make their fortunes; pert French brigantines; Indian merchantmen crewed by wiry Malays and Thais; old-fashioned, flat-bottomed Dutch galliots; and low-slung Guinea Coast brigs armed with ancient swivel guns to fend off pirates. Standing impassively aside, but keeping a watchful eye for miscreants, was a Royal Navy 80-gun warship, HMS *Majestic*.

The *North American* pulled and hauled her way to a basin, a kind of antechamber, outside Prince's Dock. Then a water gate groaned open to allow entrance. A dockmaster, his despotic authority conspicuously designated by a tin sign hung over his hat, clambered aboard and bawled orders to the other ships to make space ("*Highlander* ahoy! Cast off your bowline and sheer alongside the *Neptune*!"; "*Trident* ahoy! Get out a bowline and drop astern of the *Undaunted*!"). Every ship shifted this way and that to accommodate the newcomer in her assigned berth. Eventually, miraculously, they all fit.

Some were in better shape than others; the sea exacted a heavy price on ships. Lashings of salt spray whitened funnels, which meant a paint job every couple of trips. Canvas tore, engines gave up the ghost, ropes frayed, and storms snapped masts. Liverpool provided a watery inn for stricken ships.

Bulloch knew the New York docks, but compared with their magnificent Liverpudlian counterparts, its miserable wooden wharves and slipshod piers were like some barbarian village embarrassingly nestled in the shadow of the Colosseum. When Herman Melville visited Liverpool before the war, he "beheld long China walls of masonry; vast piers of stone; and a succession of granite-rimmed docks, completely inclosed" to protect against the weather. In their vast Pharaonic scale, the seven-odd miles of docks extending along the waterfront "seemed equal to what I had read of the old Pyramids of Egypt."

Many of the enclosed docks formed their own immense fortress. Festooning the internal walls were posters announcing the imminent departure of "superior, fast-sailing, coppered" ships for distant ports and advertisements for best-price sailor's outfitters, dubious taverns, and the "Seamen's Dispensary" (a busy venereal-disease clinic). For those eager to take the Queen's shilling, there were inducements to enjoy a bout of dysentery guarding India's northwestern frontier or to stand shivery sentry on Quebec's bleak ramparts, all courtesy of the army.

Bulloch disembarked and gingerly avoided being run over by wagons carrying the numberless tons of bales, crates, boxes, sacks, and cases unloaded from the ships. An oddity of Liverpool was that the horses drawing them were treated like Roman citizens, it being forbidden to lay a lash to their backs. Once off the quay and trundled to a wide paved area, the cargoes were heaved and stacked in iron sheds by hundreds of "lumpers" (laborers who worked for a lump sum). There, scores of agents and collectors measured, weighed, and invoiced the commodities—wire, spirits, wines, hardware, wheat, rice, corn, tobacco, cotton, rare woods, sugar, hides—transiting to and from the Americas, India, Madagascar, Asia, Persia, the Caribbean, and Europe.

Every dock was an epitome of the world, and every ship, a colony of its homeland. The Liverpool waterfront formed a grand parliament of masts, observed Melville, where all the nations and creeds of earth congregated in brotherly love, yardarm touching yardarm, to serve the great gods of commerce and empire.

Bulloch left the riverside and walked up Water Street, deeper into this 1860s boomtown of grimy, brick-walled warehouses and soot-smeared churches, of twisting alleys and hissing gaslights, of smokestacks belching into the fuggy air. Everywhere, you could smell the rank of burning coal powering the clank of machinery.

He was heartened to see that the rumors of Liverpool's Southern sympathies were accurate. Confederate flags and bunting were everywhere: hung in shop windows, suspended from lampposts, strung along streets, decorating office thresholds.

A few minutes away, tucked off Rumford Street, was Rumford Place. It was quiet and discreet, a difficult little nook in which to loiter— aimlessly or otherwise—without being noticed.

He stopped outside No. 10, an unprepossessing three-story building marked only by a small brass plate reading "Fraser, Trenholm & Co." Before knocking, he cautiously scanned the street, but no one was watching.

The door opened. Waiting inside was an elegantly dressed man in his mid-thirties. In a soft Carolinian accent, he introduced himself as Charles Prioleau.

IV

Prioleau was urbane and charming, qualities that had helped clear his path upward. His father had been a lawyer who went into local politics, and Charles had joined the old mercantile house of John Fraser & Company of Charleston as a clerk.

He had risen quickly through the ranks, mostly by dint of his efficiency with the accounts, but partly by his attachment to George Trenholm, the firm's senior partner. The latter had taken over the company in 1838 from the elderly Mr. Fraser and had expanded it since. At its peak, the firm handled twenty thousand bales of Southern cotton each morning and shipped them to Liverpool. To supervise the company's business there, the Old Man had established a branch named Fraser, Trenholm & Company that was run by Prioleau.

Prioleau had moved to Liverpool in 1856 and ingratiated himself with the city's elite by marrying a wealthy shipper's daughter, Mary Wright, thirteen years younger than he and rumored to be the most beautiful of all the Liverpudlian belles. That Prioleau was descended, or so he flattered himself, from the Priuli doges of Renaissance Venice certainly impressed the more gullible of Liverpool's merchant kings. Mary's father owned Allerton Hall, an impressive Palladian mansion just outside the city, and the Prioleaus rented it from him, setting themselves up in the grand style befitting a Charleston clerk made good. These days, Prioleau liked to fly the Confederate flag from the mansion's rooftop.

The ambitious Prioleau had an eye to buying Allerton Hall but could not yet afford it. He earnestly hoped that would change. Prioleau may have only been a junior partner of the firm—he was entitled to 5 percent of the profits—but given the size and nature of the company business, that small holding was capable of turning into a fortune, thanks to the war.

Trenholm, who enjoyed deep connections with the Confederate government, had already prepared the ground by offering to place his companies at Jefferson Davis's disposal. Thus, the Trenholm empire had become the dark financiers of the Confederacy's clandestine navy program. Patriotism and profit now marched hand in hand, all greased by Fraser Trenholm's half-percent commission on every transaction.

In theory, at least. The reality, as both Bulloch and Prioleau realized at their first meeting, was messier. Bulloch had been sent to Britain armed with Secretary Mallory's promise that the navy would be good for his bills, but he was shocked to hear from Prioleau that "no funds had yet reached them." Neither had the Carolinian any idea when they would arrive.

It turned out that the finances of the Confederate government were rather more straitened than Bulloch had been led to believe. The little hard cash Richmond had was earmarked for the army, but Prioleau had heard a rumor that Mallory had managed to extract $600,000, which was apparently on the way. Even so, it wouldn't last long: A large steamer alone cost at least $140,000, and a new ironclad was estimated at $2.5 million. Who was going to pony up the down payments shipbuilders required to start work? In Liverpool, "no contracts or purchases could be made without cash actually in hand," Prioleau informed an unpleasantly surprised Bulloch, and some firms would want the *entire* sum up front. Bulloch needed more money, a lot of money, urgently.

Prioleau had an answer for that. Let's take a walk, he suggested.

V

Bulloch could hear the barking and bawling grow ever louder as he and Prioleau approached the outdoor plaza fondly known as The Flags, just around the corner from Fraser Trenholm's Rumford Place office.

The Flags

It was the height of summer, yet there it was snowing. Little fluffs filled the air and covered the cobblestones of an entire market frenziedly devoted to buying and selling one thing: cotton. Agents examined samples as carefully as jewelers do diamonds, assessed their grades, and then, with a flash of fingers and a nod between the hundreds of top-hatted brokers, deals were made in seconds. Message boys rushed the scrawled transactions inside for telegraphing throughout the world. Everywhere one looked there were boards papered with the latest news and notices of prices, cargoes, freights, sailing times, barometer readings, weather reports, and schedules of inward- and outward-bound ships.

Formally called the Cotton Exchange, The Flags had until recently been a sedate gentleman's club of sorts but the outbreak of war had turned the place rabid. Attracted by fast-rising prices, speculators were avidly entering the market as mill owners raked up as much product as they could lay their hands on for fear of being caught short.

Everyone tipped their hat to the Great Prioleau as the pair passed. He represented Fraser Trenholm, and Fraser Trenholm was one of the major players. The firm not only imported cotton, sold it, and bought it, but served to underwrite a host of smaller merchants, making Prioleau a combination of merchant, broker, creditor, and banker. It was a highly profitable line of work but also a risky one. Since Fraser Trenholm traded on its own account and indulged in the new sport of futures trading while at the same time taking on debt and extending credit, it was possible to get disastrously trapped on the wrong side of the ledger if the cotton market turned against it.

But that could never happen, boasted Prioleau. Why? Because cotton was the once-and-future king, the savior of the South, the slayer of the Union.

VI

Cotton was blood. On the fertile plantations of the South, four million slaves backbreakingly picked the raw plant, after which it was ripped in gins to remove the seeds from the fiber.

Cotton was money. Baled together and sent to Liverpool, it was sold to mills in nearby Lancashire to be turned into cloth and spun into yarn. These finished textiles were re-exported and sold to the world at high markups, the profits returning home and used to build grand civic buildings, railways, and canals. And thus Dixie cotton was wondrously alchemized into white gold.

Cotton was addictive. Up to five million people—a fifth of the British population—relied directly and indirectly on the cotton industry for their daily bread. Forty percent of Britain's total exports consisted of cotton products, not surprising when between 1800 and 1860, the country's clamor for the stuff increased by 1,000 percent, reaching an annual 400,000 tons. More than 80 percent of that was supplied by the South, whose product was regarded as of the highest quality. As *The Economist* worried in 1853, should "any great social or physical convulsion visit the United States"—like a civil war, for instance—Britain would feel the shock if the cotton was cut off. "A thousand of our merchant ships would rot idly in dock, two thousand mills must stop their busy looms; [millions of] mouths must starve for lack of food."

And cotton, above all, was king. Among politicians, planters, newspapermen, and merchants, this was a law as venerable as the commandments of Moses or the code of Hammurabi. Not a man among them denied, as the South Carolinian senator James Hammond—an incestuous ephebophile, busy slave-rapist, and inadvertently amusing egomaniac ("the 4th July was celebrated this year to toast me")—famously declared in 1858, that "we could bring the whole world to our feet" by stopping the supply of cotton. "What would happen if no cotton was furnished for three years?" he asked. "England would topple headlong and carry the whole civilized world with her, save the South. No, you dare not make war on cotton. No power on earth dares to make war upon it. Cotton is king!"

Following Hammond's cue, with the outbreak of war the South weaponized cotton by embargoing its *own* shipments to Britain to create an artificial shortage. In the ports, there were "Committees of Public Safety" that physically blocked cotton exports and publicly humiliated planters who did not hold back their crops. While in June 1861 an already low 133,679 bales would find their way to Liverpool, by September, a mere thirty-five did.

The idea was that the British could only save themselves from an economic heart attack if they disavowed neutrality and threw in their lot with the South. Whether it was wise, though, to threaten a superpower by withholding vital resources was a fraught question. Backers of the embargo assured nervous planters that it would be only a few months before Britain saw sense, but for Bulloch the turning off of the spigot could not have come at a worse time.

Between the Northern blockade, British neutrality, and the Southern embargo, Bulloch's once simple Stage One mission—acquire blockade-runners—had turned dauntingly complex. Worse than that, actually. With no money, it was impossible.

To raise cash, Prioleau proposed a scheme involving a modest steamer named the *Bermuda*, recently purchased by Fraser Trenholm. Sometime in August, she would be loaded to the gunwales with pricey English items like billiards tables, chandeliers, jewelry, tapestries, wallpaper, perfumes, lace, and drugs (quinine, ether, morphine, laudanum) that could be auctioned in the South. Rich people would pay a fortune for their luxuries, now difficult to acquire thanks to the blockade.

At a stroke, Prioleau would make a lavish profit while solidifying Fraser Trenholm's predominant market position. The firm currently owned at least five other steamers, and if the *Bermuda* escapade succeeded, he would divert all of them to running Lincoln's insolent blockade and showing it up as absurdly porous.

Then, once the Fraser Trenholm ships had offloaded their wares in Charleston or Savannah, they would take on a cargo of cotton for the return trip to Liverpool. This cotton would be sold by Prioleau at The Flags, with most of the proceeds in cash and credit secretly funneled to Bulloch so he could forge ahead while awaiting the arrival of Mallory's promised funds.

The trick was how to evade the embargo forbidding the exportation of cotton from Southern ports. The Committees of Public Safety had lately taken it upon themselves to harass and punish those they suspected of trying to ignore the rules, sometimes going so far as to burn warehouses full of valuable cotton. Prioleau's solution was to ask Old Man Trenholm to put a word in certain ears within the government. Miraculously, the firm soon received a permit to export limited amounts of cotton covertly earmarked for Bulloch's use.

And with that, Bulloch and Prioleau congratulated themselves on a job well done. Prioleau was so confident that everything was going to work out perfectly, not only for the Confederacy but for Fraser Trenholm (and himself), that he purchased 19 Abercromby Square, one of Liverpool's fanciest addresses. He even applied for special permission to raise the height of his mansion a few feet above those of the rest of the square to accommodate his collection of South Carolinian palmetto trees, imported through the blockade alongside a cargo of white gold.

THREE

The Black Crow

I

By the beginning of June, the United States Legation in London was very worried. Neither hide nor hair of the mysterious James Bulloch had been seen since his disappearance from New York a month earlier. The *North American* had arrived in Liverpool, certainly, but Bulloch had gone to ground.

Then Henry Shelton Sanford showed up and said he'd find him, by hook or by crook.

One of those grand nineteenth-century eccentrics whose kind has since vanished from this earth, Sanford was an archetypal Victorian, the sort of man who, when cautioned that some venture was perilous, would have replied, "Splendid!"

Sanford was two days younger than Bulloch and likewise came from an affluent family, but there the similarities ended. He was from Connecticut, not Georgia. He was wealthy thanks to a large inheritance. And whereas Bulloch preferred to blend into the background, Sanford made himself the subject of every portrait.

Measuring six foot one, with chestnut hair, hazel eyes, and geometric cheekbones, Sanford enjoyed living up to his nickname of the "Black Crow," which he himself might have invented. He wore only black suits

Henry Sanford, master of the dark arts

run up by the finest tailors. His shoes, fitted precisely by master boot makers, gleamed, as did the dandyish, gold-headed walking stick with which he swaggered around. His only flaw, if one could call it that, was his expensive pince-nez—a legacy of an eye infection—but Sanford was convinced they made him look stylishly intellectual.

His self-conceit and self-promotion were legendary among the diplomats he'd formerly worked with in St. Petersburg, Berlin, and Paris, where he'd left behind a trail of aggrieved ministers who disliked both his arrogant assumption that the rules didn't apply to him and his predilection for taking shortcuts through gray areas. Sanford, however, wasn't concerned with what lesser mortals thought of him. Geniuses like him never are. But Sanford's problem was that he wasn't a genius. He was merely intelligent—which would make him almost as dangerous as a fool in the spying game.

Yet Sanford had many friends, not least owing to his unceasing devotion to defending the virtue of the Great Republic. On the eve of war, Sanford had ingratiated himself among Republicans by inviting them to lavish dinner parties and promising that he would spy the daylights out of any Confederates who dared show their faces in Europe.

All those dinner parties paid off when he was granted the position of de facto chief of Union intelligence in Britain. As official cover, he was appointed "minister to Belgium," a ruse necessitated by Her Majesty's Government's dislike of foreigners conducting espionage within the realm. He was directed by Secretary of State William Seward "to counteract by all proper means the efforts" of Southern agents abroad.

Seward unfortunately left the definition of "proper means" unclear. To the secretary of state it meant that Sanford would be responsible for what was called the Black List, a compilation of descriptions and departure dates for any blockade-runners leaving Britain. He was to send this list to the Legation in London, which would pass the intelligence on to the navy. Armed with this information, the blockading squadrons would intercept and seize the runners in American or international waters. *Under absolutely no circumstances* was Sanford, who was to keep strictly within the law to avoid antagonizing his hosts, to imperil Minister Adams's diplomatic efforts to keep Britain neutral.

To Sanford, however, "proper means" meant exactly what it said. When it came to unearthing Confederates and frustrating their knavish plans, *every* means was proper. "How it will be done, whether through a pretty mistress, or an intelligent servant, or a spying landlord is nobody's business," he pledged. Nothing was off the table, according to his expansive definition, which included sabotage, piracy, kidnapping, and, possibly, assassination. "I go on the doctrine that in war as in love every thing is fair that will lead to success."

As soon as he stepped foot in London, Sanford quickly rubbed Benjamin Moran, the assistant secretary at the Legation, the wrong way. Moran pegged him as "an unprincipled fellow, and treacherous," who spoke "rapidly, pertly, and with an air of insolent authority."

Worse, Sanford was proposing to use someone as equally (in Moran's eyes) dubious as himself to hunt the elusive Bulloch: Paddington Pollaky.

II

Ignaz or Ignatz or Ignatius Pollaky was born in Pressburg or Malacky in what was then Hungary but is now Slovakia, in 1819, 1822, 1824, 1828, or 1829, the son of either a synagogue watchman or a minor government official. He was probably Jewish but was baptized a Catholic—and would marry an Anglican (twice). Pollaky seems to have involved himself in the Hungarian Revolution in 1848, and, with the Habsburg secret police hot on his heels, escaped to Britain later that year—or maybe in 1850, 1851, or 1852. With Pollaky, nothing was ever quite certain.

A man of parts and halves, of shadows and shadings, Pollaky traded in rumor and subterfuge. Once in London, Pollaky deployed his linguistic talents—he was fluent in seven languages—to bring, as he said, "Criminals (Foreigners) to justice" by serving as a police informer.

Occasionally, too, as a spy. The British government once hired him to travel to Romania and Egypt to gather intelligence on arms smuggling to Russia, and later sent him on another secret mission, this time to Zurich, to contact a fugitive Italian prince with apparently vital information.

Between these murky episodes, Pollaky gained a useful acquaintance with the criminal underworld that allowed him to set up his own private-detective agency, one of the world's first. He specialized in tracking thieves on the lam, chasing embezzlers traveling under fake names, tailing errant spouses for evidence in divorce trials, and "retrieving" incriminating letters from blackmailers—not always by asking nicely.

By the outbreak of the Civil War, and still (probably) only in his early thirties, Pollaky was an expert in surveillance, disguise, and finding people who did not want to be found. People, for example, like Confederate secret agents.

Pollaky wasn't cheap, but he did work quickly. He was hired on June 29, and within a fortnight he had tracked down Bulloch, who had departed Liverpool some weeks earlier. With no little relief, the Legation informed Seward that "this man is here and his movements are observed."

Bulloch's renting of a comfortable apartment on the second floor at 58 Jermyn Street, one of London's posher thoroughfares, had certainly made Pollaky's task easier. The Union men assumed, dangerously, that Bulloch had been there since he'd arrived in Britain and were unaware of his connection to Prioleau, let alone the *Bermuda* blockade-running scheme they had cooked up.

Sanford, in fact, was more interested in Pollaky's discovery that Bulloch was not 58 Jermyn Street's only resident. Staying at what was nicknamed the "Casemate," too, were Captain Caleb Huse and Major Edward Anderson, both there to purchase guns for the Confederate Army. Huse, a former superintendent of a military academy in Alabama, was something of a worthy bore. Anderson, meanwhile, was a wealthy Georgia planter and former navy officer, gregarious and entertaining. Bulloch got on well with, and thought highly of, both of them, though Anderson was his clear favorite.

At the beginning of the war, the Confederate arsenal consisted of just 159,000 muskets, rifles, and pistols, about 3 million cartridges, sufficient gunpowder (mostly left over from the Mexican War) to fill another 1.5 million, and 9 musicians' ceremonial swords. At best, the South could distribute an average of 28 rounds per firearm—barely sufficient for a soldier to fight a single battle—while its factories could manufacture a mere 1,500 firearms per month. It was imperative, therefore, to amass as much gunpowder and as many weapons in Britain as quickly as possible to offset the North's industrial advantage.

That summer of 1861, the trio became the toast of London's arms dealers. Free tickets to the theater and invitations to agreeable country houses showered upon them, as did offers of kickbacks and bribes— which Anderson amusingly called "the English way of doing business." The Southerners were too honest to accept the money, and it was only after one gunmaker complained that his bookkeepers would be most inconvenienced if they couldn't account for the "commission" that they relented—but scrupulously donated the money to the Confederate government.

Two firms in particular were the major suppliers: The London Armoury Company, run by Archibald Hamilton and Frederick Bond, and S. Isaac, Campbell & Company, located across the street from the Casemate at 71 Jermyn.

Samuel Isaac, proprietor of the latter, was *very* flexible when it came to arranging deals with representatives of a foreign power, partly because he was banned from supplying the British Army after an official inquiry had discovered certain "irregularities" in his financial affairs. Still, he was happy to extend credit to Huse (for a 2.5 percent commission) and he could source large quantities in short order. In a single month, for instance, Huse contracted for no fewer than 21,000 older muskets and 24,000 new Enfield rifles.

While Archibald Hamilton always "haggle[d] over a ha'penny" when it came to business, Frederick Bond was different. He and Anderson rattled along splendidly. Bond used to take his friend on no-expense-spared visits to the Holborn Casino, a glamorous dance hall in rackety Covent Garden where there were many pretty, artfully powdered ladies wearing kid gloves, frilly ruffs, and high-heeled boots, as one observer archly noted.

Broad shouldered and olive complexioned, twenty-year-old Frederick had guns in his blood. His parents, uncle, brother, and sister-in-law were gunmakers. His father had even loyally committed suicide with one. Aside from selling Anderson every firearm he had in stock, Bond's importance lay in his introducing the major to the man we can call Agent X, the Confederates' spy within the British government.

III

Sanford and Pollaky thus initially dismissed Bulloch as only a bit player, and they quickly lost interest in him in favor of tailing Huse and Anderson. Bulloch was not at Jermyn Street that often, and he certainly did not seem as busy as the other two, who were constantly scuttling in and out of London's arms-dealing emporiums.

It was only by doggedly tracking Huse's purchases to Liverpool for export that Pollaky first stumbled across the *Bermuda* in the late summer. By surreptitiously examining the shipping labels and trademarks stamped on crates delivered by train, he discovered that what he (exaggeratedly) estimated as being up to eighty light cannons and 457 crates of guns had been brought on board.

Though he did not realize it at the time, Pollaky had stumbled across the final preparations for Prioleau's *Bermuda* run to smuggle in embargoed cotton from the South for Bulloch's use. There had actually been a slight change of plan: Since moving to London, Bulloch had persuaded Prioleau to reserve part of the *Bermuda*'s hold for Huse's and Anderson's weapons. In exchange, Prioleau had insisted on charging the Confederate government an exorbitant rate for the "freight." His rationale—that to run guns meant that he had to leave some pianos and chandeliers behind in Liverpool—had not found much sympathy with the disapproving Bulloch, who thought Prioleau's luxury-smuggling sideline was putting profit before patriotism. To fill your pockets by shipping critical war materiel at a major markup was crass, but Bulloch could do nothing more about it.

In hindsight, Prioleau would have been better off leaving the guns and taking the chandeliers, for Pollaky would never otherwise have turned his attention to Liverpool, where it was easy enough for him to trace ownership of the *Bermuda* using the Customs House registration records. A cursory check revealed the name of a certain Charles Prioleau, rumoredly connected to the Confederate government. And who was seen regularly entering and exiting the Fraser Trenholm offices? One James Bulloch—the once spectral presence now emerging as the real mastermind behind Confederate operations in Britain.

IV

The detective Pollaky and the spymaster Sanford now focused all their attention on Bulloch, their new quarry. Pollaky even adopted a new code name for himself in his reports to Sanford: "Mephisto," after the demon serving the Devil in the German legend of Dr. Faust. He evidently saw Bulloch as a Faustian figure—a brilliant man too enamored of his own genius—and believed that he, Lucifer's agent, would concoct Bulloch's downfall. Though blessed with a less vivid literary imagination, Sanford agreed that Bulloch was their greatest adversary, reporting that "he is the most dangerous man the South have here and fully up to his business."

Bulloch soon became an obsession for Sanford, who started proposing ever more bizarre schemes to destroy his nemesis. At first, he wanted Bulloch to be arrested "on some charge or another and as he would have no papers, he would get no diplomatic protection & might *be sent home for examination*"—Sanford's euphemism for hard interrogation.

Then, entirely ignoring his responsibility to maintain the Black List for the Legation, Sanford suggested stationing warships just off the English coast that would swoop once any suspicious ship, like the *Bermuda*, departed. Armed marines would board and search every crevice. "If her hold is free of contraband she will be safe from us here," promised Sanford, but if not, "I will go for *taking* her no matter what her papers. We can discuss the matter with the English afterwards."

Minister Adams instantly vetoed that idea. Forcibly stopping and scuttling British-registered, British-flagged ships, even if they *were* carrying guns, would trigger a major diplomatic crisis, the very kind Seward had cautioned him against.

But desperate times called for desperate measures, Sanford believed. If Adams was too squeamish to do what was required, then he would take matters into his own hands. Sanford's preference was to pay some of Pollaky's criminal acquaintances £5,000 to blow up ships. After all, he commented wryly, "*accidents* are so common in the Channel, you know!"

Thankfully, nothing came of the proposal, and Sanford instead directed Pollaky to engage in a little light bribery of a public servant, paying the local postman £1 a week to tell him the names and addresses of Bulloch's correspondents. Every day, Pollaky reported, Bulloch received letters addressed to a "Mr. Barnett" care of Hatchett's Hotel on Piccadilly, a coaching inn two minutes' walk from Jermyn Street. Most of these were sent from Scotland and Liverpool under a variety of anodyne aliases and made-up streets.

Sanford desperately wanted to know the contents of the letters and would gladly have paid much more for the chance to steam them open, but the postman proved lamentably honest in that regard. Even Pollaky, who usually had few qualms about flouting legal niceties, had to caution Sanford. In Britain, getting tipped off about letters coming and going was one thing; interfering with the Royal Mail was a serious crime.

Surveillance was instead greatly increased, but Bulloch and his colleagues soon cottoned on to the tails. One day, Major Anderson noticed "a rough looking fellow standing across the street" disguised as a "a plain, countrified looking man." Subsequently, he saw the very same detective "accoutred in a neat suit of black clothing like a gentleman," then as a stable hand in brown shorts. Sometimes he wore a mustache and whiskers. Other times, he was clean-shaven. Anderson was amused at the man's presumption, but still, Pollaky and his men were cramping the Confederates' movements. When he was in London, Bulloch now had to leave 58 Jermyn Street at odd hours and hop into a random cab, then change to another mid-trip to throw off the detectives before he could catch a train to Liverpool.

To force them to back off, Bulloch counterattacked by having a couple of tame newspaper journalists reveal to their horrified readers "a system of political espionage and terrorism" directed at several innocent Southern gentlemen. These poor fellows had been harassed by detectives sordidly "shuffling about [in doorways]," questioning their servants, peering through their windows, tampering with their private letters, and vindictively interfering in their business affairs. These "foreign" methods, Bulloch or his amanuenses concluded with a flourish, were abhorrent "to English ideas of everything that is fair, honorable, or manly."

As a result, and much to Minister Adams's embarrassment, the British authorities suddenly began to take an interest in the Union's counterintelligence activities happening on their soil. Sanford had by now long outworn his welcome with Adams, who wanted the rogue spymaster gone. But it was at just that moment that the minister needed Sanford, and Pollaky's network of detectives, most.

As August turned to September, Bulloch had gone underground. He stopped communicating via mail and would pop up only briefly, every few weeks.

Then he did not pop up at all.

V

On September 2, shortly after the *Bermuda* had departed, Bulloch, Major Anderson, and Prioleau met at one o'clock in a tavern called The Angel on Dale Street, near the Liverpool Cotton Exchange.

It was here, at a place popular with brokers merrily getting sozzled at lunchtime, and where no one paid much mind to the trio talking quietly at a corner table and ordering only soup and a little wine, that Bulloch raised the question of how to smuggle an enormous cache of arms and ammunition out of the country, past the Union blockade.

At the time, Prioleau's *Bermuda* was two weeks away from Savannah on her proof-of-concept run, and all the other Fraser Trenholm boats were being closely watched by Pollaky's men, making it impossible to load the stockpile of weapons Huse and Anderson had since amassed. There was no time to waste. At some point, a stevedore would blab and the detectives would bribe a guard to let them into the warehouse where the arsenal was hidden.

Bulloch needed a ship urgently, one that wasn't known to the Union. He'd heard from one of his Scottish contacts that a steamer named the *Fingal* was for sale at a knockdown price. Even better, she was docked well away from prying eyes at Greenock, on the western coast of Scotland.

At 7:00 P.M., armed with an emergency loan from Prioleau that drained the coffers, Bulloch was on the train to Glasgow. Within ten days, he'd purchased the *Fingal*. He, almost literally, bought her lock, stock, and barrel. Included in the price were six dozen toddy glasses, "each heavy enough to serve for grape-shot," Bulloch joked. More usefully, the *Fingal* also came with a thirty-man crew and a captain: John Anderson.

Though he still had important business in Britain, it was clear that Bulloch would have to go on the trip. Captain Anderson was not only a little too obviously fond of his tipple, but as a local captain, he did not know the Atlantic, let alone the Confederate ports and signals. Bulloch accordingly had to clean up his affairs in London while evading the intrusive Pollaky. To keep an eye on things in Greenock in the meantime, he sent John Low.

Born in Aberdeen, orphaned young, sent to sea at sixteen, and now twenty-five, Low had only recently arrived in Britain from Savannah, where he'd been working for his uncle, Andrew Low, one of the city's wealthiest men and a longtime acquaintance of Bulloch's. Uncle Andrew had been only too pleased to suggest to Secretary Mallory that his nephew join Bulloch as his assistant. He was about to prove his worth.

VI

By early October, Pollaky was desperate to find Bulloch. Finally, he had a break. A Pollaky-paid clerk working for the arms dealer Samuel Isaac one day supplied a detailed manifest of the weapons and munitions that were to be loaded onto a Bulloch-purchased ship named the *Fingal*.

Pollaky now had the name of a previously unknown ship, and he knew that Bulloch was intending to transport Confederate arms to Dixie. Now all he had to do was find her. Find her—and he would find him. Pollaky did not have much time. The clerk had hinted that the *Fingal* was due to depart soon. But where was she?

Wherever she was, it wasn't Liverpool. Pollaky's men fanned out across the country and fruitlessly scoured the port of Hartlepool, the wharves at Stockton-on-Tees, and the harbor at Scarborough. Then on October 8, Ed Brennan, one of Pollaky's veteran snoops who'd traveled to Greenock on a hunch, came through with gold: He'd found the *Fingal*. After taking a sketch, Brennan reported that the ship was loading, though he had "seen nothing of B[ulloch] or friends."

Sanford immediately demanded that the *Fingal*'s hold be searched. Following protocol, the Legation contacted the Foreign Office to request an emergency inspection by customs officials on the grounds that the *Fingal* was suspected of carrying contraband. If they found any, they might detain the ship indefinitely or confiscate the weapons. At

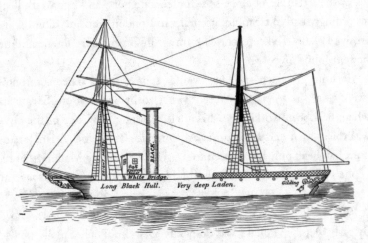

Detective Brennan's sketch of the elusive Fingal

the very least, Bulloch, Huse, and Anderson would be exposed as gun-runners to the British government.

Soon afterward in Liverpool, where he had been keeping his head down, Bulloch received an urgent telegram from Major Anderson in London: *The Union is preparing to swoop*. He went into high alert. John Low happened to be visiting from Greenock, so Bulloch transferred the title of the ship and its cargo to him, now designated a "Liverpool merchant," for the princely sum of one shilling. Immediately afterward, he bustled Low onto an express train for Scotland.

Low, being new, was completely unknown to Sanford or Pollaky. As a British-born national, he could serve admirably as a cut-out to delay a customs inspection. After arriving in Greenock, Low filed the new ownership papers with the authorities, secreted himself on board, and told Captain Anderson to get the *Fingal* ready to go.

Detective Brennan noted the sudden burst of activity in a hastily scribbled note to Pollaky that evening of October 9: The *Fingal*, oddly, had left the harbor and anchored downstream, "evidently waiting for somebody or thing as she has her fires banked up, ready for a moment['s] start." There had been no sign of Bulloch, but a check at the Customs House revealed that the *Fingal* was owned by somebody named John Low of Liverpool. Brennan had no idea who this John Low was, but it was too late to find out. At 8:00 A.M. on October 10, the *Fingal* departed. She was on the run.

Afterward, Sanford and Pollaky couldn't understand what had happened. Clearly, something had spooked "John Low," which they assumed was a Bulloch alias, into urgently taking the *Fingal* out to sea. It was almost as if he had known the Union was ready to pounce. *But Bulloch couldn't have known.* That was impossible.

They couldn't guess the simple truth: The Confederates had an inside man—Agent X—at the Foreign Office. Alerted by the Legation's request for a customs inspection of the *Fingal,* it was he who had supplied the tip that sparked Bulloch into action. This spy—a friend of Frederick Bond, the arms dealer—had been recruited just a week earlier by the avuncular Major Anderson and would continue to prove his utility. It would not be until early December, when some articles based on confidential information appeared in the *Observer* newspaper about Union espionage, that the Legation even began to suspect there was a mole. Benjamin Moran, ever shrewd, immediately pinned it on "some person either in the Foreign Office, or [Prime Minister] Lord Palmerston's confidence," but had no inkling who it could be.

For the time being, the bigger problem was that the *Fingal* had escaped, and Bulloch's whereabouts remained unknown. Brennan was adamant that he had not seen Bulloch board the ship, making it almost certain that he was still in Britain. As it turned out, Brennan had not seen Bulloch aboard the *Fingal* because he had not been on her. And neither, by the time Sanford received the detective's reports, was he even in the country.

VII

Wary of being tracked, Bulloch had stayed in Liverpool before slipping out of the city and heading to Holyhead on the northwestern tip of

Wales, where he had arranged to rendezvous with Major Anderson. The major's secondment to Britain was up and he was going home.

Lodging at the Royal Hotel, Bulloch and Anderson impatiently awaited the *Fingal*'s arrival from Greenock, as it would only be so long until the Union men figured out where they were. Anderson and Bulloch resolved that, if they caught sight of a Pollaky detective, they would kidnap him and give him a surprise trip to Dixie.

At last, at four in the morning of October 15, Bulloch was awoken by a desperate knocking at his door and "a sepulchral voice . . . like the last tremulous quivering of a thunderclap" calling his name. He found John Low dressed in a sou'wester and long canvas coat—drenched to the skin. He now spoke so fast Bulloch could barely understand him. All he caught were the words *Fingal . . . brig . . . collision . . . sunk*. Bulloch assumed he meant the *Fingal* had sunk in a collision with a brig, which gave him horrible visions of his precious ship lying at the bottom of the harbor "with the fishes swimming among the shattered Enfields, sipping the mixture of sea-water and gunpowder through their gills."

It was not quite so bad as that, but neither was the news good. Low said that Captain Anderson had gotten drunk and had run his ship into an anchored Austrian coal brig called the *Siccardi*. With the *Siccardi* sinking, her crew were making their way in boats to Holyhead, and it was a matter of hours before nettled customs officials would detain the *Fingal* to investigate. No doubt, Sanford's people would be there soon afterward. If Bulloch wanted to save his ship, they had to leave right *now*.

Bulloch roused Major Anderson and scrawled a note to Prioleau asking him to settle any claims with the *Siccardi*'s owners as quietly as possible. When they clambered aboard the *Fingal*, however, they found a particularly early-rising customs officer already there taking notes.

Thinking fast, Bulloch told the officer that he needed to move the ship into the inner harbor to avoid another accident. Would he be so kind as to cast off his own boat, roped below, and meet them there? Once the poor man thanked them for their thoughtfulness and pulled away, the *Fingal* raised her sails, cracked on steam, and raced out to sea.

VIII

The *Fingal* Affair led to a crisis right at the top of Union intelligence in London. Since the moment she had disappeared, Sanford's card was marked. Benjamin Moran was particularly pleased that the "bouncing, ill-mannered Yankee" was finally, he thought, about to have his comeuppance. His "system of espionage" had been "both useless and injurious, without being in any way creditable."

On November 2, as Moran rubbed his hands with glee, Minister Adams summoned Sanford to dress him down for the serial failures that had led to Bulloch's escape. Sanford, startled at the outburst, promised that he would from now on "confine himself to observation of shipping movements" via the Black List and played, uncharacteristically, meek. According to Adams, "this shallow and imprudent man . . . bore my remonstrance with a good deal of equanimity, and left apparently very cordial. But I imagine he will never forgive me."

He was right about that. Sanford was not going down without a fight, and within hours of leaving Adams's office he had embarked on a deep-black operation to show Adams who was the *real* chief of intelligence.

In his time, Sanford had made a lot of strange friends in London. He seemed to collect them, these kindred souls with a predilection for the dark arts. Chief among them were Edwin Eastman, a thirty-year-old, six-foot-tall, robustly built New England merchant captain, who, like Sanford, preferred to take action and maybe untruthfully answer a few questions later. Then there was George Francis Train, a fervent Unionist raising funds to build a tram system in London, and a man widely regarded as half lunatic, half genius. He agreed with Sanford that "war between the U.S. and England was evident and the sooner the better," so why not chivvy along the inevitable by creating a crisis? Also numbered among Sanford's cronies was "Captain de Rohan," a pseudonym for William Dahlgren, an American mercenary-adventurer who had served in the Turkish, Argentinian, and Chilean navies. Most recently, he had worked with Sanford running guns to Garibaldi, the Italian liberator. (Sanford had fingers in a lot of pies.)

Together, this quartet conceived a breathtakingly audacious, some might say mad, scheme to storm a Fraser Trenholm–owned steamer named the *Gladiator*, believed to be carrying some 22,000 Enfield rifles purchased by Caleb Huse. She was docked in the Thames and soon due to leave.

The plan was for Eastman and perhaps Rohan to get themselves hired as crew, then for Sanford to bribe the *Gladiator*'s pilot to run the ship aground on a mud bank, at which point Eastman and Rohan would take the officers prisoner as Sanford and Train persuaded Captain John Marchand—short, tubby, good-natured—of USS *James Adger*, currently docked at Southampton taking on coal, to race up the Thames, capture the contraband, and then head out to sea like a Barbary pirate before the British could react.

There was no chance of success, of course. For one thing, notwithstanding Sanford's hand-waving assurances, Captain Marchand was skeptical that it was legal to seize a British-owned vessel in British waters literally within sight of the British Parliament, and he went to see Adams on November 7 to confirm that the mission had his approval. The minister, according to an understated Marchand, "emphatically said no," and seemed surprised to hear that Sanford had repeatedly told the captain that he was fine with it.

The *Gladiator* eventually left, unmolested, on November 10. Sanford's fate was sealed two days later, when the Legation received a letter from Lord Palmerston, the prime minister, politely summoning Adams to visit him at home after lunch. When Adams appeared at Cambridge House at 94 Piccadilly, where, it was said, Palmerston liked to cut and shuffle the cards to play the game of State, his host casually mentioned that a drunken Captain Marchand had been overheard at Morley's Hotel blabbering about the *Gladiator* business.

It would be most impolitic, Palmerston smoothly advised as they sipped tea, for the Americans to ever attack a ship within Britain's hospitable waters, though *of course* the minister could not have known anything of these nefarious plans. Adams, understanding the veiled menace behind Palmerston's words, promised that the United States would always strive to avoid "opening questions" with Britain.

Adams left Cambridge House a shaken man. Sanford had come close to implicating him in an illegal covert operation that would have caused a major diplomatic, probably military, crisis. Within hours, the Black Crow was told to pack his bags. Pollaky, too, was unceremoniously released from his duties.

With their exit, there was no Union intelligence apparatus operating in the United Kingdom, the most important country on the planet, the very navel of the world. Bulloch, almost single-handedly, had rendered the North deaf and blind.

IX

At one thirty in the morning on November 12, 1861—the same day that Palmerston had asked Adams to Cambridge House—the *Fingal* lay about twenty miles off the Georgia coast. The night was clear—not ideal, considering the U.S. Navy was on the prowl. Thankfully, a murky fog was rolling in. As it enshrouded the *Fingal,* her crew felt the dew slowly drenching their clothing, leaving the deck looking as if it had just been swabbed. The fog was so thick a man could barely see another just a few yards away. They couldn't have asked for better weather.

The *Fingal* had to run silent and dark on her approach into the Confederate port of Savannah. The engines were set to dead slow, and every light, aside from a small covered one illuminating the compass, was doused. All were banned from talking, or even whispering, as the *Fingal* invisibly drifted past any wandering sentinels enforcing the blockade. At the first sign of daybreak, as the fog began to burn off, the *Fingal* would roar her engines and drive relentlessly toward her destination.

When tensions were at fever pitch, in that dangerous dawn as the first rosy-fingered rays of sun appeared, a "shrill prolonged quavering shriek" suddenly tore the sky. Every man jack on board jumped out of his skin at the unearthly sound, which could have been heard by any blockader within a five-mile radius.

Frantically searching the ship, they discovered the culprit hiding in the hen coop. One sailor grabbed an unhappy fowl and wrung its neck. But it was the wrong one, and the chanticleer crowed defiantly again amid the now agitated hennery. The man took another guess, but this time the rooster mounted a daring escape and had to be chased around the deck before meeting his doom.

There was again a profound stillness, despite everyone's nerves a-jangling at the prospect of enemy shot or shell ripping from out of nowhere to send red-hot metal fragments or lethal shards of timber into their bodies. But none came.

Dawn broke. Bulloch clambered to the crow's nest and saw the bushy tops of the tall pine trees first emerge. Then came their trunks, and finally the low sandy beach with a gentle surf just creaming its edge. Bulloch ordered the engines fired up and the Confederate colors raised as the *Fingal* began her dash into the Savannah River. Bulloch anchored at four that afternoon to the kind of wild acclaim once reserved for triumphant Caesar returning to Rome.

And with good reason. Bulloch had come home with an arsenal of 14,000 new Enfield rifles, 1 million cartridges, enough percussion caps to make 2 million more, 3,000 cavalry sabers, 500 revolvers, 4 cannons, 8,000 artillery shells, and 400 barrels of precious gunpowder. It was the largest haul ever brought into the Confederacy. The Enfields alone were sufficient to arm between ten and fifteen regiments, while the sabers could equip an entire cavalry brigade.

Back in Britain, the Union men had to deal with the dire fallout from Bulloch's *Fingal* escapade. Despite his being kept under close surveillance, like some Houdini shaking off a straitjacket before an audience, Bulloch had somehow slithered free with a mother lode of weaponry smuggled aboard a ship he'd purchased with no one noticing. He had pulled off a near miraculous trick, leaving his audience not only stunned but utterly humiliated.

It was time for a shake-up or else risk losing the war on the waters. A week later, Thomas Dudley, innocent of the drama and the stakes, stepped off a steamship in Liverpool.

FOUR

The Crowning City

I

O nce away from the horrors of the Liverpool waterfront, Thomas Dudley put his family up at Mrs. Blodgett's respectable boarding-house at 153 Duke Street. He then took a ten-minute walk to the United States consulate, a three-story, smoke-stained building at 51 Paradise Street with a giant four-hundred-pound gilded eagle surmounting its door.

Paradise Street was a busy commercial thoroughfare near the docks, neither salubrious nor sketchy. The consulate's current neighbors included tobacconists, hatters, tailors, and boot makers, with other merchants catering to maritimers (victuallers, an immigration agency, a ship's-store dealer, a tallow chandler), as well as a busy pawnbroker and the usual bordellos.

The eagle was certainly impressive, but nothing else at the consulate could be described as such. It comprised a few spartan rooms, the consul's own office being a grimy space barely five paces from end to end, whose soot-fudged, cobwebbed windows admitted little sunlight. It was always cold and damp, and the noise from the nearby docks was incessant.

Decorating its walls were a large, outdated map of the (once–) United States and some cheap prints of America's naval victories in the War of 1812, while a bust of Andrew Jackson, ferociously frowning at any Englishman daring to cross the threshold, presided over one of several creaky wooden bookcases containing digests of the revenue laws, manuals of commercial regulations, and shelves of old, unread congressional reports.

In Dudley's battered desk, a drawer held the tools of his trade: the official seal, a passport stamp, a press to make letter copies, and a greasy, black-leather-bound copy of the New Testament for administering oaths to, as a previous occupant put it, the parade of perjurers, desperadoes, imposters, vagabonds, jailbirds, cheats, and a few reasonably honest men who needed something from Washington's official representative.

It was a fittingly utilitarian arsenal for one such as Thomas Dudley. For him, there could be nothing ornamental, nothing superfluous, to distract him from executing his chosen task. Unlike Bulloch, with his designedly aristocratic style—all effortless superiority, relaxed charm, and worldly detachment—Dudley lacked any discernible sense of humor, and social ease was not one of his virtues. His Quaker rectitude, stiff-necked temperance, and remorseless work ethic would in time make him a figure of fun among his better-bred superiors in Washington and London. They would condescendingly remark upon or sneer at his middle-class "nervousness"—that sense of constant urgency, those wearisome demands for immediate action—yet even they would come to acknowledge his competence and dedication. Indeed, to those who worked with him, like Benjamin Moran, Dudley was an entirely admirable figure. When Dudley first turned up at the Legation, for instance, Moran—a man who dismissed every other American consul in Europe as stupid, inept, or, usually, both—was pleasantly surprised. This new "modest, refined, and able" consul, he wrote, was "as intelligent as he looks[,] talk[s] with great force, [and is] a strenuous patriot."

Unsurprisingly, given his humble background and stern character, Dudley was noticeably out of place among the well-heeled movers and shakers of Liverpool. He got his first taste of the locals a couple of days after arriving, when a twenty-strong delegation from the American Chamber of Commerce called upon him at Mrs. Blodgett's.

Despite its name, Liverpool's American Chamber was composed not of Americans but of four dozen wealthy merchants with American trading ties. Most of the time it was concerned with mundane things like freight payments and customs fees, interspersed with bibulous banquets for honored guests, and traditionally met each incoming American consul for the usual glad-handing ceremony, but this time they were agitated.

Getting straight to business, George Melly, its president, launched into a vituperative attack on Washington's refusal to let the South secede. Lincoln's pointless war, his blockade in particular, was hurting their profits. Previous Liverpool consuls had generally been convivial go-along-to-get-along sorts, and these particular fellows had not yet understood that Dudley was cut from a different cloth. As Dudley understatedly recalled, "the thought immediately came to me that it was necessary to be very decided in my reply."

His broadside swept them off their feet. Very bluntly, Dudley told them that the war was not a romantic, moonlight-and-magnolias fight for freedom from Northern oppression by noble plantation owners but was in fact a rebellion *by* the oppressors "against liberty, for the purpose of perpetuating human slavery," who were determined "to destroy the best, purest, and freest government that the sun shines upon."

This rebellion was of a different character from any previous, he continued. Its very nature "grew out of slavery" and he would, he said, do his damnedest to ensure the South never expanded into a "slave empire."

The merchants started to huff and puff about states' rights, but Dudley bore indomitably on: "Do not deceive yourselves—the rebellion will be put down. The Government of the U.S. intends to suppress it" even if it takes "shedding the last drop of human blood and the expenditure of the last dollar in the treasury."

And with that, he bade them good day. Dudley was pleased at his handiwork, saying that "my remarks had not been what they expected and had not left a favorable impression upon them." But he'd made his point and fulfilled his duty as United States consul to Liverpool.

Afterward, from talking privately with Andrew Squarey, a well-respected solicitor serving as the Chamber's new pro-Union secretary, Dudley learned that the confrontation had been the work of a faction of Southern sympathizers, albeit a large one. If nothing else, they had been alerted that the new consul was a formidable adversary while Dudley had been made aware that Liverpool was hostile ground. A less intractable man would have trod carefully, but that really wasn't his wont.

II

Keen to get to grips with his new job, Dudley placed himself under the tutelage of Henry Wilding, a middle-aged, sickly Englishman who had uncomplainingly served as vice-consul for a decade at a pittance. Said the writer Nathaniel Hawthorne, one of Dudley's predecessors, Wilding's mixture of "English integrity" and "American intellect, quick-wittedness, and diversity of talent" would have ensured him success had he been lucky enough to have been born in the Great Republic, but as it was he was doomed by class and tradition to "wear out his life at a desk" and to count himself blessed being handed the occasional raise.

For a time, it looked as if Dudley's training would be all for naught. He had arrived at a singularly low moment in Anglo-American relations, and it was all too likely that he would be returning home in just a month or two.

On November 8, 1861, during Dudley's voyage over on the *Africa*, the steam frigate USS *San Jacinto* under Captain Charles Wilkes had intercepted a British mail packet, RMS *Trent*, carrying two Confederate diplomats, James Mason and John Slidell. They were on their way to press London and Paris to intervene on the Southern side.

Wilkes, a notorious martinet with a habit of court-martialing junior officers who disagreed with him, had termed the pair "contraband of war" and forcibly arrested them. It had not gone smoothly. In splendid fettle, Rosina, Slidell's daughter, had slapped a lieutenant's face when he "laid hands" on her father, crying, "Back, back, you [*censored*] cowardly poltroon!"

When details of the seizure were published in America on November 16, three days before Dudley stepped foot in Liverpool, Wilkes was hailed as a national hero. On the same day as Dudley's contentious meeting with the American Chamber, November 27, the *Trent* news first reached Britain. The subsequent storm at Wilkes's high-handedness, his blatant violation of neutral rights, and his tarnishing of British honor prompted nearly every newspaper to clamor for war against the Union.

Lord Palmerston, the prime minister, was particularly angry. Had he not warned the Americans about interfering with British commerce during his talk with Adams at Cambridge House on November 12, just two weeks earlier? First it was the *Gladiator*, now it was the *Trent*. The Yankees clearly needed to be put back in their place. Britain was in a position, he judged, "to inflict a severe blow upon and to read a lesson to the United States which will not soon be forgotten." Thousands of troops, to invade the North from Canada, were embarked on ships bound for Halifax and the navy prepared to bombard Washington.

All over Britain, support for the Confederacy surged. The regimental bands sending off the redcoats played "I Wish I Was in Dixie," pro-Southern posters hung in railway stations, street sellers hawked Jeff Davis badges, Dixie flags were raised outside theaters, and cabs flew Union Jack pennants entwined with the Confederate ensign. In Liverpool, members of the Cotton Exchange passed a resolution demanding "reparation" for Wilkes's insult to British honor, and if not immediately received, there must be war.

The Confederates and their friends in Britain had been ecstatic from the moment they heard Wilkes had taken the *Trent*. This was it, the great crisis that would convince Britain to unite with the South to undo the Yankees. William Yancey, a Confederate commissioner in London, knew he could count on the support of the South's many backers in Parliament to push for military intervention. There, the Union had the strong backing of just eighteen MPs compared with the Confederacy's sixty-six—plus another thirteen peers in the House of Lords.

Alas, the Confederacy's friends celebrated too soon. Russell, the foreign secretary, was much less enthusiastic for a war than Palmerston. Like

Minister Adams, he chose to "infer nothing, assume nothing, imagine nothing" from the ginned-up outrage. Crucially, just as reluctant was the ailing Prince Albert, Queen Victoria's influential husband.

When Russell sent the Queen a draft of a particularly bellicose letter from Palmerston to Secretary of State Seward, Albert, always a rock of good sense, took a pencil and edited out its more noisome parts. His view, like Russell's, was that the *Trent* was an accident, a misunderstanding, and that the Americans had to be given a chance to make things right with a graceful retreat. If Lincoln apologized and released the Confederate envoys, the problem would go away. (Russell privately told Lord Lyons, the British ambassador in Washington, that the key thing was the prisoner release; the apology could be overlooked.)

The *Europa*, carrying this new version of the dispatch, arrived in Washington on December 18. Following some tense discussions at the White House over the next fortnight, Lincoln decided that maintaining British neutrality was more important than anything else. He ordered Mason and Slidell freed while refraining from a formal apology.

British fury was assuaged by Lincoln's climb-down. News that the Lion had roared and retreated to its den was greeted with enormous relief in Washington, but Lincoln was nevertheless all too aware that war had been avoided by a whisker. It was clear that Britain had to be handled exceedingly carefully in the future to prevent a sudden, violent tilt to the South.

In this light, it's easy to see why Adams was so furious over Sanford's abortive *Gladiator* escapade. Had he been compromised, the *Trent* Affair coming to a head just weeks later would have destroyed any hope of a diplomatic solution.

Despite how much fun Sanford had had playing spy, Adams wisely understood that covert action always held the potential for fatal blowback. So the new rule, made of iron, was: For God's sake, no off-the-books adventuring, no blowing things up, no black operations.

Dudley had not the slightest inclination to break it. He was merely a modest lawyer, not some secret agent. And in any case, as 1861 rolled into 1862, there wasn't much call for clandestine work.

Bulloch, an apparently mythical figure, was long gone on the *Fingal*, assuredly never to return. His colleague Major Anderson, too, had departed, and the arms buyer Caleb Huse's wings had recently been clipped in an unexpected bonus for the Union. On November 30, at the very height of the *Trent* Affair, the government announced that exporting "arms, ammunition, and gunpowder" from the United Kingdom to either side was now prohibited. Since the South needed foreign weapons more than the North did, the ruling affected Richmond more adversely than it did Washington.

Aside from his humdrum consular responsibilities, Dudley's job, then, was only to contribute to the Legation's Black List of blockade-runners, if even there were any. Indeed, so uncommonly quiet was Liverpool that Dudley moved out of Mrs. Blodgett's and settled his family into a pleasant house at 3 Wellesley Terrace, a forty-five-minute walk to the consulate. From the looks of things, he wouldn't be putting in long hours at the office.

He couldn't have been more wrong.

III

Dudley was soon disabused of his notion that the export prohibition ended Confederate arms trafficking. If anything, Huse's purchases became *more* ambitious and his methods cleverer. In Liverpool, guns were boxed up and disguised as common household goods, then separated and stacked in any of a hundred dockside warehouses. In 1862 alone, Huse would purchase no fewer than 184,000 rifles and carbines, 127,000 pounds of gunpowder, 6 million cartridges, and more than 13 million percussion caps.

Someone had to arrange for all this to be sent to the South, and that someone was Prioleau, who also had his luxury lace-and-chandelier business to think about. To that end, Prioleau amassed a private blockade-running fleet on the most modern lines. He smartly avoided using sailing ships and plumped instead for steamers. The latter were more expensive to buy and operate, but they paid rich dividends in terms of speed and maneuverability. During 1862, Union blockaders would capture or destroy fifty-four sailing vessels owned by smugglers too miserly to upgrade but caught just four steamers.

To further improve his odds, Prioleau shifted away from direct trans-atlantic runs in favor of two-part voyages. Originally, a ship like the *Bermuda* would leave Liverpool and rush headlong for, say, Savannah. But under his new system, a large, British-flagged freighter would head from Liverpool to an intermediary port like Nassau. After docking there, the cargo would be "transshipped" by dividing it among several small, swift, Confederate-flagged dodgers for the run to the South.

For the Atlantic leg, two classes of ships were used. Dozens of sidewheel-paddle ferries, originally built to cross the Irish Sea or the English Channel, had their passenger saloons torn out to make room for cargo and their bows and decks strengthened. Cheaper and slower, but larger and sturdier, were *Fingal*-type propeller-driven "coasters."

For the dash from the Caribbean into the South, Prioleau insisted on a new, specialized sort of vessel. They had to be supremely fast and light drafted to excel in charting a course through shallow waters and un-guarded inlets. With time, they would be radically modified to eke every possible advantage in the cat-and-mouse game with the U.S. Navy.

Noisy engines were muffled by situating them lower in the hull and building the cargo holds around them for further insulation. Masts were mostly removed, any hint of ornamentation above deck was sawn off, and hulls were painted a dull gray to camouflage them. Many had their funnels raked backward to reduce their silhouette, and some of these were telescoping or hinged, meaning they could be lowered to the deck to disguise their telltale smoke. Steam was exhausted through a sub-merged pipe. As such, these upgraded steamers were difficult to spot in daylight at more than two hundred yards' distance.

It was the obsession with greater speed, however, that truly distin-guished the sleek runners from anything before. Since longer, narrower ships travel relatively faster through water than shorter, broader ones, the blockade-runners first greatly increased their length relative to their beam. Then a "turtle-back" shell built over the forward deck allowed them to drive through waves, rather than having to ride over them. Finally, engines were overpowered, the number of propellers doubled to two, and boilers specially tuned to work at higher operating pressure. So vital became the chief engineer to success that his pay was increased to ten times more than that of a regular crewman. Only the pilot and captain made more.

Armaments were minimal. The blockade-runner's objective was to sneak close to the coast, exploit the weather and the darkness of night, and then sprint for port—not to be dragged into a battle with a patrol that would, inevitably, be lost.

The blockader may have enjoyed the advantage of greater combat power, but he lacked the ability to choose the time and place of an encounter. Instead, long days and nights were filled with nervous anxiety, incessant watchfulness, and boredom, interrupted occasionally by a few minutes of excitement if a runner was spotted.

A blockade-runner's chances hinged on seeing the blockader first. It was common practice for the lookout man in the crow's nest to be given a bonus of a dollar for every ship he sighted. But if it was seen from the deck before he called down, he was fined five. In that instance, the captain would order the stern turned to the blockader and the engines revved to maximum until the predator vanished, hopefully, below the horizon.

If it didn't vanish, then the chase was on. Typically, the patrol would fire a flare in the direction of its quarry to signal others to comb the area. In reply, enterprising runner captains shot their stock of flares in several directions, sending pursuers on wild-goose chases.

After that came the most pulse-pounding stage. "Hunting, pig-sticking, steeple-chasing, big-game shooting, polo—I have done a little of each," boasted the veteran Thomas Taylor, and "all have their thrilling moments, but none can approach 'running a blockade.'" After days of little sleep and having threaded their way through the swarm of cruisers, they had to hit the mouth of a river only half a mile wide in total darkness.

Occasionally, a Union captain would lurk as close offshore as he safely could, about two hundred yards, in order to surprise a runner with a broadside. To avoid capture, the runner captain then had no other choice but to put on speed and drive directly at the attacker to present the opponent with a smaller target. Sometimes, the ships came so close their jousting commanders would trade insults with each other in a manner similar to "two penny steamboat captains on the Thames," recalled one sailor. Once the runner passed the cruiser, an annoyed fusillade of short-range, man-maiming grape and canister would follow in her trail, forcing the crew to fall flat on their stomachs to avoid the whizzing metal fragments.

From there, the runner would race coastward, leaving the cruiser in her wake. Soon afterward, the blockader would have to give up the pursuit, wary of running aground on a bar or reef. In any case, it was almost impossible to hear a modified engine over the pounding of the surf or to see a ship against the backdrop of darkened hills.

That still left the small gunboats stationed nearby to give it their best. Half a dozen would rush out, angrily firing their guns as dawn broke. They had only a minute or two to hit the runner before the coastal forts guarding the port opened up with their warning shots—the symphony of shore guns frightening off insolent Union gunboats was music to every blockade-runner's ears.

It meant they had made it.

IV

Prioleau chose Nassau, the only town on the barren island of New Providence, as his base of operations. Until recently, said a blockade-runner after the war, Nassau had been "the obscurest of colonial capitals," whose affairs occupied only a "dusty pigeon-hole somewhere in the Colonial Office." Around 3,500 people were resident, a large number, like the bishop and the chief justice, idling away the time before they could return to the Mother Country. The settlement was so boring that even the pirates who had once yo-ho-hoed their way through the Caribbean had settled down and turned sponge fisher and turtle hunter.

But for Prioleau's purposes, Nassau was ideal: Located as it was about 550 miles from Savannah, Charleston, and Wilmington, a fast runner could get to the Confederacy in less than three days. Before the war, the port had played host to just a handful of vessels a year, but now Prioleau stationed Fraser Trenholm's growing runner fleet there.

With their arrival, Nassau boomed as an offshore haven. The town's fine harbor, once almost deserted, was ringed with wharves, quays, and warehouses crammed full of merchandise, legal and illegal. One newspaperman noticed that "every available place large enough to hold half a dozen bales [of cotton] is crammed full and running over. It is piled up six and eight bales deep on all the wharves, vacant lots, and even on some of the lawns."

In Nassau, rhapsodized Thomas Taylor of his time there, "money flowed like water, men lived for the day and never thought of the morrow, and in that small place was accumulated a mixture of mankind seldom seen before." Serving as a kind of neutral ground, a wartime Switzerland, every night in Nassau there were parties where Confederate officers traded gossip with visiting Union diplomats, blockade-running captains chatted amicably with their Northern antagonists, "calculating, far-seeing" financiers made cotton deals, sharpers searched for suckers, and "Yankee spies" posing as journalists picked up excellent color copy. Everywhere, said one captain, "the almighty dollar was spent as freely as the humble cent had been before this golden era in the annals of Nassau."

There were also a number of rackety, retired Royal Navy captains eager to make some cash by trading their seamanship skills for a slice of the profits from running the blockade. Chortled the remarkable adventurer Augustus Charles Hobart-Hampden—an earl's son who assumed the alias "Captain Roberts" before later becoming "Hobart Pasha," grand admiral of the imperial Ottoman fleet—he once earned 1,100 percent on a cargo of women's corsets.

Fraser Trenholm enjoyed first-mover status and dominated the market, but any number of hopefuls alike tried their luck at the blockade-running business. In short order, there were five companies based in Charleston alone, for instance. Of these, William Bee's Importing & Exporting Company was the most successful. Bee specialized in things like "fancy neckties," "spring skirts," and "pearl shirt buttons" that commanded impressive markups when auctioned. (Those skirts cost eighty-three cents each in Britain and sold in Charleston for six dollars.) For special items, like General P. G. T. Beauregard's order of fine Bordeaux, figs, and French cheese, which sustained him during this hard war, Bee named his own price. On just two runs, Bee made a colossal profit of $200,000, his operation eventually expanding to six ships.

As Bee's windfall indicates, there was a lot of money to be made importing enjoyable fripperies—much more than for vital war materiel. Captain Steele of the *Banshee*, for instance, noted that he earned £50 per ton from shipping much-needed firearms into Wilmington for the army, but from tobacco, £70—and for the same risk.

This discrepancy lay at the heart of the South's logistical problems—its yawning gap between weapon imports and military requirements—but the *Banshee*'s owners didn't care. Over the subsequent eight voyages, even as Southern soldiers hoarded their cartridges and went without shoes, Steele would earn his bosses a 700 percent return on their investment.

V

On their return trips, blockade-runners brought cotton to Liverpool. Fraser Trenholm, of course, had a government permit to import limited amounts (in contravention of the embargo) to finance Bulloch's naval mission. But it was nowhere near sufficient for all the new demands on Prioleau's purse. In 1862, seven-eighths of the cotton shipped to Liverpool may have belonged to Fraser Trenholm, but that was seven-eighths of a pittance. Even after Prioleau finally received a portion of what he needed from the treasury ($1,261,600 in gold), much of it was earmarked to clear Huse's enormous, exorbitant-interest debts (the modern equivalent of about $140 million) for his arms purchases.

To pay the bills and maintain liquidity, Prioleau was forced to rely ever more heavily on issuing cotton certificates to creditors. These certificates were essentially Fraser Trenholm bonds given to contractors and shipbuilders in lieu of cash and were redeemable for a given quantity of the South's stockpiled cotton at a temptingly low price when the war was over. In exchange for their forbearance, certificate holders would later be able to sell the white gold in Liverpool for a large profit.

This kind of financing on the never-never and its snowballing debt would soon weigh down Prioleau's once balanced books. Just as alarmingly, where the devil was Bulloch? Their cotton-for-ships scheme was only supposed to have been a temporary measure to raise some short-term money, yet it was beginning to look like he'd been left holding the bag.

Worse yet, this new American consul was getting in the way.

FIVE

A River in Sicily

I

Dudley could make neither heads nor tails of Liverpool. Blessed with their distinctive Scouse accents, named after a cheap stew eaten by sailors, and enriched with Irish, Scottish, and Welsh dialects, the locals were difficult to understand for a New Jersey man. The colloquialisms and sweary slang didn't help, either.

Their language may have been the same as Dudley's, but the things they spoke of—shipbuilding techniques, cotton financing, maritime law (and lore), the port's ancient customs—were utterly alien. He had to learn how Liverpool worked.

Until he did, tasks that should have been simple were inordinately hard. For instance, compiling the Black List was, at least according to the instructions, a straightforward matter: Go to the Customs House, check the registry of owners, record the ships' names and cargo, note their departure and destination, and report the information to London for distribution to the blockading squadrons.

Except that the wily Prioleau operated no vessels under his own name, ships' names were often changed, distinguishing features commonly removed, and false destinations and fake manifests always filed. A Fraser Trenholm clerk, one Richard Bushby, was clearly a coconspirator—he apparently "owned" several Prioleau ships—but it was not illegal for a clerk to maintain a small fleet, even if it was highly improbable.

Understandably, given the tangled web Prioleau had woven, Dudley was hopelessly confused. For instance, a recently arrived steamer called the *Prince Albert* was "under the control of a Mr. Klingender," he reported a couple of weeks after starting work in December 1861. She was rumored to be heading out to Savannah, but the ship had just been sold to a Spanish company and "I cannot find anyone who knows who the purchasers really are." So was the *Prince Albert* a blockade-runner or a legitimate merchant ship? (Only much later did Dudley discover the answer: She was a runner, Melchior Klingender was a Fraser Trenholm front man claiming to be based in Gibraltar, and the Spanish owners didn't exist.)

With only isolated, misleading, and random clues to go on, Dudley was forced to guess at the enemy's designs but made little headway. When someone, probably an ally in the American Chamber of Commerce like Squarey, told him that he had overheard Prioleau saying "that he had made a fortune by the *Bermuda* venture, and should send her again," that was useful but not actionable information. Dudley had to know where the *Bermuda* was, for a start.

He often had only the wispiest of evidence to hand. When Dudley spotted a suitcase being taken on board the *Consul* that was stamped "E.C.A.," he had a hunch (correct) that it belonged to Major Edward Clifford Anderson, who had left with Bulloch months earlier in the *Fingal*. Probable, then, that the *Consul* was going to run the blockade, but when and where and with what aboard remained a mystery.

But worst of all, Dudley was a Daniel alone in the lions' den amid his enemies. Liverpool was, Dudley despondently wrote, crammed with Southern partisans and "the great mass of the residents of the place is and has been against the North." A large number of firms "are openly engaged in aiding the South in sending arms while many others [are] sympathetic and aid them secretly."

Blockade-runner owners believed themselves so untouchable they publicly touted their services. One advertisement in the *Liverpool Journal of Commerce* publicized the *R.D. Shepherd* under Captain Gale as being "well known for the delivery of her cargoes in good order" to New Orleans. Fraser Trenholm, of course, led the charge. Nearly every consular dispatch Dudley sent to Adams and Seward mentioned the firm.

Dudley needed help. The consulate was staffed only by himself, Wilding the deputy, two clerks, and a couple of messengers. Dudley, who also had to carry out regular consular activities, could not watch ships all day by himself. Wilding was not cut out for the work, and the others were backroom employees, not spies.

Wilding advised Dudley to hire Matthew Maguire, a private detective with whom he had earlier worked. The consul was initially hesitant. People like Maguire, the upright Quaker lawyer informed Seward, "are not as a general thing very estimable men, but are the only persons we can get to engage in this business[—]not a very pleasant one."

Given Dudley's sniffiness, their first meeting might have been an awkward one, but they soon rubbed along. Maguire, a memorable figure with a shock of red hair and blooming pork-chop sideburns, was forty-six years old, a hardened drinker, and Dublin born. After emigrating in the 1830s or '40s, he'd joined the police in Hull in northeast England, rising to superintendent before moving to Liverpool. He and Dudley shared a common experience in that Maguire had once survived a terrible accident at sea in similar circumstances to the consul's in Philadelphia.

In 1853, a ferry, the *Queen Victoria*, wrecked upon the rocks during a snowstorm. Maguire had been standing at the bow when the collision happened and survived by leaping into the freezing water, the shrieks and lamentations of those who chose to stay behind ringing in his ears. More than half of the 112 aboard perished. Maguire was lucky that some crewmen helped him clamber up the slippery crags.

After several years with the Liverpool detective force, Maguire had left to set up shop as an investigator (*Private Enquiry and Absconding Debtors Office*, announced his letterhead on genteel lavender paper) in a poky little room at 6 Dorans Lane, five minutes' walk from the consulate. Dorans Lane, which was named after an old slave-trading family, was really nothing more than an alley. But it was a busy one, nevertheless.

Maguire's neighbors included an estate agent, a watchmaker, a book-keeper, a tea and coffee dealer, the inevitable pub, and a few merchants and cotton brokers. (A discreet brothel, too, no doubt.)

He'd since made something of a name for himself. It was Maguire, for instance, who had trailed a bankrupt fugitive, the perfectly Dickensian-named Jeremiah Winks, all the way to Australia and hauled him back to face justice. His bread and butter, though, were the little, everyday cases: dragging a reluctant Mrs. Glen "through the streets" to a lawyer's office to extract an affidavit in a complex case of a contested will, or being hired by an embittered ex-partner to entrap Thomas Cope, tobacconist, by buying a box of fraudulent Havana cigars from him.

As an ex-copper, Maguire knew this dark city—its streets and taverns, its wharves and yards, its lingo and customs, its scams and scandals, and, most important, where the bodies were buried and who had buried them. Dudley, an uncertain and quivering Dante, now had a Virgil to guide him through the depths of the Inferno.

II

The spectacular squalor of the dockside slums garnered all the attention, of course, but the first thing you really needed to know about Liverpool, Maguire informed Dudley, was that it had long been ruled by "the Families" in a manner resembling the doges and magnificos of Renaissance Venice.

Many of the great cotton lords were literally descended from the slaving merchants who had built Liverpool's wealth. Beginning in 1700, when the perversely named *Blessing* embarked from Liverpool to Guinea on the first slave voyage, over three-quarters of the roughly 11,000 British ships that transported some three million slaves to America during the eighteenth century were fitted out on Merseyside. It all came to an end in July 1807, when *Kitty's Amelia,* the last of the Liverpool slavers, departed for Africa just after Parliament abolished the trade within the Empire.

With their profits cut off, some former slavers went into tobacco, rum, and sugar. Many others merely pivoted to cotton, effectively doing business with the same Southerners as before, just trading white gold rather than the humans harvesting it. The connections between Liverpool and the Confederacy, then, were not newly forged but passed down generationally.

The shipbuilding dynasties formed a haughty class of their own. Chief among them was Laird Brothers, a family partnership that had made a fortune as iron ships replaced wooden ones, and as sailing vessels evolved into steamers.

The first of his name to come to Liverpool had been thirty-year-old William Laird, sent there in 1810 to represent his father's Scottish rope-making business, but who eventually expanded into shipbuilding. Liverpool proper was too expensive and crowded to open a new yard, so Laird looked across the Mersey and noticed Birkenhead, then a hamlet of some fifty people living near the ruins of a medieval Benedictine priory. There was room there in abundance, thought Laird farsightedly, and in 1824 he started buying land, digging sewers, and laying down gas lines. Laird was just the first shipbuilder to see the future: By 1861, Birkenhead, whose population now stood at 36,000, would form a friendly rival to Liverpool, a ten-minute ferry ride away.

In 1828, Laird's son, John, joined the firm, which soon after completed its first shipbuilding contract—for a sixty-foot-long, fifty-ton lighter named the *Wye*. Much of the reason for the company's rapid success was that William had entered the business late in life and thus had no sentimental attachment to the ancient, handcrafted methods by which artisans used rules of thumb and rock of eye to build ships.

Lairds (as the company was popularly known) instead specialized in modern steamships, designed on scientifically sound hydrodynamic principles with powerful engines, watertight bulkheads, and efficient propellers. In fact, of the fifty-five vessels Lairds built between 1833 and 1844, just three were sailing ships. They were also masters of iron. In 1850, when 95 percent of Britain's ships were still made of wood, four out of five of Lairds' were of metal.

That feat alone made Lairds the most technologically advanced shipbuilder in the world. When Jules Verne, the author of *Twenty Thousand*

Lairds shipyard, capital of an iron kingdom

Leagues Under the Sea, wanted Captain Nemo of the *Nautilus* to impress Professor Aronnax, who else could he choose but Lairds as the company that had supplied the fantastical submarine's iron plating?

In 1857, his founder-father having died, John Laird opened the "New Yard" with a shore frontage of 650 feet, and which included boiler- and engine-works to keep everything in-house. Until then, that particular spot had been a bucolic idyll where birds chirped and woodland creatures frolicked amidst the trees. After the forest was razed, only the clangor of iron striking iron, the roar of giant furnaces, and the metallic din of red-hot riveting could be heard, resounding from Lairds' dark Satanic Mill.

The workforce had, by that time, risen to two thousand, soon to rise to three, and John's sons (William, John Jr., and Henry) had joined the company. They were being trained to take over, for John Sr. had recently retired to become Member of Parliament for Birkenhead, where his was among the most prominent of pro-Confederate voices.

The new-generation triumvirate intended to make a lot of money off the Civil War, and each had his own fiefdom. William ran the technical and manufacturing operations. He seemed to have kept to himself, his sole concern being to get things done. John Jr. was the business boss of the firm, a ruthless opportunist widely considered to be a cross between Mr. Gradgrind and Ebenezer Scrooge, with a little Wackford Squeers thrown in. And Henry, the most creative, was in charge of the drawing and design department.

The gated and guarded precincts of the Lairds yard were off-limits, but if one wanted to observe Liverpool's powers that be in their native habitat Maguire might have taken Dudley on a stroll to Abercromby Square, a twenty-odd-minute walk from the consulate.

The square was Liverpool's most expensive and fashionable address. Surrounding its verdant manicured lawn and tended flower beds, bisected by a stone path, were elegant, three-story, Georgian-style houses. It formed the Confederate nexus of Liverpool's cotton, shipbuilding, blockade-running, political, and trade power.

Over the course of the war, it would be home to the likes of Prioleau at the grandest mansion of all, No. 19; James Spence (the head of the Southern Independence Association, whose members were almost interchangeable with those of the American Chamber of Commerce) at No. 10; Thomas Hunter Holderness (who designed blockade-runners) next door; Elias Arnaud (the port's former collector of customs, who could mysteriously afford to live there) at No. 13; Robert Preston (chairman of Fawcett Preston, engine builders and arms makers for the Confederacy); and Charles Mozley (whose family had made a packet in the slave trade and who served as Liverpool's mayor).

To Dudley, Abercromby Square represented everything he detested. Leading their cosseted existences and profiteering through a vile war, these vipers would be unearthed and destroyed, he vowed.

III

Under Maguire's tutelage, and increasingly familiar with Liverpool's ins and outs, Dudley rapidly improved his intelligence skills. From January 1862, his reports became much more precise when it came to describing known and suspected runners. Before, Dudley had said only that a "ship" was in port—not much use—but thanks to Maguire's sharp observations, blockading captains could now keep a sharp lookout for, say, the *Ella,* which had a "black hull, figure of a female on stern painted in color, lower masts and yards black, top masts bright."

Maguire's morning routine was to scour two Liverpool trade papers, the *Shipping Telegraph* and the *Journal of Commerce,* which listed vessels' comings and goings and carried advertisements for scheduled blockade runs. Thus armed, he would head to the waterside and roam from dock to dock searching for suspicious ships arriving from or bound for the Caribbean, Nassau in particular. If any seemed especially promising, he would commission Mr. Bullen, a "photographist from Castle Street," to take a surreptitious snap.

Maguire filled in blanks by working human sources for exploitable intelligence. The detective was an assiduous collector of dockside gossip and an active briber of sailors, a talkative lot once you got a few drinks inside them. The invoices for "Treating Money" he submitted to Dudley

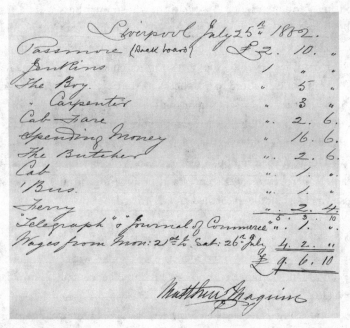

One of Maguire's expense reports, noting some informants

told the story: Among many others, he paid a rigger, a butcher, a ship's carpenter, two boatmen, and a cabin boy for information.

Given the nature of the intelligence trade, a portion of what Maguire's informants passed on was wishfully speculative or drunkenly embroidered, but when panning for gold there is always sediment and sludge to sift. It was by such methods, for instance, that Maguire learned that Edwin Haigh, an otherwise respectable cotton broker, was nowadays being paid by Prioleau to claim that he owned the *Bermuda*. That small grain turned into a large nugget when Maguire paid one Michael Brady (or Brody), a newly signed cook on the *Bermuda,* to tell him what was being loaded into her hold. The informant, perhaps a former artillerist as he seemed to know his guns, reported there were 12 field pieces, 19 cases of small arms, "100 cases of 5.5-inch shells, 100 cases of 3-inch shells, 325 cases 7.5-inch shells, three rifled cannon 7.5-inch bore, two rifled cannon 5.5-inch bore, two rifled cannon three inch bore, and three breech loading rifled cannon."

Things got so busy, intelligence-wise, that in January 1862 Dudley transferred his personal office from the Paradise Street consulate to the Tower Building, a large, long, four-story Italianate block constructed a few years earlier on Water Street across from the busy Prince's and George's Docks. Partly motivated by Dudley's fear that his British hosts might not take kindly to his conducting of espionage from a diplomatic consulate address, at the Tower Building Dudley could watch ships come and go. More important, *sources* could also come and go— discreetly. It was easy for the Confederates to place a man to spy on the Paradise Street entrance, but with the Tower Building's dozens of marine, legal, and commercial offices, an observer would never know who was visiting whom there.

IV

That same month, on January 24, to be exact, Dudley made the first mention in his correspondence of a ship named the *Oritis*. According to Maguire, she was almost finished, "built of iron and is 700 tons," and had recently emerged from the William C. Miller & Sons shipyard with her engines installed by Fawcett Preston, a pro-Confederate manufacturer reputed to have made the gun that fired the first shot at Fort Sumter.

The most curious thing, though, was that she didn't look like a typical blockade-runner. With "eight port holes for guns on each side," the *Oritis* had the lines and aspect of a "gun boat," one built for lethality rather than speed. Said Dudley, "she is a very complete and perfect vessel, no pains or expense having been spared in her construction and will when fully armed and equipped . . . be a formidable and dangerous craft."

Maybe it was nothing, Dudley cautioned. After all, "she is reported [as being] for the Italian Government." That did not seem outlandish: Italy had been unified the year before, so it made sense that its government might have wanted to build up a national navy. And the *Oritis*—Dudley soon corrected the name to *Oreto*—was named after a river in Sicily.

Still, there was something off about the *Oreto*. That Fawcett Preston was involved "make[s] me suspicious, and cause[s] me to believe she is intended for the South."

Dudley tried to delve deeper into this mysterious ship but got only so far. After paying a visit to the Italian consul in Liverpool, who informed him "that he knows nothing about it, has no knowledge whatever of any vessels being built for his government," little more could be ascertained owing to heightened security at the Miller yard. "There is much secrecy observed about her," reported Dudley, "and I have been unable to get any thing definite."

It was clear, nevertheless, that the *Oreto* was getting ready to depart. Coal was being taken on board, though there was no sign of her being equipped with armaments. The very fact that the *Oreto* was a gunboat without any guns was "of itself . . . somewhat suspicious," thought Dudley. Along with the Italian denial, it was this dog-that-didn't-bark-in-the-night omission that convinced him that the *Oreto* was for the Confederacy. "When she sails," he told Minister Adams, "it will be to burn and destroy whatever she meets with bearing the American flag."

To find out more, in mid-February Dudley managed to talk to William Miller, the owner of the shipyard that had built the hull. His, like Lairds, was a close-knit firm: Three of his children as well as his son-in-law, James Duguid, worked alongside him. Miller had done very well for himself. He'd built the *Racehorse*, a wooden paddle steamer for the Royal Navy, then four gunboats, and while his ships weren't Lairds-class cutting edge, they were good enough to have made him a leading light in Liverpool business circles.

He had no intention of helping this Yankee any more than politeness required. When Dudley asked him about the *Oreto*, Miller had his answer down pat: He knew nothing about her aside from the fact that she was owned by Fawcett Preston, who had given "him the contract and have paid him for his labor."

Dudley would have to talk to them, shrugged Miller, knowing that it would be a dead end. A consul wasn't a policeman, meaning that neither he nor Fawcett Preston were obligated to answer his questions. And even if Dudley fancied himself as one, well, in Liverpool confidentiality was sacrosanct. As John Laird himself had once put it, in the shipping trade "a builder has no right to make public the orders or instructions of his employers."

Miller may have hoped his obtuseness would dissuade Dudley from proceeding any further, but he did not know his man. Dudley kept going. If Miller and Fawcett Preston were going to be unhelpful, he would find the truth through other means. While Maguire set about digging up informants inside the firms, Dudley had a breakthrough when one William Parry visited him at the Tower Building.

Parry introduced himself as the *Oreto*'s pilot, the man charged with taking the ship out of the Mersey before her captain took over. Soon code-named "Federal" by Dudley, he was a Union sympathizer, a rare thing indeed in Liverpool. Most of Dudley's very few allies were radicals, often religiously Nonconformist with abolitionist ideas, and while they were generally middle class, there was also a modest community of textile workers and cotton-mill employees. Among the port's maritimers, though, pro-Unionism was vanishingly small, and its few supporters kept their views to themselves. Parry, then, was a very valuable source.

It was Federal who told Dudley that "there is no doubt of [the *Oreto*] being for the Confed. G'mt" and that she was to be armed with eight rifled cannons and two swiveling guns. But his biggest bombshell was identifying her real owner. He'd even brought proof: a note signed by Prioleau himself confirming that, as Dudley said, "the money up to this time that has been paid to Fawcett Preston & Co. on account of her construction has been advanced by Fraser Trenholm & Co."

On February 17, Dudley excitedly related to Adams the smoking-gun evidence that Federal had produced. Adams agreed that the *Oreto* was a clandestine Confederate ship and sent a formal letter stating such to Russell at the Foreign Office the next day. The day after that, February 19, Russell asked the treasury, which oversaw customs, to investigate the matter.

Two days later, Samuel Price Edwards, the collector of customs in Liverpool, dispatched an inspector for a surprise search of the *Oreto*. All he found was that "she was a splendid steamer . . . pierced for guns, but has not any on board . . . Coals and ballast are all that the holds contain." Edwards poured cold water on any idea that the *Oreto* was a Southern ship.

On March 4, another of Edwards's men, a customs officer named Mr. Mudie, boarded the *Oreto* for a routine departure check. Again, the *Oreto* came up completely clean. Mudie reported that "she had no gunpowder, nor even a signal gun." The *Oreto*'s cargo consisted only of rum, brandy, gin, wine, tea, coffee, tobacco, and twelve boxes of raisins, among other sundries. All her paperwork, too, was in order. Only the day before, in fact, her ownership had been transferred to John Henry Thomas, a Liverpool merchant. He was born of British parents in Palermo, it was said, and managed the local branch of a Sicily-based firm, Thomas Brothers.

For all intents and purposes, then, the *Oreto* was exactly what she purported to be: a merchant vessel, albeit with a few unused gunports,

owned by an upstanding Palermo firm represented by John Henry
Thomas of this parish. Collector Edwards immediately cleared her to
leave. When he heard the news, Dudley was angrily astonished that
anyone could be so naive.

V

The problem, however, was more of a legal one than anything else.
Until then only dimly aware of its existence, Dudley had walked smack-
bang into the Foreign Enlistment Act of 1819, an obscure law originally
passed to stop British mercenaries from volunteering their services to
native rebels fighting Spanish rule in South America. These days it was
used to dissuade Britons from enlisting in the Union or Confederate
armies in order to preserve neutrality.

Bulloch had also grappled with the act's provisions when he had first
arrived in Britain in June 1861. But he turned them to his advantage
once he cannily realized that no one, aside from him, had paid any
attention to Section Seven—which dealt with ships rather than soldiers.
Half a century earlier, it had been added as an afterthought and since
then there had never been a legal case related to it. The subject had just
never come up.

Bulloch, sitting in his office at 10 Rumford Place, had studied Section
Seven with beetle-browed intensity. It was densely written and tediously
prolix, but Bulloch had read and reread and then read again each and
every word, clause, and sentence.

And he had found a loophole you could sail a fleet through.

Section Seven stated that no person "within any part of the United
Kingdom" shall knowingly "equip, furnish, fit out, or arm" any vessel
intended to attack another foreign power friendly to Britain. At first
glance, Section Seven would seem to have torpedoed Bulloch's mission
to acquire offensive commerce raiders and ironclads at the very outset—
except that there was a missing word.

One couldn't equip, furnish, fit out, or arm a vessel as a military ship
in Britain, but Section Seven said nothing about building a civilian

ship that might later be converted to military use. The only crime lay in anyone's *knowingly* turning that merchant ship into a warship *within British jurisdiction.*

Still unsure whether he had understood the legislation accurately, Bulloch had retained Frederick Hull, a Liverpool solicitor as sleekly cunning as he was clever. He agreed with Bulloch's novel interpretation of a seemingly bulletproof law.

So long as he refrained from informing any builder as to the true "intended" purpose of a ship and did not arm her within Her Majesty's eyesight, Hull assured his client, Bulloch was free to do as he wished once the ship was on the high seas.

Thus, Bulloch could fill the hold of a different cargo vessel, like an old freighter, with legally purchased armaments like deck guns and have it rendezvous with this newly built "civilian" ship out at sea. Once there, the guns would be transferred from the freighter and installed on its civilian counterpart. And so, abracadabracally, a Confederate commerce raider would appear.

Terrific, but who was going to sail the civilian ship from Liverpool and then do the equipping? The law was very firm that no British subject could knowingly "engage, contract, or agree to go" on a ship "intended to be used for any warlike purpose" while said vessel was "within the United Kingdom . . . or [anywhere] belonging to or subject to Her Majesty."

To Bulloch, ignorance was bliss. So long as British sailors were kept in the dark until the unarmed ship was in international waters—which, despite any claims to the contrary, did not belong to Queen Victoria—then they could be hired to equip and crew a Confederate vessel. He would still have to be exceedingly careful, though. Under no circumstances could Bulloch openly recruit onshore for the Confederate Navy or ever carelessly divulge his ships' true purpose.

And so long as shipbuilders like Miller and the Lairds pleaded ignorance of any intended "warlike purpose" for their products and kept ships like the *Oreto* free of weaponry in Liverpool, then they, too, were in the clear—just as Collector Edwards had decided.

VI

Despite being given a clean bill, however, the *Oreto* did not leave. Instead, she made a series of daylong trial trips, each one sending Dudley scurrying to the docks at all hours to try to discern whether this one was the real departure. Dudley could not account for her strange behavior. "She no doubt is either waiting for her guns or some person," he reported.

There was a rumor that a "Southern Naval Officer was to come over to take command after they transfer her [to Confederate control], it is possible they are waiting for his arrival." Rumor turned into fact when the *Annie Childs*, a Fraser Trenholm blockade-runner coming from Wilmington with seven hundred bales of embargoed cotton, arrived on March 10.

On board there had been five Confederates, Dudley was informed by Maguire, who'd made friends with one of her crew. He was induced to tell Maguire that the names of four of them "are Young, Low, and Maffet or Moffet, [and a man referred to as] Eddy." Apparently, "it was talked about and understood by all on board that their object in coming was to take the command of a vessel which was being built in England for the Southern Confederacy."

And the name of the fifth man? "Bullock."

Long since written off as a threat, James Bulloch had returned to Liverpool to complete his mission. His reappearance helped clear up the mystery of who the *Oreto* was waiting for. But at the same time, Dudley understood that he had been outplayed. "They have managed this business better than any thing else they have attempted at this port," he lamented.

It only now became clear to him that "John Henry Thomas"—one of the most generic names possible—had never existed. The *Oreto*'s ostensible owner, now mysteriously vanished and untraceable, was almost certainly none other than the reliable Prioleau clerk and frontman, Mr. Bushby. It went without saying that the company "Thomas Brothers" of Palermo was equally fictitious. From the very first, it seemed to Dudley, the Confederates had been several steps ahead of him.

There was nevertheless one piece of the puzzle that Dudley couldn't fit into place: that first customs visit on February 21, just four days after the agent Federal discovered the *Oreto*'s clandestine ownership and two days after the Foreign Office requested a search. The visit was intended as a surprise, and very few people had known that it was coming. Even Dudley and Adams were unsure whether it would happen. And yet, not even the wispiest piece of evidence that the *Oreto* was for the South had turned up.

It was almost as if Prioleau had known the inspector would come calling and had swept the ship clean from stem to stern.

SIX

The First Raider

I

What had seemed to be a flawless operation to Dudley was, in fact, at least from Bulloch's vantage point, a cavalcade of close shaves and frustrations.

Bulloch had commissioned the *Oreto* in June 1861—after he had relocated to Liverpool and months before he'd departed Britain on the *Fingal*—but Sanford and Pollaky hadn't even noticed. Armed with *Gore's Directory for Liverpool,* essentially the Yellow Pages of its day, Bulloch had found seventy-two "Ship and Boat Builders" listed. Digging down, he excavated just two that were suitable for his needs: William C. Miller & Sons on the Liverpool side of the Mersey and Lairds on the Birkenhead side. While the others specialized either in small vessels or civilian ships, only Miller and Lairds had previously built warcraft for the Royal Navy.

Bulloch visited both. At Lairds, he talked to Henry Laird about what he wanted, and at Miller's he found to his delight that Mr. Miller had a scale drawing of a gunboat the Royal Navy had recently commissioned from him. It would serve admirably as a blueprint for the *Oreto*.

Bulloch, however, had some specific modifications in mind. The Royal Navy gunboat had been powered by 80-horsepower engines made by Robert Napier & Sons. Bulloch replaced those with 200-horsepower

Fawcett Prestons, which would raise the ship's speed by nearly a fifth, to thirteen knots. The *Oreto* was also longer, by some forty feet amidships, in order to double the amount of coal in her bunker, allowing greater range. To accommodate the weight of the planned pair of seven-inch rifled guns and four smoothbore 32-pounders, the floor of the hull was to be flattened for better buoyancy.

It had been Bulloch's idea to camouflage the *Oreto* by using Fawcett Preston as the cutout for Fraser Trenholm and by subcontracting the hull work to Miller & Sons for an additional layer of cover. To avoid violating the Foreign Enlistment Act, Bulloch made sure not to mention the ship's purpose and real owner, and Fawcett Preston and Miller made sure not to ask. Then, "to provide an answer in advance for any inquisitive comments or surmises," Bulloch artfully christened her *Oreto* and started a rumor "among the workpeople that she would probably be sent to a mercantile firm doing business in Palermo."

Bulloch was told the ship would be ready in mid-December 1861.

That's when things had started to go wrong. Before he left in the *Fingal* in October, Bulloch gave detailed instructions to Prioleau on how to handle the *Oreto* business in his temporary absence: who to pay, his contacts, notes on the particulars of the Foreign Enlistment Act, and so forth. Bulloch assured Prioleau that he'd be back in a few months, around the time the *Oreto* was delivered, but the blockade ended up preventing his departure. That Christmas, Bulloch and the *Fingal* were still bottled up in Savannah by five Union ships lurking offshore.

While trapped in Savannah, Bulloch used his time efficiently to recruit a few trusted men to accompany him back to Liverpool, when or if he was able to make a break for it. One was Clarence Yonge. Bulloch told Secretary Mallory that he considered the recruit to be "absolutely necessary to aid me in the large [financial] disbursements" Bulloch's task required, for the "complexity of accounts and [the] quantity of correspondence" involved with the covert naval program would take up much of his time. Yonge admirably fit the bill as an assistant bookkeeper.

Bulloch placed great stock in Yonge. Georgia born, he was twenty-nine years old and a former railway clerk. For a short time he had served aboard the *Lady Davis*, a blockade-runner, but Bulloch found him laboring in the Naval Paymaster's Office in Savannah and offered him the chance for secret service abroad. His conduct, said Bulloch, "was most exemplary," and most important, he was honest to a fault when it came to keeping the ledgers.

There was also the reliable John Low, who stayed with Bulloch after the *Fingal*. Bulloch brought him on board along with the teenage acting midshipman Edward Anderson, known as Eddy. Soon joining Bulloch's merry, if immobile, band was another young midshipman: Eugene Maffitt.

There was a pattern to Bulloch's team building. Low had already proved himself, and he was the nephew of Bulloch's old friend, the Savannah merchant Andrew Low. The Yonges and the Bullochs had deep shared roots in Georgia (their two families knew each other), and Clarence was a distant kinsman, while Eddy Anderson was his former colleague Major Anderson's son.

Eugene Maffitt, similarly, was the son of Lieutenant John Maffitt, an officer a few years older than Bulloch, but one he had known for a long time. Before resigning from the navy, Bulloch had served in the Coast Survey for a time, reporting to Maffitt, who later enjoyed great success in running down slavers in the West Indies. Originally from North Carolina, he had faced the same hard decision as Bulloch at the outbreak of war and had, like his comrade, plumped for the South.

Bulloch's habit, then, was to surround himself with men he could trust and vouch for through blood, class, or service. They in turn tended to be one-man dogs, professing allegiance to Bulloch alone. A natural secret agent, Bulloch rarely, and only reluctantly, worked with those unknown to him. That one of these four young men would eventually betray him would feel sharper than a serpent's tooth.

II

Eventually, Bulloch decided that escaping Savannah by sea was impossible. Fearing that, unless he acted soon, he would have to sit out the rest of the war, Bulloch took his team to Wilmington, which was less heavily guarded. It still took some time, but finally, on February 5, 1862, they left aboard the blockade-runner *Annie Childs*.

Bulloch was impatient but in no particular hurry. Having heard no news of the *Oreto* since October, he had assumed the best. Scheduled for December, she must have been completed by now and long since set sail. Once in Liverpool, his first stop was not, then, to 10 Rumford Place to see Prioleau, but to 2 Marine Terrace. His wife, Harriott, had recently rented the place, and Bulloch was understandably eager to see his family for the first time in five months.

The next morning, March 11, he was leisurely walking along the waterfront. To his horror, he saw the *Oreto* still conspicuously anchored at Toxteth Dock. After rushing to Rumford Place, he found Prioleau, who was in a terrible state. Since late January, he said, this Dudley character had been asking questions while some detective named Maguire had been trawling the taverns for information about the *Oreto*.

He, Prioleau, had adeptly handled these impertinences, but February 20 had brought an urgent note from Agent X, the Confederates' mole in the Foreign Office. His master, Lord Russell, had received a request from Minister Adams to inspect the *Oreto*. The customs man would be on his way the next day, the mole warned.

Prioleau had immediately scrubbed the *Oreto* of any possible incriminating evidence before the inspector arrived. Thankfully, the *Oreto* had been cleared by customs to leave back on March 4, but now Prioleau begged Bulloch to get her out of Liverpool as soon as possible to avoid tempting fate.

Unfortunately, there was no way the *Oreto* could leave immediately. For one thing, Bulloch needed to clear the crew for the journey.

Prioleau had done good work in recruiting some fifty-two men, but Bulloch, wary of another surprise inspection, locked himself into his office at Rumford Place to confirm their paperwork exhaustively for himself. He had to make sure every man had signed his articles in strict conformity with the law. They had to be British and contracted to serve only for a voyage from Liverpool to Palermo. In keeping with the terms of the Foreign Enlistment Act, none could enlist for service with the

Confederacy, and no one could know, it went without saying, that there was no intention of ever voyaging to Palermo. In fact, the *Oreto* would be traveling in the opposite direction—to Nassau. He wasn't worried, though, about diverting from a declared destination. Ships legitimately did it all the time, depending on weather, prices, and cargo. The *Oreto* would be one of them.

To ensure all was aboveboard, James Duguid—the shipbuilder Miller's son-in-law—was appointed captain. Duguid was a safe pair of hands, even if those hands were attached to someone with a dangerous streak. A Royal Navy veteran who'd gone into the cotton trade, now aged forty-five and with thirty years at sea under his belt, Duguid was known for "carrying on"—he kept a press of canvas on the yards in high winds when others furled sails rather than risk their masts. Once, in what seems to have been the fastest time on record, he'd commanded the *Advance* on an eighteen-day run from Mobile to Liverpool. If anyone could get the *Oreto* to the Caribbean, it was James Duguid.

That raised the question of who was to be the *Oreto*'s real captain once she reached Nassau. There was one ideal candidate: Bulloch's old friend and Coast Survey comrade, Lieutenant John Maffitt, currently overseeing two Fraser Trenholm blockade-runners shipping cotton into Nassau and guns out to Charleston and Wilmington. Maffitt had a reputation for fearless rashness, or perhaps rash fearlessness, acquired by taking it upon himself to attack the Union fleet almost single-handedly in the gunboat CSS *Savannah* in late 1861.

With his ship heavily damaged and his superiors less than impressed, Maffitt was soon after "disattached" from the Confederate Navy as punishment and reassigned to the blockade trade.

Blockade-running was a lot of fun, but Maffitt wanted to get back into the fight. The problem was finding him. Captain Duguid wouldn't have the foggiest idea of where Maffitt was. John Low and his Confederate connections, however, would. On March 21, Bulloch added Low as a kind of secret supercargo on the *Oreto*. His task was to assume charge of the ship in Nassau from Duguid and deliver her by any means possible to Maffitt.

A rakish John Maffitt

That might take some time, Bulloch conceded. He advised Low that, if he needed money in Nassau, he was to call on George Harris and Augustus Adderley, young partners in the local firm of Henry Adderley & Co., a pro-Confederate British company long used by Prioleau to handle his transfers, coal supplies, and warehousing. (The old man himself, Henry Adderley, was known as "King Conch," slang for his Southern sympathies.) For anything else, Low should contact Louis Heyliger, the Confederate "Agent of the Treasury" there, another friend of Prioleau's. Outside of them, however, he was "to appear always as a private gentleman traveling on his own affairs." As soon as Maffitt took command of the *Oreto,* Low was to hand him Bulloch's secret instructions—they were sewn into the seams of Low's coat— and then immediately return to Liverpool "as I have duties of great importance for you here."

The next day, March 22, after Bulloch reiterated to Low that above all else the *Oreto* had to be armed and equipped in international waters, *not* in British-held Nassau, to avoid violating the Foreign Enlistment Act, she quietly departed.

Dudley watched the ship leave from the dockside. Bulloch had won this round, he granted, but there soon would be another, for a couple of weeks earlier he'd learned of "a second gun boat . . . being built here."

This one would not escape.

III

Thirty-seven days later, on April 28, the *Oreto* docked at Nassau. Low took a room at the upmarket Royal Victoria Hotel and called upon Heyliger, the Confederate agent. He was told that Maffitt was reportedly on his way from Wilmington on the *Gordon* with a cargo of cotton and should be there on May 4.

To make the *Oreto* less conspicuous, Low ordered Captain Duguid to move her nine miles away, to what was known as Cochrane's Anchorage. He also formally consigned the *Oreto* to Adderley & Co., meaning that responsibility for the ship passed from faraway Fawcett Preston to a hometown firm enjoying on-the-ground political and legal protection.

Adderley & Co. was a connected company in Nassau, so much so that two partners (Harris and Adderley) served in the government and its chief counsel was G. C. Anderson, who happened to be not only the colony's attorney general but a zealous Confederate partisan. That did not mean the *Oreto* was entirely safe from seizure if found to be in violation of the Foreign Enlistment Act. The governor of the Bahamas, Charles Bayley, was not in the Confederacy's pocket, and neither were the Royal Navy officers stationed there.

Thankfully, Maffitt's *Gordon* hove into Nassau at 4:00 P.M. on May 4, right on time. At eleven that night, he huddled with Low at the Royal Victoria to be given his orders from Bulloch and to be briefed on his new command—if he could get her out of Cochrane's Anchorage, that is.

For the time being, he lacked a Southern crew. But the more immediate concern was that the American consul in Nassau, Samuel Whiting, was making trouble. Soon after the *Oreto* had docked, he'd received a letter from his colleague in Liverpool. Dudley explained the situation and asked Whiting to intervene with the British authorities. On May 9, Whiting politely asked Governor Bayley whether the *Oreto* was "preserving the strict neutrality so earnestly enjoined" by Her Majesty. Bayley was sympathetic, but Attorney General Anderson waded in, saying that he would need "positive facts," not "repute or belief," to approve a search or seizure. Bayley let the matter drop.

On May 25, the *Bahama,* under the trusty Fraser Trenholm captain Tessier, finally dropped anchor in Nassau, a few weeks later than expected. She was carrying the armaments for the *Oreto,* as well as several Confederate naval officers traveling home from Europe. One of these officers, Lieutenant John Stribling, volunteered to stay in Nassau to help Maffitt with the *Oreto*. His first task was to sneak the guns off the *Bahama* and take them to a bonded warehouse owned by Adderley & Co., putting them out of reach of the government.

All this suspicious activity caused Commander McKillop's ears to prick up. As the senior Royal Navy officer at Nassau, he took HMS *Bulldog* on May 27 to pay a surprise visit to the *Oreto*. More suspiciously still, after the crew was mustered, several of them complained to McKillop that the ship was "fitting and preparing for a vessel of war." Three of them, who were refusing further duty, were detained and brought to the local clink, where they were questioned by Consul Whiting. On June 4, boatswain Edward Jones—derided by Maffitt as "a low, dirty, Liverpool dock-rat"—attested to Whiting that the *Oreto* was modeled on a British gunboat, contained a "magazine, shot-lockers, ports, and bolts for twenty guns" and was, in short, "a perfect man-of-war."

On June 7, Attorney General Anderson, really earning his pay, again intervened and dismissed Jones's statement as mere hearsay. McKillop disagreed and again sniffed around the *Oreto,* but of course found neither guns nor ammunition. And there the investigation stopped, for, as it happened, McKillop's posting in the Bahamas was at its end. He left the *Oreto* problem in the hands of his successor, Commander Hickley of HMS *Greyhound*.

When the latter visited the *Oreto* on June 13, he discovered an unhappy ship indeed. The entire crew had mutinied and were refusing to raise the anchor until they knew the ship's destination. For this act of rebellion, Captain Duguid blamed John Low, accusing him of undermining his authority by publicly complaining that he treated his sailors worse than slaves on a plantation, which was saying something.

Despite Low's criticism, the sailors' main gripe was not in fact over the harshness of Duguid's regime. It was that they had signed on for Palermo, and yet were now being pressured to stay on for months without extra pay in the Caribbean.

What Low and his Confederate partners had not taken into account was that these were old Liverpool lags who knew their rights. Nothing had changed in the intervening decades since an American master of a clipper had complained of his Liverpudlian contingent that they were "tough, roustabout sailormen and difficult to handle, so that it was sometimes a toss-up whether they or the captain and officers would have charge of the ship."

Described as "a species of wild men, strong, coarse-built, thick-set; their hairy bodies and limbs tattooed with grotesque and often obscene devices in red and blue India ink; men wallowing in the slush of depravity, who could be ruled only with a hand of iron," Liverpool sailors were not the kind of people to be trifled with, especially if they thought they were being scammed by sneaky Southerners. After all, while their own code prohibited drawing a knife on each other, "to cut and stab an officer or shipmate not of their own gang was regarded as an heroic exploit."

Being a Liverpool local, Captain Duguid was rather more aware of this risk than young Low, hence his stringent discipline to keep the lads in line. He believed Low's naivete had potentially placed them both in danger of having their throats slit and their bodies vanishing deep into the azure waters.

To calm the situation, Adderley & Co. offered the sailors their wages in full and a bonus of £5 to remain with the *Oreto*. Most refused, however, saying they had been deceived and demanding a guarantee that they would not be forced to serve the Confederacy.

Several eventually went back to work, but the rest deserted and confessed everything they knew to Hickley on the *Greyhound*. With their evidence in hand, Hickley unilaterally seized the *Oreto* on June 15, saying that "allowing such a vessel as the *Oreto* to pass to sea as a British merchant vessel and a peaceful trader would compromise my convictions so entirely as to be a neglect of duty."

Two days later, ignoring Attorney General Anderson's attempted intervention, Governor Bayley left the *Oreto*'s fate in the hands of the Vice-Admiralty Court. By any definition, this decision was a disaster for the Confederates. The court could rule either way, and would take its sweet time conducting the trial. After consulting the Confederate agent Heyliger, on July 1 John Low decided he needed to return to Liverpool to update Bulloch, leaving Maffitt, Stribling, and fewer than a dozen men to protect the *Oreto*.

IV

August 2, 1862, midday: After a month and a half's delay and a week's worth of testimony, Justice Lees gave his decision in the *Oreto* case. To Maffitt's surprise, the *Oreto* was free to leave as soon as August 7 and was cleared for Saint John, New Brunswick—another false destination—carrying a cargo of lead, rum, tobacco, sugar, pepper, and coffee.

Though Lees was highly suspicious of the *Oreto*, he had based his decision on the fact that the government could not prove that the *Oreto* had done anything illegal (for instance, taking on arms or installing cannon) in Nassau. Indeed, the only thing tangibly connecting the *Oreto* with the Confederacy at all was "a gentleman named Lowe." And he was, conveniently, long gone.

Fortunately, Maffitt's name had never come up during the trial. If it had, Lees might not have gone so easy. As far as anyone was concerned, Maffitt was merely a civilian captain taking a lengthy break in Nassau at a nice hotel. Though Maffitt, who had never gone near the *Oreto*, later

The only known photograph of CSS Florida

admitted that he had "governed (privately)" Captain Duguid's actions, it was Duguid's signature on all the documents, and Duguid had sworn on oath that the *Oreto* had no Confederate links.

Maffitt wasted no time. Within hours of the *Oreto*'s clearance, he took command of the undermanned ship. After that, Adderley & Co. purchased the *Prince Alfred*, a common-as-muck Nassau schooner to transport the armaments brought by the *Bahama* and still secretly stored in their bonded warehouse. At 1:00 A.M. on August 8, the *Prince Alfred*, under the Confederate lieutenant Stribling, rendezvoused with Maffitt's *Oreto* at sea and headed for Green Cay, a small uninhabited island sixty miles south of Nassau.

They arrived at 3:00 P.M. and then, said Maffitt, "commenced one of the most physically exhausting jobs ever undertaken by naval officers." Every man "undressed to the buff" and, sweating and swearing the whole time in the horrendous heat of a Caribbean summer, hauled out of the *Prince Alfred*'s hold the precious guns and tons of powder, shells, and shot. It was all then transferred to the *Oreto*, which slowly began to assume the aspect of a Confederate warship. It took an entire week to move the lot. The skeleton crew was absolutely exhausted, and one had died by sunstroke. But the task was finished on August 16.

The next day, Maffitt hoisted the Confederate flag to cheers and (re)christened the *Oreto* as CSS *Florida*, the first of Bulloch's raiders.

SEVEN

The War Rules

I

When Bulloch commissioned William C. Miller to build the *Oreto* in June 1861, he had also taken a ferry across the Mersey to audition the Laird brothers for a major job: the *Oreto*'s sister ship and fellow raider. As a potential client, Bulloch was given the grand tour, and no wonder: There was so much to show off. By this time, Lairds was so large that it could simultaneously build eighteen thousand tons' worth of shipping, a third more than its nearest competitor.

Bulloch was standing in the royal capital of an iron kingdom, home to the maritime cathedrals of the industrial age. But as he told Henry Laird, head of the firm's design and drawing departments, he didn't want an iron ship—at least not yet. He was here to commission a wooden one. Could Lairds do it?

The Confederate agent had a dream warship in mind. Upon showing Laird his sketches, the designer thought them a little out of his wheelhouse—the company was not famed for its expertise in wood—but he took another look and changed his mind. There would inevitably be a few problems: He'd have to hire some skilled joiners, find a good timber supplier, and of course talk to his brothers. But yes, it could be done. Indeed, sir, it would be Messrs. Laird's pleasure to assist such a worthy cause—not that Bulloch ever mentioned who he truly represented, but when a Southern gentleman of good breeding appeared at a shipyard it was patently obvious.

Bulloch had not randomly turned up at Lairds. After finding their address in *Gore's Directory,* he had been assured by his friends Archibald Hamilton and Frederick Bond, the pro-Confederate arms dealers of The London Armoury Company, that he would be warmly welcomed there. Hamilton happened to be the second cousin of the senior John Laird, and Bond had once worked for his brother Macgregor at the African Steam Ship Company. The Anglo-Confederate world was a small one, and both Hamilton and Bond had vouched for Bulloch.

For his part, Henry Laird did not act solely from political sympathy. Financially speaking, this one-off order could easily turn into several, and potentially for pricier ironclads, as Bulloch was hinting. Truth to tell, too, Bulloch's concept was an intriguing one. It would be an interesting change from the merchant ships and coastal ferries they were cranking out.

On August 1, 1861, Bulloch signed a contract with Lairds under his own name as a private individual to conceal the ship's real ownership. Judging by its litany of details, the Confederate was an exacting customer. Calling for a 3-masted screw steam vessel 220 feet long and 32 in the beam, making her some 30 feet longer and 5 wider than the *Florida,* and faster as well (13 knots compared with 12) thanks to her twin 300-horsepower engines, the contract specified the sizes, shapes, and types of wood (English oak, American elm, teak, greenheart, mahogany, Danzig fir) to be used for its various components, like the futtocks, keel, stem, apron, and trusses.

There was no mention, of course, of guns. Even so, the contract specified installing shot racks, magazine bulkheads, and shell rooms. In the event, so long as the ship contained no actual munitions, there was no possibility of a legal violation, though a curious person might have wondered why this ostensible trading vessel needed shot racks and shell rooms when cargo space was at a premium.

Additional suspicions might have been raised by Bulloch's insistence on a telescoping funnel, the inclusion of an enormous bunker for 350 tons of coal, the addition of a large launch boat, a cutter, and a whale-boat potentially suitable for boarding operations. And why was the ship to be rigged according to "East India Outfit," the highest mercantile grade, meaning an expanded set of sails and stores (ropes, chandlery, anchors, cables, hawsers) suitable "for a long Voyage"? Not to mention Bulloch's hinting to leave sufficient room on deck for some "additional equipment," which might just happen to occupy the same area as, say, a battery of half a dozen 6-inch 32-pounders and 2 pivot guns, one a 7-inch rifle and the other an 8-inch smoothbore.

Despite being a new and untested client, who would normally have been required to advance at least half the total with the rest payable on completion, Bulloch received remarkably relaxed financial terms—a testament to how much Lairds valued his (future) custom, their Southern sympathies, and Fraser Trenholm's sterling credit at the time. For the price of £47,500, modest for a ship of this size and nature, he was permitted five easy-pay installments of £9,500, due at successive stages.

Lairds promised to complete and deliver the ship in nine months. She was called *290*, for being the 290th hull the firm had laid down, though more colorfully it was rumored that she was being built by 290 Englishmen sympathetic to the Confederacy.

II

After getting the *Florida* safely out of Liverpool in late March 1862, Bulloch finally had time to check on *290*'s progress. He was disheartened, but not surprised, by Henry Laird's apology that they were running late. For his part, Laird was relieved that Bulloch had even showed up. He hadn't been heard from for six months, and Laird had been anxiously wondering whether he would have to auction off the apparently abandoned ship.

Shouldn't be long now, Laird assured Bulloch, explaining that it had been more onerous than anticipated to acquire the requisite quality and quantity of timber.

On a beautiful May 14, good as his word, Laird arranged to launch *290* at 10:45 A.M., timed for high tide. The private ceremony was attended by Bulloch; his wife, Harriott; Prioleau; and several other friends of the Confederacy. On strict orders, no one uninvited was allowed into the yard. After a brief prayer for *290*'s good fortune, Mrs. Bulloch performed the honor of christening her with a bottle of wine cracked against her bow "in a comely manner."

In a near replay of his *Oreto* trick, Bulloch obscured *290*'s true purpose by disguising her destination, only instead of Italian owners this time she was to be a Spanish señorita. In one of his little jokes, Bulloch Hispanized "Harriott" to *Enrica*—"a flexible and mellifluous equivalent," he gallantly boasted.

Unfortunately, when Henry Laird ordered the pegs restraining *Enrica* to the inclined shipway to be struck away, she remained resolutely stuck. This happened occasionally, and it was a little embarrassing, but no matter: A foreman standing on the bow cried, "Dance!" to his gang and dance they did, jumping up and down enough to loosen the hull. Inch by inch, then foot by foot, the *Enrica* slid down toward the sea, the tallow-grease smeared on the rails beginning to smoke with the friction.

III

A couple of weeks before Bulloch returned to Liverpool from the South and sneaked the *Oreto* out, Dudley had heard the first rumor of another Confederate boat being built, this time in Birkenhead. On March 1, he promised Secretary Seward that he would pursue the matter, but after a month of investigation Maguire had come up dry. The detective had visited Lairds but could elicit nothing, Dudley reported on March 28, and tailing Bulloch had led nowhere.

Then, on April 23, Maguire noticed that twenty-odd Confederate sailors from CSS *Sumter*, at the time trapped at Gibraltar by USS *Kearsarge* and USS *Chippewa*, had turned up in Liverpool on their way back to the South. He had eavesdropped on two of them, a "Lieutenant Beauford & Gunner Caddy"—he meant Beaufort, a sailmaker, and Cuddy—gossiping in a tavern about a new ship Lairds was building. But Maguire gleaned no more than the tidbit that she was still a long way from completion.

So Dudley was more surprised than anyone when Maguire informed him on May 15 that this apparently unfinished ship had just been launched. The consul rushed to the dockside to witness this "very superior boat" in the flesh and was staggered by what he saw. Just by looking at the *Enrica*, even a landsman like Dudley could tell she was the apex of the shipwright's art. Maguire confirmed that a foreman at Lairds had boasted to him that "no boat was ever built stronger or better than she. The order when given was to build her of the very best material . . . without regard to expense."

Concluded an alarmed Dudley, "There is no doubt but that she is intended for the Rebels," a fact "admitted [to Maguire] by one of the leading workmen in the yard," who said "she was to be the sister to the *Oreto*."

Dudley's consternation was understandable. A heavily armed *Enrica* would surely present a critical threat to vulnerable American merchant-men. To protect them, Union warships would have to be diverted from blockade duty, thereby rending even more holes in the screen for the blockade-runners to exploit and leveraging pressure on Lincoln to negotiate a settlement with the South at a time when the North's fortunes were wavering.

With the unveiling of the *Enrica*, everything suddenly began to make sense. In April, Dudley had first noticed a curious burst of blockade-runner activity, with no fewer than thirty-nine ships departing Liverpool for Nassau. New vessels were being financed, built, and launched almost every day, but the consul had no idea why. He initially thought it might partly be owed to a relaxation of the embargo and the concordant increase in cotton imports, and he was right, but the real reason, it had become clear, was that the Confederates were coordinating their efforts in order to undermine both the blockade and Lincoln.

But who was behind the coordinating, and who was paying for the ships? The fog cleared a little when Dudley learned, probably through his ally Squarey in the American Chamber of Commerce, that a large number of Liverpool merchants had started a subscription, serving as a kind of loan, "to aid the Rebellion" by buying ships, arms, and munitions.

Though the identities of the participants were studiously kept secret, Dudley heard rumors that they had quickly raised at least £50,000 but probably much more. And the amount kept increasing—£750,000 by year's end, apparently. As Dudley reported, this incessant flow of funds accounts "for the number of vessels that have been [recently] fitted out at this port to aid the Confederates and for the great activity manifested by them."

Dudley dug deeper, heedless of cost. At one point, he was spending a third of his entire consular budget on informants and loose tongues, but it was worth the price. Prioleau, it slowly emerged from his investigations, was heading the campaign, it being common knowledge within shipping circles that Fraser Trenholm "act[s] as the agents [and] procure[s] the subscribers." The funds were then sent to "a Mr. Hotz" in London, who gave the subscribers, or lenders rather, short-term Confederate bonds: IOUs payable every three months in cotton smuggled through the blockade.

Even Dudley grudgingly admired the cleverness of Prioleau's pyramid-like scheme. Because no subscriber knew the names of the others, how much had been raised, or even how many participants there were, the debt could be continually rolled over and more credit leveraged until the total increased "to an indefinite sum and no one would be any the wiser except the Messrs. Fraser Trenholm and Co. and Hotz."

IV

This shadowy "Mr. Hotz" was actually Henry Hotze, one of the war's stranger and more diabolical characters.

Born in Switzerland in 1834, the son of an army captain, he immigrated to the United States and became a naturalized citizen in 1856. Settling in Mobile, Alabama, he quickly became more fervently "Southern" than even native Southerners. After ingratiating himself with the plantation and city gentry with his fancy European manners, Hotze was made assistant editor of the *Mobile Advertiser & Register*, where he received an invaluable apprenticeship in journalism and how to manipulate facts to suit convenient truths. Even for the time, Hotze's output was eye-

A deceptively cherubic Henry Hotze

poppingly racist, partly thanks to his submersion in the swampier depths of Franco-German "scientific" race theory. Through name-dropping and using big words, Hotze impressed readers with his pseudo-intellectual articles—so much classier in tone than the customary perfervid splutterings one heard in his circles.

Shortly before war broke out, the baby-faced, wavy-haired, five-foot-eight Hotze joined a gentlemanly volunteer unit, where he had lots of fun dressing up and pretending to be a soldier. After a couple of months, though, the parades and party going began to pall, and the twenty-nine-year-old conjured up the idea of his establishing a newspaper in London to circulate Confederate propaganda.

He outlined his scheme to Confederate secretary of state Robert Hunter, who sent him on a two-week scouting mission to Britain in early October 1861. Besides researching the British press, he was to bring secret dispatches from Richmond to the clandestine Confederate operatives in London. His contact would be Bulloch's colleague Major Anderson.

At 11:00 P.M. on October 4, Hotze went round to Anderson's place. They talked for two hours. It was then that Anderson inducted Hotze into the mother of all secrets: his recent recruitment of Agent X as a mole in the Foreign Office. He suggested that Hotze meet Frederick Bond of The London Armoury Company, who had first put Anderson in touch with Agent X, to arrange an introduction as he, Anderson, would soon be departing for the Confederacy with Bulloch on the *Fingal*. When Hotze returned to London in the new year, he would take over running Agent X.

On January 29, 1862, Hotze began his sideline as a case officer under the official cover of "Commercial Agent." Three weeks later—February 20—when Agent X alerted him that Adams had written to Foreign Secretary Russell and that a customs inspection of the *Oreto* was imminent, it was Hotze who almost certainly transmitted the warning to Prioleau.

Hotze unveiled his baby on May 1: *The Index*, a broadsheet weekly based at 13 Bouverie Street, just off Fleet Street. Sold for sixpence and consisting of sixteen pages, *The Index* devoted most of them to Southern news and analysis ("Are the Confederates Rebels?") but also carried an interesting variety of pieces on literature, the arts, history, high-society gossip, and finance—all subtly slanted to a pleasingly Confederate worldview. In *The Index*, the blatant racism more acceptable in Alabama than in London vanished and was replaced by a blithe assertion that slavery had nothing whatsoever to do with the war, which was instead a struggle for liberty, independence, and civilization. At least half the articles, boasted Hotze, were contributed by his stable of hacks, whom he encouraged to recycle their wares in "the journals and magazines with which they are connected," such as *The Times* or the *Morning Post*, to get paid twice while amplifying Hotze's invisible reach.

The Index never made a profit, but it was never intended to. Hotze was interested only in a select audience of movers and shakers. His rag, which he called his "little kingdom," never enjoyed more than 2,250 subscribers. But that club included some very big names indeed: at least eight peers in the House of Lords and fourteen MPs, and some other familiar ones—not least Prioleau and the friendly arms dealer Mr. Isaac of S. Isaac, Campbell & Company, which also advertised widely in the paper. Other keen readers included dozens of newspaper editors, mayors, army officers, scientists, shipowners, lawyers, manufacturers, senior clergymen, and, of course, a certain spy in the Foreign Office.

V

Dudley soon realized that in discovering the existence of Prioleau's subscription scheme, its connections to blockade-running, and the thread to Hotze, he had stumbled onto a major scoop. He had come very far since his days as a naive consul bumbling around, cataloging ships for the Black List. Bouncing back from the humiliation of the *Oreto*'s escape, in May Dudley set about uncovering the identities of Prioleau's subscribers. Understanding the Confederate financing system would bring him one step closer to Bulloch, the fox-like mastermind behind the mysterious *Enrica*.

Prioleau secreted his subscribers' list in a heavy safe at 10 Rumford Place. Maguire no doubt knew a safecracker or two from his days on the beat, but breaking into a commercial office and stealing the list was out of the question. Not only was it against Adams's directive to avoid Sanford-style covert operations, but the Confederates and their friends would be handed a huge propaganda victory if Dudley was caught and sent home in disgrace. The consul possessed a leonine bravery, that was uncontested, but in this case he would take to heart the teaching of the ancient Greek historian Plutarch, who advised, "Where the lion's skin will not reach, it must be patched out with the fox's." He had to be cleverer than his foes. Prioleau remained every bit the wily devil, but his accomplices had become cocksure. They had gotten careless and that made them vulnerable.

Working in his cramped, ill-lit office for nights on end, Dudley followed the bread crumbs they had inadvertently left behind. By cross-referencing their own customs records with newspaper clippings,

Maguire's observations, chatter among brokers and shipbuilders, publicly reported bank transactions, and cotton receipts, Dudley compiled his own personal register of the most prominent participants.

By early June, he had untangled so much of Prioleau's network of companies, cutouts, sympathizers, and fronts that he sent Washington an extraordinary catalog of "the most active houses at Liverpool engaged in assisting the Rebels and fitting out vessels and to run the blockade." Lurking at the center of the web, of course, was Prioleau and Fraser Trenholm, who were, Dudley bluntly noted, "engaged in every thing."

Aside from those congenial miscreants, there were at least forty-one other firms and individuals up to their necks in the business. Some were arms dealers like Henry Lafone and the questionable William Grazebrook—Major Anderson had once caught him selling the same

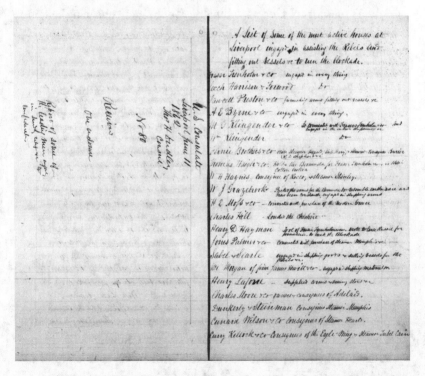

The first page of Dudley's remarkable list of pro-Confederates in Liverpool

guns to both sides—who had lately gone into blockade-running. Others, like Melchior Klingender, whom Dudley had long suspected of working for Fraser Trenholm, was now a confirmed Prioleau agent. Also making an appearance were the brothers Thomas and Edwin Haigh. The first served as Prioleau's false-front broker to cover up cotton-import trades, while Edwin was often used as a fake registrant for Fraser Trenholm's ships. Interestingly, there was a Mr. Ashbridge, a merchant from New Orleans whose office was being used as the headquarters of the Southern Club, a new and very secretive group of businessmen covertly funded by Fraser Trenholm. The likes of a U.S. consul, unsurprisingly, found it impossible to penetrate these club meetings, but Dudley was nevertheless convinced that it was "a most powerful agent in aiding the Rebellion."

As he forayed deeper into the labyrinth of contracts, links, and records, Dudley would expand this initial list. Staggeringly, he soon identified more than two hundred "merchants, individuals, and companies known or suspected to be trading with the Confederacy." He even came quite close to identifying the members of the Southern Club when his old antagonists at the American Chamber of Commerce gathered to petition the government to recognize the Confederacy. Dudley, putting two and two together, estimated that at least "four-fifths" of them were aiding Dixie, making it all but certain that they were also on the Southern Club books.

Dudley had connected an incredible number of dots by delving into the paperwork and checking the files. But a list went only so far. What Dudley had not been able to do was link Bulloch to the Prioleau and Fraser Trenholm nexus. Bulloch's name appeared nowhere, and neither did the *Enrica*'s. After all that work, Dudley still had nothing tying Bulloch and the *Enrica* to this larger, concerted campaign to finance runners, break the blockade, and force Lincoln to negotiate an armistice.

VI

You couldn't ask as many questions around Liverpool as Dudley had been without word getting back to Prioleau and Bulloch. That spring and summer, Bulloch was made aware that "spies were lurking about, and tampering with the workmen at Messrs. Laird's, and that a private detective named Maguire was taking a deep and abiding interest in my personal movements." Yet, perhaps a little overconfident after his *Oreto* vanishing trick, Bulloch didn't take Dudley's probing too seriously. He instead made fun of Dudley's "wakeful and agitated condition," and thought it amusing that his games always so "grieved and vexed" his foe.

As long as he played by the war rules and ensured that the *Enrica* was as free of armaments as the *Oreto* had been, he knew that Dudley might seethe but not act. To that end, he purchased the guns separately and had them sent covertly to London, where they were packed aboard the *Agrippina*, a thoroughly unremarkable tender Archibald Hamilton of The London Armoury Company had purchased to ensure no direct connection could be made to Bulloch. The plan was for the *Agrippina* to rendezvous with the *Enrica* in international waters.

In early July, Secretary Mallory informed Bulloch that Raphael Semmes was to command the *Enrica* on her cruise. Semmes was a fine sailor, Bulloch knew, but he was currently in Nassau and not expected to arrive in Liverpool until early August. That left several weeks to keep the *Enrica* safe—longer than Bulloch had expected.

To have her ready to go as soon as Semmes showed up, Bulloch wrangled a skeleton crew of thirty to forty men. Wary as always of tripping the Foreign Enlistment Act wire, he made sure to hire only British civilian seamen. Most were in their mid- to late twenties and born to the sea, men like the sailmaker Henry Alcott (of whom it was said that he was "slow of speech but profound of thought, and hard to convince that canvas was not the most important part" of a steamship), a somewhat troublesome Scot named Samuel Henry (later subjected to two courts-martial), and a Crimean War veteran named George Horwood.

Most important of them was Matthew Butcher, who was placed in nominal command. Butcher, twenty-nine years old and serving as an officer on a Cunard steamship, had been recommended to Bulloch by Prioleau. To obscure Bulloch's involvement, it was Prioleau who asked

Butcher to come round to 10 Rumford Place because, as Butcher recalled, "he wished to see me on business of a special nature." Butcher assumed it was for a position on a blockade-runner. Why else would anyone go to the Fraser Trenholm office? Once there, he found himself being interviewed for a much bigger job.

Bulloch had told Prioleau that he needed a man of "professional competency, prudence . . . and absolute integrity," but most of all, one in "control over the tongue." Getting the *Enrica* past Dudley meant "an indiscreet remark, or a hint . . . to a careless gossiping acquaintance, would [spoil] all of our well-laid plans." Only if Prioleau trusted Butcher could he tell him what the *Enrica*'s real mission was at their meeting. It seems he did, for Butcher quickly accepted the offer for its "very liberal remuneration."

The next day, Butcher finally met the real power behind the throne: Bulloch. It turned out that they had previously met in Havana before the war, during one of Bulloch's mail-packet runs there. After a half-hour chat, Bulloch took him to see the *Enrica* and introduced him to Henry Laird. "I at once took charge and hastened the outfit as much as possible," said Butcher, "for even at that time we were aware that danger might arise from delay."

VII

Dudley was finding it almost impossible to pierce Bulloch's wall of secrecy. In mid-June, the Liverpool papers had reprinted some articles from the New York press mentioning his dispatches to Seward concerning suspicious ships. Some fool at the State Department had obviously been too chatty with a reporter. Ever since, security had been noticeably tightened at Lairds and around the *Enrica*. Bulloch was now keeping the ship locked up at the Victoria Wharf in the Great Float (a broad branch of the Mersey) at Birkenhead, making it impossible to get a look at her without arousing suspicion. When the *Enrica* had undertaken a trial excursion that month, reported Dudley, "no one was admitted on board without a ticket. They were issued only to the persons actively engaged in aiding the rebellion."

Dudley grew despondent. But a nugget from Maguire gave him renewed hope. The detective said he'd befriended a lad from New Orleans named Robinson in one of the sketchy dockside taverns he liked to frequent. The fresh-faced Robinson couldn't hold his liquor and had blabbed to Maguire, who could, that he had come over on the blockade-runner *Julia Usher*. As Maguire played gracious host and stood round after round, Robinson grew ever more loquacious. On the way over, he said, the captain and officers had spoken freely of a new gunboat being built by Lairds that was to carry eleven guns and be commanded by some fellow named Bulloch. She was going to be a long-range commerce raider and never have to enter a Southern port. Moreover, all the money was being put up by Fraser Trenholm.

During all this, the cunning detective had allowed poor, callow Robinson to labor under the misapprehension that he, Maguire, was working for Bulloch. As the boy was excited about the prospect of being taken on as crew, Maguire promised to put a good word in for him.

The next day, Maguire took Robinson to see not Bulloch but Dudley. It must have come as an unpleasant shock to the hungover youth. The consul beckoned him to sit down and explained the unfortunate pickle in which the lad had found himself. His fellow Southerners might not be overly pleased at discovering his indiscretion, and this was Liverpool, after all. Here, the very best he could hope for was to be abandoned, penniless and alone, in a strange country. Or at the worst, well, people mysteriously disappeared in Liverpool all the time. But Dudley was a friend, and in return for his information he would pay for Robinson to attend "a school in London" to "keep him from being tampered with" by the Confederates.

Once the boy had been put on a train south by Maguire, Dudley ruminated on Robinson's revelations. What he'd said was very interesting, certainly, but it was not conclusive evidence, not by a long shot. Still, Dudley was able to put a few pieces together. He had Maguire's earlier, overheard conversation involving "Lieutenant Beauford & Gunner Caddy," and the yard workman saying the *Enrica* was the *Oreto*'s sister.

And now he had Robinson's drunken admission—plus the *Enrica*'s recent trial run with Bulloch's Confederate friends on board. Add it all up, and Dudley believed he now had enough to again approach Samuel Price Edwards, Liverpool's collector of customs, to demand a search and her possible detainment as a vessel of war.

Taking such a radical step required clearance from Adams. On Friday, June 20, Dudley traveled to London to see the minister. Adams, naturally, was fearful of a repeat of the *Oreto* episode, when Collector Edwards unilaterally decided she was not in violation of the Foreign Enlistment Act. Instead, he proposed approaching Russell at the Foreign Office to request detention. Edwards would never dare to ignore a direct order from Russell to hold the ship until her innocence was proven.

On Monday, June 23, Adams dropped off a lengthy report from Dudley before asking the foreign secretary to "stop the projected expedition" of the *Enrica* from Liverpool. Just in case, Adams also summoned from Spain the Union cruiser *Tuscarora* under Captain Tunis Craven. If the British did not play along, he would order Craven to sink the *Enrica* somewhere in the Atlantic when no one was looking.

Unfortunately, Adams, an otherwise astute man, seemed to have misunderstood the nature of the British state apparatus and its ancient traditions, legal and bureaucratic. Even with the best of intentions, the foreign secretary could not simply order the *Enrica* "stopped" by some kind of magical presidential fiat. There were committees and departments and boards and reviews. There were *processes*.

Which is why Russell sent Dudley's report to both the law officers of the Crown and the lords commissioners of the treasury for their advisory opinions. A week later, the law officers advised him that if Dudley's allegations were true, then the *Enrica* was in manifest violation of the Foreign Enlistment Act. They thought Russell should request Edwards to begin an investigation immediately.

A couple of days later, on July 1, the lords commissioners said that their subordinate Board of Customs believed that the *Enrica could* possibly become a warship. However, since she had no armaments, detaining her was unwarranted. The commissioners suggested that Dudley take his evidence to Edwards and let him decide if he wanted to proceed.

Russell agreed with the Board of Customs and sent Adams a letter to that effect on July 4. The upshot was that Dudley had to do exactly what he originally had wanted to do—only he'd lost nearly two weeks' valuable time.

Upon presenting Edwards at the Customs House in Liverpool with the evidence on July 9, Dudley was told a week later that "there does not appear to be *prima facie* proof sufficient in the statement of the consul to justify the seizure of the vessel." Interpreting Edwards's adverse decision as having been dragged out deliberately, a furious Dudley accused him of being bribed by Bulloch.

This was a case of Dudley's occasional overstatement—that "nervousness" others remarked upon—which rarely did him good. Filled with righteous zeal, he was convinced that anyone who obstructed his crusade to destroy the Confederacy was corrupt and evil. What he failed to see was that Edwards, described as "a staid and somewhat obese gentleman, attired in a blue frock-coat and gilt buttons," was merely a time-serving bureaucrat whose job was to clear ships in and out of Liverpool as efficiently as possible, not fight Dudley's war for him. That he was a Confederate sympathizer who dithered, placed a thumb on the South's scale, asked few questions, and buck-passed when it suited him is also true. But he wasn't on Bulloch's payroll. He had never even met the Confederate agent. Even Adams, exasperated as he was by Edwards's behavior, considered him "honest but obtuse," not bought and paid for.

In this light, Dudley would have been better served by trying to persuade Edwards rather than attacking him and complaining loudly that Americans could not "expect anything like impartiality and fairness" from Her Majesty's Government. And to give Edwards his due, moreover, Dudley *hadn't* provided *prima facie* proof of anything in his report—just nebulous hearsay picked up from shipyards and taverns by a dodgy detective.

The good news was that, having learned that pointing a finger and expecting others to jump was not an optimal approach, a somewhat chastened Dudley then did what he should have done earlier: He got a lawyer. The solicitor he chose was Andrew Squarey, the sympathetic secretary of the American Chamber of Commerce and a man "reputed to be a man of honor as well as ability." Dudley instructed him to prepare a case supported by legal affidavits "without regard to expense," which certainly concentrated the solicitor's attention.

Within three days, Dudley and Squarey had assembled no fewer than six sworn affidavits. On July 21, they confidently marched to Edwards's office, where Squarey bored him by solemnly reading out the relevant clauses of the Foreign Enlistment Act before making a formal request to detain the *Enrica*. Edwards replied that he could do no such thing without written instructions from London but promised to read the affidavits, probably to persuade Dudley to go away.

Dudley left, confident that Edwards would be bowled over by the sheer weight of evidence he had presented.

VIII

Edwards was not impressed. Not at all. These affidavits were weak tea, indeed. One was from a clerk employed by Squarey stating that the *Enrica* was a screw steamer commanded by Captain Butcher—so what? Another was from a shipping master saying that Bulloch was linked to the *Oreto*, an unarmed merchant ship at the time still in Nassau doing nothing untoward. Two others were from Dudley and Maguire themselves, who could hardly be counted as disinterested observers, highlighting Bulloch's alleged connections to the *Enrica* and the Confederacy—nothing questionable about either since Bulloch was a Southerner who had contracted for the ship under his own name. And another, signed jointly by Maguire and Henry Wilding, Dudley's vice-consul, cited information given to them by Richard Brogan, a young Lairds apprentice, who had told them that Bulloch often visited the Lairds yard and that Matthew Butcher had tried to recruit him to the crew as a carpenter. All a bit ho-hum.

It was the final affidavit that gave Edwards greater pause for thought. William Passmore, a former Royal Navy man and Crimean War veteran, said that he had applied to Captain Butcher to serve as a signalman on the *Enrica*, and that he had been hired at £4 10s. per month. Butcher had then told him that the ship was "going out to the Government of the Confederate States of America" and that if he signed articles in international waters he could fight for the South. That amounted to fairly incriminating evidence, but Passmore could also have been a Dudley agent sent in to entrap Butcher. It was *he*, after all, who approached Butcher. And there was no proof Butcher had said anything of the sort to him.

Had Edwards known that, in fact, Dudley was paying not only Passmore but also Brogan as well for their affidavits—behavior generally frowned upon in the legal profession—he might well have chosen to interpret these as financial inducements to frame Butcher. But Dudley was learning how to be the fox.

Which is why, suspecting that Edwards would do nothing owing to "his sympathy for the Rebels," Dudley was on a train to London a few hours after leaving the collector's office. There, he gave copies of the six affidavits to Adams to forward to the Foreign Office for transmission to the more sympathetic law officers before hurrying back to Liverpool. Within a few days, to help make up the law officers' minds, Dudley submitted three more affidavits freshly procured by Maguire, whose skill at greasing palms had induced the proper spirit of voluntarism among the witnesses.

Edward Roberts, a ship's carpenter, said it was common knowledge on board that the *Enrica* was a Confederate vessel. Robert Taylor's statement was more damning. Born in England, Taylor had immigrated to Alabama and had recently been captured attempting to run the blockade. He'd since been released and gone to Liverpool, burning to avenge himself on the Northerners because they "had robbed me of my clothes when I was captured, and I wanted to have satisfaction." He was very specific that Mr. Rickarby of Liverpool, the brother of the blockade-runner's owner, had advised him to go see Captain Butcher.

Taylor told Butcher he wanted to exact his revenge and the captain replied "that if I went with him in his vessel I should very shortly have that opportunity." Taylor joined the crew but quit, for reasons unknown, a few days before being deposed.

It was the third affidavit that proved the most convincing, mostly owing to the seniority of the witness and his lack of conflicting motive. Henry Redden was a veteran boatswain of some fifteen years' standing who had been engaged by Butcher at an impressive £10 per month. He said the crew would probably number around a hundred, that Butcher had listed the *Enrica* as bound for Nassau but had no intention of stopping there, and that "the rules on board are similar to those in use on a man-of-war, and the men are not allowed to sing as they do on a merchantman." As for Bulloch, he was overseeing everything, and all knew the ship was for the Confederacy.

These two sets of affidavits arrived at the Foreign Office on Thursday, July 24, and Friday the twenty-fifth. But they were not consulted by the department dealing with "China, Japan, Siam, and United States" (for unknown reasons, America was counted as a minor Asian country) until Saturday afternoon, the twenty-sixth, when its chief, Senior Clerk Francis Alston, met with his juniors, Charles Abbott, William Cockerell, Victor Buckley, and Charles Kennedy, to review them. One of these five men was Agent X.

The feeling around the table was that Russell wanted to move upon the *Enrica* and that, even if some of them were a little shaky, nine affidavits provided enough of a push to recommend immediate action first thing Monday morning.

But the final legal decision whether to detain the *Enrica* lay in the hands of one man: Sir John Harding, the Queen's Advocate and thus senior law officer. Copies of the affidavits had arrived at his home that Saturday, but Harding was visiting his brother-in-law William Atkins, who, with the approval of Lady Harding, "forcibly and treacherously seized" her husband and placed him "in strict solitary confinement, with two keepers in a private house in the Regent's Park." For some time, Harding had been experiencing delusions and seems to have been suffering from early-onset dementia, and his despairing wife had taken the only avenue she could think of to save him from embarrassment. For that reason, she had not informed the authorities of his incapacitation. As such, Dudley's thick bundle of papers lay, unopened, in his hallway that entire weekend.

It was not until Monday, July 28, then, that someone realized that Sir John was in absentia and a messenger was dispatched to retrieve the documents. Harding's law officer colleagues, the attorney general (Sir William Atherton, a staunch advocate of British neutrality), and the solicitor general, Sir Roundell Palmer, took over the case that evening and urgently read over the affidavits in the Earl Marshal's office in the House of Lords. The next day, July 29, they issued their decision.

Their view was that the *Enrica* was almost certainly a Confederate military vessel, though they pointed out that she had not violated the terms of the Foreign Enlistment Act, which forbade the equipping, furnishing, fitting out, or arming of a vessel in British waters. *But*— and this was a blow to Bulloch's craftiness in adhering strictly to the letter of the law rather than accounting for its spirit—"we think, however, that such a narrow construction ought not to be adopted; and, if allowed, would fritter away the act, and give impunity to open and flagrant violations of its provisions." In sum, having rumbled Bulloch's scheme, they recommended that "without loss of time the vessel be seized by the proper authorities."

On July 31, at 11:35 A.M., Collector Edwards was instructed by treasury telegram to board and seize the *Enrica*.

The only problem was that the *Enrica* was no longer in Liverpool.

EIGHT

The Magician

I

By getting the *Enrica* away, Bulloch had outplayed Dudley, pipping him at the very last post. As Dudley gasped at his antagonist's wondrous feat, Bulloch, like any good magician, left his audience in the dark as to how he had made the ship disappear before their very eyes. But the trick was very simple: Bulloch had known Dudley's every move before he made it.

Since at least June, Bulloch had seen all of Maguire's confidential reports for Dudley that the consul had forwarded to Squarey the solicitor. The papers appear to have been surreptitiously copied by one of Squarey's clerks and slipped to Bulloch, presumably in return for payment. This intelligence coup permitted Bulloch to see in near real-time what information Dudley had gathered on the *Enrica*, how he gathered it, and from whom it was gathered. Of the greatest interest were Maguire's successful efforts to infiltrate the security cordon surrounding the ship. On June 27, for instance, Bulloch discovered that Maguire had paid a Lairds gateman to keep him abreast about possible sailing dates. This man had offered "to get to know more for me [Maguire] from the watchman on board."

More worryingly, on July 4 Maguire had actually managed to get into the Lairds yard and board the vessel. Perhaps the Irishman was wearing

Intelligence supplied by Bulloch's inside man

a disguise, for he claimed to have seen Bulloch himself there "giving orders to the men, who saluted him." He'd even gone belowdecks for a look-around and supplied a detailed description of the *Enrica*'s insides. Quite a scoop for Consul Dudley.

Just as troubling was the revelation of July 15 that Maguire had a young spy at Lairds named Richard Broderick. Bulloch might even have dimly recalled him from the launching of the *Enrica* two months earlier. It was then that Mrs. Bulloch accidentally dropped her bonnet from an office window and Broderick, the little creep, had gallantly "lifted it and passed it up to her." Now he was, rather less gallantly, betraying everything he knew to Dudley, including that the *Enrica* was a Confederate ship. He had once met with Maguire in a hotel and said, "as sure as you are sitting there, Captain Bulloch is the owner of the gunboat."

A week later, something clicked in Bulloch's mind. He reread Dudley's six original affidavits (the ones sent to the Foreign Office), which had been helpfully supplied by his Squarey insider, and found what he was looking for: Richard *Brogan*'s deposition saying he'd often seen Bulloch at Lairds. Much of what Brogan claimed then sounded awfully familiar to what Richard *Broderick* was saying now. Obviously, "Brogan" was a pseudonym for Broderick, to protect the source's identity.

Brogan, probably illiterate, had not signed his affidavit. Maguire and Vice-Consul Wilding had done so in his place, inadvertently giving Bulloch a small but valuable victory. And that was, Maguire and Wilding had knowingly stood surety for a witness who had sworn upon oath that "Richard Brogan" was his real name. As such, his testimony had been rendered legally invalid. Such a pity that it didn't have Dudley's own signature at the bottom of the page . . .

Nevertheless, to be forewarned is to be forearmed, and Bulloch chose not to have Broderick dismissed. He wanted him kept on at Lairds, though obviously sidelined from anything more to do with the *Enrica*, in order to avoid raising any suspicion on the consul's part that his asset had been compromised.

But Bulloch still had a problem. His intelligence may have revealed Dudley's activities in Liverpool but not what was happening in London, where the decision whether to hold or clear the *Enrica* was being decided by the powers that be.

And yet, on that fateful Saturday afternoon of July 26, he had somehow known the answer before anyone else.

II

As soon as the Foreign Office meeting ended that day and his colleagues had gone home, Agent X—Victor Buckley—scribbled a note, very brief and to the point: "The order will be issued 'immediately' for Liverpool staying your protégé." He called for a messenger and instructed him to deliver it immediately to Henry Hotze at his lodgings at 17 Savile Row.

Twenty-odd minutes later, Hotze read it and headed to *The Index* office, where there was a private telegraph. There wasn't a moment to lose. Buckley was only an occasional agent, but his material was always gold—not surprising, given his influential position overseeing the American Desk of the Foreign Office.

Buckley was habitually cautious. He always worked through an intermediary, either Anderson or Hotze, to maintain plausible deniability. Under no circumstances would he contact Bulloch or Prioleau directly, which would have established a connection between them. This one time, though, he slipped up. In his haste to get the message to Hotze, he had used his real name on the note, no doubt assuming that Hotze would destroy it upon receipt.

Buckley was otherwise a perfect spy, one completely above suspicion. He was born to the plush, if not the purple: His father was the dashing Waterloo veteran General Edward Buckley, equerry to Queen Victoria, and his mother a daughter of the Earl of Radnor.

Victor came along in 1838, sixth of six offspring, and was granted the honor of becoming the young queen's first godchild. When he was twelve, Victor was sent, of course, to Eton, where he left no memorable impression on anyone. After that, the usual route was the army or the church, but Victor, with his pale, slight figure, fondness for silk cravats, and habit of rakishly swinging his cane, did not come across as a military man, and sipping tea at the vicarage with the local dowager was a fate too grim to bear.

In 1857, gainful employment was found for him as a third-class junior clerk in the Foreign Office, a place where, as one staffer put it, "as a house of call to gossip and smoke and read the morning papers, [it] is a most admirable institution. It so nicely takes up the time between the one o'clock lunch hour and the seven o'clock dinner." While the meager pay was suitable for most noble sons biding their time until they inherited an estate, Victor, as the youngest son, had no chance of ever coming into money.

He would have to be a Foreign Office lifer, and to his credit, Buckley took his job seriously. After passing a difficult qualifying examination, he was promoted, to second-class junior clerk, within the year.

After that, it was going to be a long, slow, tedious trudge up the ladder to first-class junior clerk, then assistant clerk, maybe senior clerk, and perhaps, if he were extraordinarily lucky (the current incumbent had joined the Foreign Office in *1812*), chief clerk. By sheer happenstance, he was allotted the American Desk, as very little of interest was happening there in the late 1850s, at least in the lordly eyes of the Foreign Office. When war broke out in 1861, making the continent rather more pressing from a diplomatic point of view, Buckley found himself occupying a prime position. He handled, for instance, every letter that passed between Minister Adams and Russell.

As a young, single, and aristocratic, if penurious, boulevardier, Buckley was invited to lots of smart parties. And in 1861, the smartest parties were organized by the Confederacy's friends, which is how Buckley met Frederick Bond of The London Armoury Company and a close pal of Major Anderson. Oiled by liquor, cash, and charm, Bond quickly made fast friends with the impressed Buckley, even calling him his "near kinsman."

It's difficult to condemn Buckley for having his head turned by his new crony. Bond, unlike himself, led a monied and glamorous existence, and he no doubt introduced his sheltered friend to the various fleshpots of London, as he had with Anderson when he took him to the Holborn Casino. Ultimately, however, Buckley had eyes only for one: Mary Stirling, a daughter of Vice-Admiral Sir James Stirling and Ellen Mangles, of a shipping family.

Buckley and Mary had met in 1858, but the nature of their relationship was an odd one, not least because, at twenty-five, she was six years older than he. Given her age and the enticing prospect of having an earl's daughter as her mother-in-law, marriage should normally have been a rapid affair. But it wasn't.

Three years later, she and Buckley still hadn't wed. The hitch was a lack of money. Mary was one of eleven children, making a meaningful dowry unlikely, and Buckley was getting by on a pitiful salary of about £175 a year, half of what, for example, even the Foreign Office chaplain in Austria made. To be upper class yet doomed to live a straitened, middle-class existence was unacceptable.

So when, in October 1861, Major Anderson offered Buckley the chance to be a "partner" in the Fraser Trenholm blockade-running scheme, "making it certain to him that he should not be a loser," Buckley—already romantically sympathetic to the South—started work as Agent X. Buckley probably thought his career as a mole would be a one-time deal. After all, in those halcyon days, nearly everyone believed Britain would rouse herself to the defense of the Confederacy and that the war would be a short one.

But as the fighting dragged on, the money proved too good to quit. It not only allowed him to affiance Mary but also gave him the wherewithal to speculate in cotton. One day soon, he'd be rich.

III

Sometime in the early evening of that Saturday, July 26, Bulloch received the warning telegram from Hotze. Once Her Majesty's Government opened for business on Monday, the detention order would be dispatched to Edwards, the Liverpool collector, to hold the *Enrica* pending an investigation.

In the event, the Confederates would be granted a slight postponement because Buckley had not known of Sir John Harding's travails, which delayed the other two law officers' judgment until Tuesday, July 29, with the final order not being delivered to Edwards until Thursday morning, July 31.

Bulloch was unaware of that at the time, of course, and so had to move extraordinarily fast. Within hours of the telegram, he had a plan. The first thing he did was notify Lairds that it was time to go. At the shipyard, he arranged to messenger a note to Captain Butcher "requesting my immediate attendance," as the latter recalled. Once Butcher arrived at Lairds, Bulloch told him that the *Enrica* had to be ready to leave come Monday's tide. It was a tall order, especially since the next day was the Sabbath. This one would not be of rest. A full crew had still not been recruited, all the necessary coal and stores were not yet on board, and Captain Semmes was somewhere in the Atlantic and would have no idea of the change of plan.

Butcher scoured Liverpool looking for likely lads willing to sign up and urging the stevedores to put their backs into loading the coal and bringing on supplies. William Passmore, one of Dudley's most effective informants, noticed something was up. He immediately reported to Maguire that he had just seen about thirty sailors marching to the docks and playing "Dixie's Land" on a fife, a concertina, and a cornet.

In the meantime, after Bulloch engaged the taciturn George Bond as pilot—his abiding attraction was that he "never asked an inquisitive question"—he called in the ever-trusty John Low to give him a special mission. He would be sailing on the *Enrica* but first he needed him to find a tender to follow the ship out of Liverpool. Low quickly rustled up the *Hercules,* a small steam tug that would carry any bits and pieces (brass engine fittings, spare spars, etc.) unavoidably left behind in the rush.

Bulloch then told his assistant Clarence Yonge, who had come over with him and Low back in March on the *Annie Childs,* that he, too, would be leaving "at a minute's notice" and appointed him paymaster of the *Enrica.*

According to the orders Bulloch handed him, while at sea Yonge was to soften up the crew for possible service as Confederate sailors. His task was to "mix freely with the 'warrant and petty officers,' show interest in their comfort and welfare [and] talk to them of the Southern States, and how they are fighting against great odds for only what every Englishman enjoys—*liberty!*" He was to hint that once "a distinguished officer of the Confederate States Navy" came aboard they would have an opportunity to "have the most active service, and be well taken care of."

Next up, Captain Butcher. His orders were to take the *Enrica* to the "bay of Praya [Praia da Vitória], in the island of Terceira, one of the Azores." Bulloch predicted Dudley would assume Nassau would be the rendezvous point for the *Enrica* and the *Agrippina*, the steamer still docked inconspicuously in London carrying the *Enrica*'s guns. That port was a known friendly, but Maffitt and the *Florida* had run into so much legal trouble there that Bulloch wanted to avoid a repetition. To confound Dudley, he selected the Azores, an out-of-the-way, North Atlantic archipelago of nine islands under Portuguese control.

Butcher was to consider himself "my confidential agent" and Bulloch "rel[ied] upon you as one gentleman may upon another" to execute the laborious task of transferring the guns to the *Enrica* after meeting the *Agrippina*, captained by Alexander McQueen. Once done, he was to "send me a line" before "get[ting] out of the reach of the telegraphic stations as soon as possible" to prevent any nosy American consul there transmitting information back to Liverpool. At some point, Captain Semmes of the Confederate States Navy would find him and take command.

In writing these incriminating words down and signing the letters under his real name, Bulloch made an uncharacteristic mistake, one prompted by haste, necessity, and desperation. He had violated the Foreign Enlistment Act outright on several counts, not least in planning to induce British civilian sailors into knowingly signing up for a belligerent navy and designating the *Enrica* as a Confederate warship to be armed with British-supplied guns.

Even so, it was time for a party.

IV

Come Monday morning, Bulloch shielded the *Enrica* from a surprise visit by Edwards's customs men by anchoring her in the middle of the Mersey. As a precaution, her boiler was kept heated and the engines gently turned over to ease a rapid escape if need be. To relieve any suspicion, Bulloch informed the authorities that he was holding a celebration to mark that day's planned trial run out to the famous Bell-Buoy and back.

The next day at 9:00 A.M., the smooth water and light breeze making for a fine day's outing, the *Enrica* was gaily festooned with pennants. Picnic tables and hampers, along with the requisite refreshments, had been brought on board. Dudley and Maguire, uninvited to the festivities, stood onshore watching the theatrics but were powerless to intervene.

Bulloch's guests, brought over by the tug *Hercules,* arrived. The Laird brothers were there, accompanied by five or six ladies, including two of their sisters, and Prioleau, too, no doubt. They were all there "as a blind," said one sailor. "When we sailed it was not our intention to return, but it was with the intention of going to sea, and so understood by us all."

At 3:00 P.M., with the *Enrica* puffing away near the Bell-Buoy, Bulloch kept up the charade by announcing that as Captain Butcher needed to keep the ship out all night to complete the trial, he and his guests would be returning to Liverpool on the *Hercules,* which had stationed herself nearby. Before he clambered into the boat, Bulloch directed the pilot Bond to make for Moelfre Bay, a small harbor in north Wales about sixty miles away.

So far, so good. But then things got complicated. Bulloch told Butcher that he would meet him there the next day in the *Hercules,* which would be transporting another forty or so men signed up too late to make the *Enrica*'s departure. At 7:00 A.M. on July 30, a rainy gray day, Bulloch showed up at the wharf to find not just the extra crew but their wives and girlfriends, who, the shipping master told him, were there not only to bid adieu to their Jacks but to make sure they collected a month's pay in advance. Bulloch had not included this large figure in his calculations, and he had no cash on him. Saying there was money aplenty aboard the *Enrica,* he promised to pay it once he returned, but the women, no strangers to shipowners' wiles, told him they would come with him to get it. Bulloch bowed to the inevitable and took everyone on a pleasant day trip to Wales.

That afternoon, the *Hercules* got alongside the *Enrica.* Once all were aboard the steamer, Bulloch called for a bumper supper for everyone, including bounteous grog "to add zest and cheerfulness to the meal." After pipes had been smoked, the men were called aft and told they would be heading to Havana. Bulloch, described by a sailor there as "a low-sized, stoutish man, with black bushy whiskers, moustache and beard, apparently a foreigner," declared that "he wanted men not cowards" for the voyage. Demonstrating that not everyone believed Havana was the real destination, one of the men asked whether they would run the blockade, with Bulloch guardedly replying that "he would let them know." Afterward, one by one, each man, accompanied by his watchful beloved, signed his articles in Butcher's cabin and received his month's advance wages, counted and rapidly tucked into a purse.

With that matter settled, the ladies and any sailors who refused to sign (twenty or so) were taken back to Liverpool that night. Bulloch had good reason to get them off the ship quickly. A few days earlier, he'd heard through an anonymous "judicious friend" at Southampton that the sloop USS *Tuscarora*, under Captain Craven and earlier summoned by Minister Adams from Spain, had been ordered to "catch the pirate at all hazard." The likeliest place Craven would come looking would be Wales and then Queenstown, on the south coast of Ireland—the natural, shortest route for the *Enrica* to take into the Atlantic.

There was no love lost between Craven and Bulloch. Before the war, the two of them had been in the Coast Survey, but what had provoked the bad blood is impossible to say. Bulloch regarded him as "a very credulous officer, as well as a very rude man." He would enjoy making him look a fool, too.

At 2:30 A.M. on July 31, Bulloch instructed Bond, the pilot, to go "north about," to head not for Queenstown but toward Belfast. With a hard wind from the southwest and a pelting rain, it was a terrible night to venture into the Irish Sea, but Bulloch had no other choice. To tarry another day at Moelfre Bay for better weather would mean capture.

The gamble paid off. As Craven fruitlessly patrolled St. George's Channel between Wales and southern Ireland, the *Enrica* arrived off the Giant's Causeway at 6:00 P.M. on July 31. Bulloch took a boat to a snug hotel, where the wind skirled and snifted about the gables, sipped Coleraine malt, and congratulated himself on a good job well done.

The next morning, a beautiful bright day with a gentle westerly blowing, Bulloch stood on the shore amid the dramatic setting of thousands of hexagonal stone columns poking surreally skyward and watched Captain Butcher depart on his adventure. Then he took a train to Belfast and returned to Liverpool, not knowing that Dudley had a man on board the *Enrica*.

But, then, neither did Dudley.

NINE

The Dead Letter

I

Bulloch was entirely justified in being pleased with himself. Despite Dudley's surveillance, his "shameless false witnesses" (as Bulloch indignantly called his informants), his stack of affidavits, and Adams's pressure upon the British authorities, the *Enrica* had flown the coop. And he had pulled it off with panache. The obstreperous consul hadn't even seen that what was coming had been coming, whereas Bulloch seemed to have a supernatural ability to peek around corners and peer through walls.

Two worries, nevertheless, niggled at him. First, Dudley had come very close indeed, closer than even the consul knew, to foiling the scheme. Bulloch, after all, had been forced to send the *Enrica* out weeks before he'd intended. If it hadn't been for Buckley at the Foreign Office, quite frankly, she would have fallen into Collector Edwards's hands.

The second worry: Where was Captain Semmes?

Bulloch got his answer on August 8, when Semmes and a number of Confederate officers unexpectedly appeared in Liverpool. Their arrival brought another headache for Bulloch. He had to keep them squirreled away out of Dudley's sight until Prioleau could arrange for his ship, the *Bahama*, to take them to Praya Bay in the Azores five days later. In the meantime, Bulloch put them all up at his modest house, where he and his charming wife, Harriott, said an admiring Semmes, lived "in a very plain, simple style."

Wanting to make sure the handover from Captain Butcher to Semmes went smoothly, Bulloch volunteered to leave with them. A week later, the *Bahama* reached the Azores and rendezvoused with the *Enrica* and the *Agrippina*. The work of transferring the armaments had not yet been completed because, as Butcher explained, when the *Enrica* arrived, a Portuguese customs officer had decided to nose around on board asking impertinent questions. It was only after Butcher's supplying him with wine, cigars, and a bribe that he "became quite friendly [and] assured me that we should not be molested."

The crews had then worked with a will, at one point heaving a gun weighing five tons between ships and coming close to dropping it in the sea as the chains strained mightily to hold it. The blessed arrival of the *Bahama* certainly lightened the load. Aided by the *Bahama* men, the scattered crates of shot and barrels of pork littering the deck were stowed away, and the last gun was installed on Friday, August 22. Another day of hard labor, and all 250 tons of coal were stowed in the *Enrica*'s bunker by 10:00 P.M. on a rainy Saturday. The *Agrippina* left soon after.

On Sunday morning, which dawned bright, cloudless, and beautiful, the *Enrica* and the *Bahama* steamed one marine league—three nautical miles—outside Portugal's jurisdiction boundary, safely putting them in international waters and beyond the reach, said Bulloch, "of foreign enlistment acts and neutrality proclamations." There, Butcher relinquished formal command to Semmes, who raised "the flag of the new-born Confederate States" at the ship's peak before clambering atop one of the broadside guns to address the crew.

He roused them with a stirring speech asking them to sign on for military service. As he later recalled, he said, adding a touch of gauzy romance, any man who did not want to go would be taken home on the *Bahama*, but for those who stayed, the coming cruise "would be one of excitement and adventure." Not only would they be heroically fighting "the battles of the oppressed against the oppressor," they would be richly rewarded for it. Each would receive double the wages of a Royal Navy man and "lots of prize money" for each ship they ravaged, payable at war's end.

One sailor there remembered his speech being significantly more wild-eyed: When Semmes spoke, he cried that "he was deranged in his mind to see his country going to ruin, and had to steal out of Liverpool like a thief. That instead of them watching him he was now going after them. He wanted all of us to join him; that he was going to sink, burn, and destroy all his enemies' property."

There were about ninety men present and of those all but ten or so wanted to stay with Semmes, which still left him undermanned (a full complement was 120). After the Britons-turned-Confederates signed their new articles, the Confederate officers, garbed in their dress uniforms of gray and gold braid, removed their hats as Semmes read out his official orders from President Davis and Secretary Mallory. In an impressively choreographed display, when Semmes finished, a gunner fired a cannon, a quartermaster struck the English colors, an ad hoc band tooted "Dixie," and a deafening cheer tore the sky as Semmes christened the new Confederate States' ship the *Alabama*.

For Bulloch, it was a bittersweet moment. His younger half brother Irvine, after distinguished service on the *Savannah* and the *Nashville*, was already serving as a Semmes lieutenant and sailing master. His presence, and his news from Georgia, had been cheering. Bulloch also had to bid adieu to John Low, who was becoming a lieutenant, and the loyal Clarence Yonge, too, staying on as paymaster. They were to go to sea and take part in the upcoming venture while he had to return to Liverpool and face the inevitable fallout from the escape of the *Alabama*.

Still, it was worth it. At eleven o'clock that night, with the heavens brilliant with stars and a blazing comet streaking across the firmament, Bulloch shook hands with Semmes and wished him happy hunting before departing on the *Bahama*. As for Semmes, once Bulloch had gone, he ordered the engineers to bank their fires and raise the screw while the riggers set the fore and aft sails. With just a fresh wind driving her forward under easy canvas, the *Alabama* headed northeast while her captain bunked down in his cabin and "slept as comfortably as the rolling of the ship, and a strong smell of bilge-water would permit."

II

Dudley was livid at Bulloch's snatching victory from his hands. So, too, were Adams and Benjamin Moran at the Legation. The latter characterized the *Enrica* debacle as one of British "indifference and connivance" combining with Confederate "falsehood" and "perjury." A month passed. Tempers cooled, but questions became more heated. In early September, Adams addressed several strident letters to Russell requesting an explanation for the *Alabama*'s mysterious disappearance from Liverpool. The foreign secretary pretended he hadn't received them, but finally, three weeks later, replied that he had ordered an investigation into the matter.

Adams could smell a government euphemism for "doing nothing" as well as anyone, and over the coming weeks he pursued Russell relentlessly for a real answer. But the foreign secretary stuck to his guns. To Adams's remonstrances that Confederate agents were still at work building warships, Russell, hoping to make Adams go away, airily waved his concerns aside by reminding him that as "much as Her Majesty's Government desire to prevent such occurrences, they are unable to go beyond the law."

Rather cheekily, Adams retorted that in that case some unbiased observers *might* say "the law is little better than a dead letter" since the foreign secretary had just acknowledged that "occurrences" (plural) of lawbreaking had indeed been detected. To which Russell, having been outmaneuvered, carefully admitted in October that, yes, the Foreign Enlistment Act could *possibly* "be evaded by very subtle contrivances," but even so, the government "cannot on that account go beyond the letter of the existing law."

This marked the first time any British official had ever admitted that maybe, just maybe, the law had been broken, not blatantly but by means of a "subtle contrivance." It was a watershed moment, soon followed by another when Russell mooted the possibility of the government "going beyond the letter" of the law in the future to prevent Confederates from using loopholes to get their ships to sea.

For the time being, Russell's hint was just the wisp of an idea. But still, there was a change in the air. Dudley could feel it.

III

Prompting Russell's cautious shift had been news reaching London in early October of President Lincoln's preliminary Emancipation Proclamation of September 22. As of January 1, 1863, Lincoln had announced, slaves in the Confederacy "shall be then, thenceforward, and forever free."

It was difficult to know, though, what to make of Lincoln's pledge. Would he actually go through with such a radical plan and risk a general mutiny within the army, many of whose soldiers were fighting for "the Union" but not black liberation? Or was it, in fact, a sign of weakness, the last throw of the dice by a cynical man to stave off the North's imminent collapse?

The foreign secretary did not know, and neither did anyone else. What he did know was that by changing the grand objective of the war from the preservation of the Union—which many in Britain could take or leave—to a humanitarian crusade to free the oppressed, Lincoln had uncompromisingly defined the South as a slave empire. Now that it had been indelibly exposed as such, fewer people were willing to be seen publicly as Confederate supporters, even if they suspected Lincoln's motives.

Sympathy for the South's fight for national self-determination was harder to come by after the proclamation. And while there remained fears of the coming American economic leviathan and the onslaught of republican democracy upon Britain's ancient political system, the abolitionist impulse was a potent one.

Neutrality nevertheless remained the British government's position. Russell had briefly looked into staging a kind of early peacekeeping operation to separate the two combatants after the horrors of Antietam in September, but he quickly dropped it when Seward bluntly said that the war would continue to the very ends of the earth, even if both sides were "mutually exterminat[ed]." This uncompromising attitude inspired Prime Minister Palmerston to remark that Britain must continue "to be lookers-on till the war shall have taken a more decided turn" and a winner emerged. Russell agreed, saying that "preach[ing] peace to them is like speaking to mad dogs" these days.

Even so, in that winter of 1862, Dudley perceived that the *meaning* of "neutrality" had subtly changed. Before, *neutrality* had been code for a soft Southernism in which Britain turned a blind eye to the Confederate naval scheme while insisting on a strictly literal reading of the Foreign Enlistment Act. *Now,* the consul noticed, by hinting that he might be amenable to a more relaxed interpretation of the act, Russell was moving toward a soft Northernism that reflected the favorable shift in public opinion toward the Union after the Emancipation Proclamation. The foreign secretary's thumb, it seemed, had been removed from the Confederate side of the scale. It now rested lightly on that of the Union.

All Dudley needed to do now was to force Russell to press down harder.

IV

On a Semmes boat, the crew soon learned, all had to be shipshape. That inspirational stump speech he had given, about the struggle for liberty, was never to be repeated. From now on, "when I wanted a man to do anything," he said, "I gave him a rather sharp order," and if that order was not instantly heeded, confinement in irons on a bread-and-water diet swiftly followed. As a salutary reminder, Semmes liked to read out the Articles of War every Sunday during muster, emphasizing with particular relish the crimes punishable by death.

The *Alabama* was a lethal military vessel, not some lubberly civilian tugboat, and Semmes demanded both men and ship look the part. After the *Alabama* was scrubbed stem to stern, Semmes cast a beady eye over the men. He had not been impressed by their raggedy turnout. "With faces begrimed with coal dust, red shirts, and blue shirts, Scotch caps, and hats, brawny chests exposed, and stalwart arms naked

A mustache and Raphael Semmes

to the elbows, they looked as little like the crew of a man-of-war as one can well conceive." They were directed to soap themselves down before being issued the snappy blue and white uniforms brought by Clarence Yonge.

Afterward, Semmes divided the crew into sections specializing in various duties, like gunnery, maintenance, assault, and defense. Then the training began and did not stop. Lieutenant Arthur Sinclair wrote that every day, no matter the weather, the officers put the gun crews through their paces, had the men practice their saber, pike, and pistol work, and perfect their boarding tactics.

Machiavelli, wise in all things worldly, may have counseled that a prince should be more feared than loved, if he could not be both, but Semmes cared only to be obeyed. That Semmes, now in his early fifties, ran the *Alabama* as a dictatorship at a time when using harsh corporal punishment at sea was fast declining marked him as an extremist.

But Semmes was an extremist in all things, a result of his orphaning as a young teenager, which bestowed both a surfeit of confidence and a dearth of doubt as he made his own way in the world. Short, introverted, solitary, prone to vowing revenge at the merest hint of a slight, Semmes read compulsively—not to challenge his strange prejudices but to confirm them. Roiling within him was an unquenchable hatred of New England Puritans and an obsessional loathing for miscegenation, but there was also a touching tenderness toward his absurdly long, painstakingly twirled mustache and a naturalist's true love for coral polyps (the "little toiler of the sea").

Despite his frightening remoteness and his weird idiosyncrasies, Semmes could afford to be a martinet because no one knew more about shipping lanes, weather, coastlines, or navigation than he, and his tactical acumen and ship-handling skills were second to none.

He immediately put them to good use.

V

On September 5, a hundred miles from Terceira Island in the Azores, the American whaler *Ocmulgee* was having a fine day. A freshly harpooned whale was being cut up, its oil, bones, and blubber worth a sweet $50,000. Deceitfully flying the United States flag, the *Alabama* moseyed up alongside. Before a surprised Captain Osborn and his men could react, a boarding party had taken them prisoner. They were politely—Semmes was good about that sort of thing, unless he saw a sizable complement of black crew—directed to pack their things, grab some provisions, and descend to the whaleboats within fifteen minutes.

As Semmes ransacked the ship's library for interesting books to consume, the *Alabama*'s crew transferred the *Ocmulgee*'s pork and beef stores before smashing its bunks for kindling. The galley was emptied of its butter and lard, and together with the sticks and straw from the mattresses, was heaped into two piles, one in the captain's cabin and the other on the forecastle. After the raiders evacuated to their own boats, a couple of men waited for the order to "Fire!" before escaping the flames. To torch a ship under Semmes's professional guidance took only a minute before the blaze was licking the topsails, dooming it to the deep.

And so began Semmes's trail of destruction. Over the next two weeks, the *Alabama* took no fewer than ten ships, burning every one; by the end of November, Semmes had boarded another fourteen. Semmes habitually changed the *Alabama*'s appearance to keep his victims unsuspecting. Sometimes she flew a U.S. flag, at others, a neutral or British one. Occasionally, he dressed her up as an old, laggardly sailing ship, but often the *Alabama* would masquerade as a steamer with a single smokestack or even two, the second effect achieved by fitting a special black sail amidships.

Semmes had started small, with whalers and schooners making easy prey, but he soon grew more ambitious. Large passenger, mail, and cargo ships like the *Emily Farnum* and the *Brilliant*, the latter worth $164,000, fell into his clutches. He ranged to Newfoundland and lurked in the Gulf Stream, all the better to harass the American grain fleets to Europe. As Bulloch had predicted, the domestic pressure on the U.S. Navy to abandon the blockade and divert to ship protection became nearly unbearable.

Yet to his disappointment, Lincoln held firm. While several gunboats were sent to the New England coast, the rest stayed exactly where they were outside Southern ports. In November, Semmes, bored of the wintry Atlantic, turned south toward the Caribbean, where the pickings were bountiful, and he thought there was a better chance of drawing off Union warships from enforcing the blockade.

At sea, Semmes's diktat reigned, but even the *Alabama* had to come into port occasionally to re-coal and parole prisoners, and it was then that he had to relax his rigid discipline. Semmes, to his credit, did not run a dry ship—twice-daily grog rations was the norm—but at Martinique on November 18, so much potent booze was smuggled on board that a mutiny nearly erupted when a drunk sailor threw a belaying pin at Lieutenant John Kell. Semmes restored order by manacling the ringleaders and dousing them with water until they almost drowned.

At Kingston in Jamaica on January 25, 1863, there were more problems, despite a new ban on bringing alcohol on board and Semmes allowing only half the crew ashore at a time. Flush with their wages and over the moon about the \$8,000 in prize money owed to each of them, the boys had a wild time. It was Clarence Yonge, though, who got himself into the most serious trouble.

Semmes had been keeping an eye on his paymaster's behavior for some time and had not liked what he'd seen. Flaunting his privileged relationship to Bulloch, Yonge regarded himself as not being subject to Semmes's commands and could not bear to be bellowed at when Semmes cracked down. Yonge's vices, now that he lacked Bulloch's fatherly supervision, grew ever more apparent as he chafed under Semmes's absolutism. Cash began to vanish, and Yonge's books looked as if they had been fudged to cover up the theft. While onshore carrying £400 to pay the *Alabama*'s bills, he was seen drunkenly consorting with Northern prisoners, and there was a rumor that he had visited the American consulate. Lieutenants Kell and Low were sent with an armed party to arrest him, and Yonge was dragged back to the *Alabama* to await Semmes's judgment.

The court-martial did not take long. Yonge was dismissed from the service, drummed humiliatingly out of the ship, and abandoned in Kingston when the *Alabama* departed that night. Semmes, giving the worthless Yonge not another thought, never dreamed of the trouble he was to bring.

VI

Since August 1862, Lieutenant Maffitt of the *Florida* had been having a terrible time. As soon as the ship was christened after being belatedly released from Nassau, he discovered that they had forgotten all the rammers and sponges for the guns. Then came an outbreak of yellow fever. Like many of his crew, Maffitt experienced "a heavy chill, pain in the back and loins, dimness of vision, and disposition to vomit," and his quarterdeck resembled a hospital. With so many ailing and so many dead, he was forced to seek refuge in Spanish Cuba.

In early September, needing new men and a refit, Maffitt was forced to leave and run the Union blockade under heavy fire at Mobile, Alabama. Against all odds, he made it in but could not get out. Four months later, his luck finally turned on the night of January 15, 1863, when a violent storm assailed the coast, scattering the Northern warships. Maffitt seized the opportunity to escape, and the *Florida* was finally free.

Eager to make up for lost time, and envious, too, of Semmes's success, Maffitt embarked on a Caribbean spree. "All the merchants of New York and Boston who [are] princes in wealth and puffy with patriotic zeal for the subjugation of the South," vowed Maffitt, "will soon cry with a loud voice, peace, peace; we are becoming ruined and the country damned!"

In the last two weeks of January, he captured three brigs, but he hit the big-time on February 12, when he took the *Jacob Bell*, a clipper returning from China carrying 1,380 tons of prime-grade China tea. Valued at a grand $2 million, a figure that put even Semmes's best score in the shade, the *Jacob Bell* alone was worth at least eight times what the *Florida* had cost to build. It was the richest haul ever taken by a Confederate vessel.

At the end of February, after taking on coal in Barbados, a local newspaper reported that the *Florida* was last seen heading south, toward Brazil, to fresh hunting grounds.

VII

The twin raiders' success filled Southern hearts with pride and Northerners' with fear. Yet the Confederate assumption that the blockade would soon collapse as Union ships were diverted from hunting runners to protecting merchant ships was flawed. This was because the U.S. Navy was becoming ever more adept at capturing blockade-runners. The North Atlantic Blockading Squadron, for instance, which covered the coast from Virginia to North Carolina, proved itself a particularly efficient sentinel once Rear Admiral Samuel Phillips Lee assumed command in September 1862.

The small changes he introduced made a big difference. First to go was the nighttime practice of blockaders' lying at anchor five miles off the coast, with two miles separating each ship. Instead, Lee ordered them to "keep steam ready to move and work, and cable ready to slip at a moment's notice," and to establish a brightly lit, tight ring around the ports from twilight to sunrise—the prime running hours.

Farther out to sea, he established an outer defensive line of his swiftest ships to snap up runners as they approached from the Caribbean, forcing the Southerners to risk two encounters on each attempt to enter port. If they evaded the outer cordon, they often found themselves trapped against the inner with no line of retreat. In just six months, between November 1862 and May 1863, Lee's squadron bagged no fewer than forty-one runners. By the end of the latter year, that total had risen to sixty-five fast, modern steamers, whose value, including their contraband, amounted to $13 million.

Against such a tally, the *Alabama* and *Florida* alone could not compete. It explains, too, why more warships were not redirected away from the blockade and toward catching Semmes and Maffitt. Despite the damage the raiders were inflicting on American shipping, the blockade was, slowly but surely, choking off the South's cotton exports and arms imports. Semmes and Maffitt were merely a nuisance, occupied primarily with stealing easily replaceable pantry goods like molasses, tea, and sugar from Northern merchantmen. The U.S. Navy, meanwhile, was achieving the greater strategic aim of stopping guns and white gold— the emergency supplies necessary for the Confederacy's very survival.

Even Fraser Trenholm, the biggest operator, managed to smuggle into Liverpool only eighteen thousand bales in 1862. By September of that year, Liverpool's entire cotton stockpile in its warehouses had fallen to a scant eighty-five thousand bales—about two weeks' supply for Britain's mills—and the price per pound had doubled from fourteen to twenty-eight pence, virtually the highest they would reach between 1821 and 1913.

Normally, market forces being what they are, such a high price would have attracted a slew of entrants into the blockade-running business, but the U.S. Navy was raising the risk of playing the game. In 1861, about one in ten ships had been captured along the entire blockade from Virginia to the Gulf of Mexico. Those good odds meant easy money. But in the following year, one in eight fell into Yankee hands, and by 1863, one in four. Neither good nor easy anymore, then.

But certainly ever more onerous, for the taking of a blockade-runner removed from the board not only the vessel and its cargo but a veteran captain and a skilled crew, who could look forward only to imprisonment. These losses added up: Of eighty-four steamers that ran the blockade between November 1861 and March 1864, fully thirty-seven were captured and another twenty-four lost at sea—an attritional rate of nearly 75 percent. Even under the most optimal circumstances, that was unsustainable, and these years were very far from being optimal. With the South's financial, manufacturing, and manpower resources buckling under the strain of war, it was almost impossible to replace either fast ship or good crew with new ones. Anaconda-like, the blockade was slowly choking the life out of the Confederacy.

It was becoming distressingly clear that the *Florida* and the *Alabama* could not themselves break its death grip. Only the application of brute force was up to that task. Fortunately, Bulloch was already moving ahead with Stage Three of his plan: building ironclads to hammer the U.S. Navy.

VIII

After Semmes abandoned Clarence Yonge in Jamaica in January 1863, the captain never bothered to tell Bulloch what had happened—an omission that would come back to haunt the latter. As Bulloch later explained to Secretary Mallory, "I suppose he thought the miserable creature would drink himself to death."

He didn't. Indeed, Yonge landed on his feet when a kindly widow took him in as a lodger. After Yonge relayed his tale of woe, appropriately edited, love, of a sort, blossomed. In short order, they were married. Unfortunately for his betrothed, Yonge forgot to mention that there was already another Mrs. Yonge and two children he'd left behind in Savannah.

Yonge had no desire to stay in Jamaica. To raise money, he callously suggested to Mrs. Yonge the Second that they take the fourteen-year-old "negro boy" who lived with her to Charleston to sell. Being mixed race herself, she refused. And in any case, she had no intention of going anywhere near the South for fear of being sold herself. So Yonge used his charms to persuade her to sell her house instead and use the proceeds to pay for their passage to Britain.

On March 25, the family showed up in Liverpool. Yonge put them up at The Angel Hotel and then absconded on a train south a few days later. Having dispensed with his inconvenient wife and the boy, Yonge went to the port of Southampton, evidently hoping to board a boat to America. But he could not afford a ticket. Now stuck in Britain, Yonge, a resourceful one, came up with the idea of selling information to the Yankees.

Yonge next popped up in London, where at 10:30 A.M. on Wednesday, April 1, he knocked on the door of the Legation, where he asked a very surprised Benjamin Moran to administer the oath of allegiance to the United States. Moran was understandably reluctant to help this Southerner with a name familiar from the notorious *Alabama* Affair, until Yonge, who admittedly had "rather good manners," claimed to know the greatest secret of them all.

Moran ushered Yonge in to see a puzzled Adams, where Yonge promised him the golden key to Bulloch's kingdom of lies—at a price. Yonge, it seems, had mused vindictively on his misfortunes since leaving Bulloch's employ and now blamed him for them. According to Moran, "it was clear that his loyalty [to us] was the result in a measure of empty pockets and partly a matter of revenge."

Then, in one of those strange coincidences that make history so interesting, it was at that precise moment that Thomas Dudley arrived from Liverpool bearing more evidence of Confederate misdeeds, including a sheaf of *Alabama*-related papers mentioning a certain Clarence Yonge, standing right there as he lived and breathed.

The encounter must have come as a shock to both consul and turncoat, especially since the papers Dudley had brought had been recently sold to him by a distraught but very angry Mrs. Yonge the Second. Her beloved husband had, she told Dudley, ungallantly ditched her in Liverpool and stolen what was left of her money.

As Yonge, still blissfully ignorant that what he had to sell had already been bought, was asked to wait outside, Dudley showed Adams and

Moran the trove he'd acquired. It was extraordinary. There were copies of confidential letters from Bulloch to Mallory, for instance, dating back to January 1862, receipts for sailors' wages received from Bulloch, and Bulloch's secret orders to Yonge just before he'd left on the *Alabama*. This last included the incriminating details as to how Bulloch had arranged her arming, his instructions to recruit a British crew for a Confederate ship, and his naming of Semmes as captain—all written and signed under his real name.

With Bulloch's secrets laid bare, Dudley finally saw his antagonist for what he was. Bulloch wasn't a masterful magician at all, just a cheap conjurer with a few tricks up his sleeve. As he had realized when, as a boy, he'd been frightened by the ghost in the graveyard, only to discover that it was merely a trapped and desperate ram, Dudley now understood that the seemingly omniscient, omnipotent Bulloch was but a phantom of the mind.

He could be beaten.

IX

After discussing with Adams what to do with this remarkable walk-in asset, Dudley took Yonge to the Golden Cross Hotel. Moran, meanwhile, scurried off to find a solicitor named Crowdy to obtain an affidavit. Before they returned, Dudley discreetly arranged to pay Yonge £6 a week plus living expenses and passage to the United States in return for his testimony and continuing assistance—an underhanded, albeit necessary, move. This was no time to play the honorable lion, not with Dudley worrying that if Yonge were left without money, his former comrades would "try to buy him off." Yonge was the sort to be bought, after all— Dudley had just done so himself. Now he needed Yonge to *stay* bought. Privately, Dudley had another insurance policy in case Yonge fled the country. His informant was still "not aware that I have his letters," though admittedly they were not as conclusive without also having the man himself on the record. Even so, it was much better than nothing.

Thus assured, Yonge sung. *Everything* tumbled out, from William C. Miller's and Fawcett Preston's roles in building the *Oreto/Florida* to

Fraser Trenholm's and Prioleau's financial involvement to the fake party Bulloch had held on the *Enrica* to the Lairds' awareness of her mission from the beginning. "There was a great deal more said and sworn to," said Moran, but most interesting was Yonge's revelation as to how Bulloch had known to get the *Enrica* out just in time. What he said only confirmed Moran's long-held suspicion that there was a mole in the Foreign Office, though Yonge was not aware of his identity. He stated definitively, nevertheless, that Bulloch had received advanced warning from an "English official."

What Yonge had divulged was incredible, but there was still the matter of his trustworthiness. He claimed to now be a Union man yet expressed sentiments to Moran showing "that he still had a good deal of the rebel in him," and he was an admitted bigamist, an accused swindler, and a known Judas. Yonge was certainly "a man of talent," Moran concluded, but "still, he is a slippery fellow," while Adams commented urbanely on the "facility with which men go from one side to the other."

With that in mind, Adams believed Yonge was a worthless character and instructed Dudley to "send him back to the United States by the next week's Steamer." He would get his citizenship and nothing more.

But the consul disobeyed what he believed to be a wrongheaded directive. Though he was "a reckless and uncertain kind of man— quite likely a bad man," Yonge was too valuable to throw away. Since arriving in Liverpool with Bulloch in March a year earlier, he had acted as Bulloch's assistant at 10 Rumford Place. As part of his sec-retarial duties, Yonge told Dudley, he had made copies of Bulloch's correspondence with Secretary Mallory, he was familiar with their handwriting, he could attest to their genuine signatures, and he himself signed pay dockets to recruits and contracts for businesses on Bulloch's authority under Fraser Trenholm's name. He also knew that the elusive John Low—whom Dudley was even at that point unsure existed—was a Confederate agent. Yonge also tied Bulloch and Major Anderson to the *Fingal* arms-running escapade, and he said that Bulloch introduced him to Prioleau and that Bulloch had an office at Fraser Trenholm, reserved only for him, to meet with Southern officers and sympathetic businessmen. In short, Yonge's inside knowledge of clandestine Confederate operations was priceless.

Instead of buying Yonge a steamer ticket, then, Dudley arranged for him to leave immediately via the consul's personal Underground Railroad—a network of his abolitionist friends—"to get him out of the way of the other side." Yonge took a train to Manchester, then stayed in the Yorkshire village of Holmfirth for several days before moving to the quiet rural outskirts of Sheffield. He was to live under the name J. Edwards Davies and use a system of drop boxes for communication with Dudley to prevent the Confederates from discovering his address.

Thanks to Yonge's windfall of intelligence, Dudley believed he now had more than enough "to convict the Lairds . . . Fraser Trenholm & Co., Fawcett Preston & Co., and Cap. James D. Bullock [*sic*] . . . under the Foreign Enlistment Act." In Yonge, at last Dudley had the weapon he needed. And, by the hand of divine Providence, the perfect opportunity to wield it against Bulloch was sitting at Toxteth Dock in Liverpool.

TEN

Traitor to His Benefactor

I

For months, assisted by Detective Maguire, who had the gateman and several apprentices on his payroll, Dudley had been accumulating evidence on a modest steamer named the *Alexandra* built by William C. Miller & Sons and "owned" by Fawcett Preston. Both firms were in Bulloch's pocket, naturally arousing Dudley's suspicions as to what they were up to.

At the *Alexandra*'s launching on March 7, 1863, a disguised Maguire had insinuated himself among the workmen. He reported to Dudley that Prioleau, Captain Tessier (the longtime commander of Fraser Trenholm's *Bahama* supply ship and runner), Captain Butcher (*Enrica*), Captain Duguid (*Oreto*), and, of course, the proud patriarch Bulloch were all present. Together, they made the ceremony seem like some kind of Confederate family gathering.

There, Charles Prioleau had loudly boasted that the *Alexandra* was a "gift" to Jefferson Davis from his loyal friends at Fraser Trenholm. By Dudley's lights, it was just another Bulloch scam to evade the Foreign Enlistment Act by presenting a "gift" that would inevitably be armed and equipped elsewhere.

On closer inspection, though, *Alexandra*'s purpose was opaque. Dudley speculated that she was intended as a sister to the *Florida* and the *Alabama*, though that would have been a stretch. At 300 tons' displacement, compared with the *Alabama*'s 1,050, and at 145 feet long, against the *Florida*'s 191, she was too small for long-range commerce raiding. Yet some who saw the *Alexandra*, like Captain Inglefield of HMS *Majestic*, stationed outside Liverpool, at the same time believed that "she was not intended for mercantile purposes," citing her oddly low bulwarks, over which pivot guns could play. On the other hand, she could just have been a particularly well-built, high-quality merchantman, perhaps even a "mail boat" or a "yacht," as Prioleau and Fawcett Preston were claiming.

In fact, according to Bulloch, the *Alexandra* was to be used as a "gunboat," albeit employed only along a coast or river. Dudley was right, then, in alleging the *Alexandra* was intended as a ship of war, even if he was off in comparing her with the *Florida* and the *Alabama*.

That March and April, two issues came to a head, allowing Dudley to seize the chance to make an example of the *Alexandra*, whatever she was. If successful, his plan would terminate Confederate operations in Britain in a single stroke. And best of all, Bulloch had no idea that Dudley had a trick up his own sleeve: Clarence Yonge. Revealing his inside man would make a pleasantly unpleasant surprise for the so-called fox.

The first issue was the Erlanger Loan, better known as the Cotton Loan. This was a Richmond-backed financial scheme, launched on March 19 by the Parisian firm Emile Erlanger & Co., to raise cash for the South, which by now was desperately short of the hard currency and gold needed to fund not only the war but the clandestine naval program.

The idea, based on the success of the secret Liverpool fundraising scheme earlier uncovered by Dudley, was to sell bonds in Europe that could be exchanged later for cotton. Early-stage investors bought them for 90 percent of their fixed face value, so £90 for each £100 bond. One such was Victor Buckley at the Foreign Office, flush from his cut of Prioleau's blockade-running, who purchased a colossal £2,000's worth on the sly, making him the potential owner of eighty thousand pounds of prime New Orleans–grade cotton. Deliverable in Dixie at just sixpence per pound, the cotton could be resold in Liverpool at the elevated market rate of about 24 pence—a nice 400 percent markup.

Buckley had high hopes of making a killing, as did many others (including several MPs, numerous peers, and two editors of *The Times*), and the bond price quickly rose to £95½ as speculators scrambled to get a piece of a sure thing. In that glorious shining moment, it seemed that Cotton was indeed King at last.

But disappointingly, within weeks bond prices fell to around £86, much to the malicious delight of Benjamin Moran, who gloated at "the English dupes who have taken up the loan." He predicted that they would drop "a good deal lower than that" as time went on. He was right.

Part of the reason was that investors realized that getting the cotton out of the South to sell in Liverpool was not as easy as they had thought. According to the loan's terms, plantation owners were responsible only for delivering the cotton to "within ten miles of a railroad, or stream navigable to the ocean." After that, it was the buyer's problem getting it to a port, loaded onto a blockade-runner, and brought to market. If your ship was lost on the way, so was your investment—a sobering thought given the U.S. Navy's success at sinking runners these days.

Worse, because there were shocking rumors that the U.S. government would not honor these enemy-issued bonds in the event of a Southern surrender, their price would rise and fall depending on how the Confederate armies were faring, like an index tracking the chances of victory. Edwin De Leon, a Confederate diplomat skeptical of the loan scheme, commented that "it soon became a gambling stock, and its fluctuations were wonderfully rapid—varying with each steamer's news [of battles]—and sometimes in the course of a week rising or falling 12 per cent."

Not for nothing was it known as "the most speculative stock ever floated on the London Stock Exchange." In early July, for example, while General Robert E. Lee was riding high after his audacious victory at Chancellorsville in May, the price had stabilized at around £90. But at the end of July, when news of his defeat at Gettysburg and the fall of Vicksburg reached Britain, the bonds crashed almost overnight to £70 and continued their plummet to £60 over the next two weeks as even hardened pro-Southerners lost their nerve. For a national bond issue, an instrument supposed to be the very acme of financial probity, this level of volatility was unprecedented.

Even so, through resales, market manipulation, and buybacks, Erlanger & Co. managed to raise the impressive amount of about $8.5 million, portions of which were urgently diverted to Bulloch through Prioleau's office. From Dudley's perspective, revenue from the Cotton Loan was refilling Bulloch's purse just as the Confederate agent was gearing up for another round of shipbuilding.

The second issue that came to a head at this time was the groundswell of support for the Union after the Emancipation Proclamation went into effect on January 1, 1863. Dudley believed that, finally, the scales had fallen from British eyes. They had been lied to for so long that slavery was not a core issue of the war, but now, he told Seward, "all over the Kingdom there are signs of a healthy reaction" that "will sweep every thing before it."

Mayor Abel Heywood of Manchester was among the first to declare his city's new commitment to the North. Following a rally at Free Trade Hall of several thousand working-class supporters, Heywood dispatched an emissary to the Legation, bringing with him an address, printed on vellum, affirming Manchester's backing for emancipation. In reply, on January 19, Lincoln sent his own effusive letter, carried to Manchester by Moran, who placed it directly in Heywood's hands. In it, Lincoln praised "the sublime Christian heroism" that had long inspired the anti-slavery campaign. Compared to the Union's soldiers gallantly fighting for "justice, humanity, and freedom," British pro-Confederates were suddenly coming across not as cavaliers dedicated to aiding plucky rebels but as partisans of a slave power whose economy was based on undercutting the wages and destroying the livelihoods of honest workingmen. Favoring Dixie, in short, was becoming socially embarrassing.

Emancipation, then, was the catalyst for a profound shift in British public opinion against the South. In 1861, there had been a mere seven anti-slavery meetings and rallies in England. That number more than doubled to sixteen the following year—impressive, certainly, but by no means a breakthrough. That would come in 1863, when no fewer than eighty-two were held, many enormous. During one rally at London's Exeter Hall, it was reported that "the name of Abraham Lincoln was received with immense applause—the audience rising and cheering, and waving their handkerchiefs," as the Confederacy was condemned for denying "human rights to the negro race."

Even Liverpool, that resolutely Confederate fortress, played host to anti-South gatherings. In mid-February, Dudley reported, 1,600 people came along to hear the Reverend Newman rail for nearly three hours against slavery. For the first time, the consul seemed less pessimistic that the entire city was against him, telling Seward, "We have now a very respectable party in Liverpool and they are quite active." A couple of days later, he went to a meeting at the Royal Amphitheatre, which "was packed from top to bottom, every hole and corner full." Just "two months ago all of these were against us," but the proclamation had "touched a chord which vibrates throughout the Kingdom."

The time was right, judged Dudley, to launch his masterstroke against Bulloch.

II

On March 28, Dudley paid a surprise visit to Collector Edwards at the Customs House. He submitted a formal application for the seizure of the *Alexandra* as a Confederate warship and provided six affidavits from various Liverpool sailors and merchants attesting to that effect. Knowing that Edwards would insist on sending the papers to London, giving Bulloch ample time to get the drop on him via the Confederates' man in the Foreign Office, Dudley helpfully mentioned that he had just sent the relevant documents to Minister Adams, who would *personally* forward them to Russell at the Foreign Office—please, no need for Mr. Edwards to exert himself!

Two days later, on March 30, Dudley's package arrived at the Foreign Office, followed the next day by a sheaf of copies of Yonge's blockbuster correspondence. Though Adams did not say how the letters were acquired—best not to bother Russell with Dudley's slightly questionable methods—they and the six affidavits conclusively connected "Bulloch as an agent of the rebel authorities" to Yonge, then to Semmes and the *Alabama*, and finally to the *Alexandra*.

The evidence was incontrovertible, as anyone could see. The law officers, to whom Russell sent the material directly by hand—Adams had probably warned him of a suspected mole inside the Foreign Office—concluded that the Confederates in Britain had clearly mounted a "deliberate attempt to establish . . . a system of action in direct hostility to the government of the United States." On April 3, accordingly, the foreign secretary instructed Edwards to hold the ship pending a trial.

Two days later, Edwards and his men entered Toxteth Dock and boarded the *Alexandra*, detaining her as being in violation of the Foreign Enlistment Act. Ignoring the complaints of those on board, they ominously painted the "broad arrow" upon her hull, a mark designating the ship as the property of Her Majesty's Government.

When he heard the news, Adams wrote an uncharacteristically peppy note to Russell telling him of his "most lively satisfaction" at the result. In Liverpool, shipyards stopped work on building blockade-runners for fear of their suffering a similar fate as the *Alexandra*. In response, Bulloch repeated his old tactic, last used to great effect against Sanford and Pollaky, of planting stories in the press designed to stoke indignation at Union harassment, but as one local newspaper remarked, Dudley's move had generated such alarmed "excitement amongst the gentlemen of Southern proclivities" in town that none took up the cause.

III

Lord Russell, a canny political operator, had felt the winds change. Given the anti-slavery agitation and the embarrassment of the Erlanger Loan—it wasn't illegal, but Russell was annoyed at London being used for what looked like financial shenanigans by dubious Frenchmen—he had grown tired of being taken for a fool by Bulloch and his friends. Coming down hard on the *Alexandra* would teach them a lesson in humility.

The ceaseless stream of newspaper reports of the "piratical" predations of the *Florida* and the *Alabama,* as well as the accusations that the government had fumbled in allowing them to leave Liverpool, demanded corrective action. As Russell told Prime Minister Palmerston on March 27, he now believed that "the fitting out and escape of the *Alabama* and *Oreto* [*Florida*] was clearly an evasion of our law." As such, the government must publicly "disapprove of all such attempts to elude our law with a view to assist one of the belligerents." Something had to be done, in other words. And it had to be *seen* to be done.

There was another reason, too, for Russell's alacrity. On the same day he wrote to Palmerston, he confessed to his friend Lord Lyons, the ambassador in Washington, that he had recently been made aware of "some scandalous act of English officials which has never been made public." Russell was referring to an internal investigation into Victor Buckley stemming from Adams's warning about a Confederate spy within the Foreign Office. The finger of suspicion had naturally fallen on the low-paid junior clerk with access to confidential correspondence who had somehow, very rapidly, acquired sufficient funds to speculate in cotton bonds.

The affair was quickly swept under the rug. Russell feared that if Buckley's improprieties came out, and if he sat on his hands while the *Alexandra* left Liverpool, his resignation was a certainty and the subsequent fall of the government a possibility. As for Buckley, he was saved from being exiled to some distant, dusty consulate by his social position—his father was MP for Salisbury and he was the Queen's godson—and the fact that there was no tangible proof, no paper evidence, that he had passed or sold secrets. Buckley was only *suspected* of doing so, and he could plausibly claim that Bulloch had either been tipped off by some *other* well-connected sympathizer, or that he had shrewdly guessed that the *Enrica* was likely to be held and so departed in a hurry. Still, Buckley had become so jittery that he refused to work any longer, depriving Bulloch of his eyes and ears in London at a critical moment.

A second blow to Bulloch's operation came with the loss of his source within the solicitor Squarey's office, the one who had passed on Maguire's reports for Dudley during the *Alabama* affair. Since the *Alexandra* deliberations were being conducted in London at the highest political and legal levels, Dudley and Maguire had little to do in Liverpool. Plain and simple, there was no information passing through Squarey's office to be sold.

Bulloch wasn't even aware, yet, of the third and final blow. The last he had heard, Clarence Yonge was cruising on the *Alabama* somewhere far away. Not only was Bulloch in the dark that Yonge had returned to England, he also had no idea that the man had turned his coat, let alone that his erstwhile wife had sold a trove of secret documents to Dudley. Altogether, Bulloch had been robbed of the early-warning system that was so key to his earlier triumphs. The result: He was completely blindsided by Russell's detention order.

On April 20, two weeks after the *Alexandra*'s seizure, Bulloch heard a rumor from Prioleau that Dudley had somehow snared Yonge. Bulloch racked his brain trying to work out what Yonge did and did not know. "I do not think," concluded Bulloch, "he was ever in the Birkenhead works [Lairds], or that he has any personal knowledge of what is going on there. He can surely have no knowledge of the *Alexandra*." But that was cold comfort when Yonge surely carried a stock of dangerous knowledge about everything else.

The following month, Bulloch's worried mind was finally put at ease. One Detective Constable Cousins, who was following up leads in Liverpool for the government investigators, naively handed the Watch Committee, a local oversight body, copies of Dudley's confidential *Alexandra* affidavits, including Yonge's. As the furious consul put it, most of the members of the Watch Committee were pals of Prioleau's and belonged to the Southern Club, which meant that now, of course, Bulloch knew "our whole case and the weak points in it."

Its weakest point, Bulloch discovered, was that Yonge's information, while damaging, was out of date. He had much to say about the *Alabama* but nothing on the more recent *Alexandra*. Since the upcoming trial was to center on the latter ship, not Bulloch's past misdeeds, this boded well for the Southern agent.

Still, as he read the affidavit, Bulloch was horribly shocked by the depth of Yonge's betrayal. When Bulloch had originally rescued Yonge from the drudgery of the Naval Paymaster's Office in Savannah and recruited him to secret service, he ruefully remembered, Yonge had been "a quiet, modest, young man." It was only afterward, in Liverpool, that Bulloch had come to realize that Yonge "was light and trivial in character and disposition," and so had (fortunately) excluded his assistant from his most confidential dealings. Even so, Bulloch "could not have supposed him capable of treason." And yet he was.

In the *Inferno*, Dante very precisely relegated "Traitors to Their Benefactors" to the Fourth Ring of the Ninth Circle of Hell, a place whose unhappy population Bulloch hoped the damnable Clarence Yonge would soon join. But here on this earth, Yonge was poised to be Dudley's star witness.

IV

More than anything, Bulloch was worried about the British government's sudden change of strategy. Back in December, Russell had mulled to Adams that he might relax the Foreign Enlistment Act just enough to prevent breaches based on "subtle contrivances" of the kind exploited by Bulloch.

In the lead-up to the *Alexandra* trial, Russell at last delivered the exact blow Bulloch had feared since the day he had discovered the "loophole" in the act allowing him to build ships in Britain so long as they were not armed, furnished, or equipped there.

Bulloch's success had always hinged on the government adhering strictly to the letter of the law. If it did, he was safe as houses, for the burden had fallen on Dudley to provide irrefutable proof—not suppositions or dockside hearsay—that Bulloch had broken the law. That, of course, had been virtually impossible, as the consul had complained endlessly.

But now Russell, tired of Bulloch's exploiting the system, changed the rules of the game. The Crown's coming case against the *Alexandra*, he determined, would instead be based on the *spirit* of the Foreign Enlistment Act—and that spirit was to maintain British evenhandedness by staying out of other people's wars. The *Alexandra*, then, was detained because of her "suspicious intent," the assumption being (as Russell put it) that she was "apparently intended" for the South. By this logic, if the *Alexandra* looked like a warship, was built like a warship, and steamed like a warship, then she probably was a warship, *whether armed or not*, and would be held until proven otherwise.

Bulloch instantly grasped the lethality of Russell's turnaround and instructed a panicky Prioleau to assure an equally unnerved Fawcett Preston "that if they would employ the best counsel and would defend the case manfully I would pay a part if not the whole of the lawyers' fees."

Dudley was at the time urging the Crown's prosecutors to try Prioleau and the other defendants on a misdemeanor charge. Bulloch, not being a British subject, was beyond reach in that regard, but Dudley planned to summon him as an "unwilling witness" to humiliate him. He was dissuaded only when the lawyers told him that a criminal trial would need to be held in Liverpool, where a jury would almost inevitably find the defendants innocent. As Russell cautioned, Liverpool was "a port specially addicted to Southern proclivities, foreign slave trade, and domestic bribery."

For that reason, the government decided to focus exclusively on obtaining the *Alexandra*'s forfeiture. Such a civil proceeding against a ship would be heard in the Court of Exchequer in London, a creaky body dating back to the twelfth century and presided over by the Lord Chief Baron of the Exchequer. While it wouldn't be as pleasurable as putting Prioleau and his cronies on trial, Dudley was assured by the government that hitting their wallets would bring down the Confederate operation much more effectively than a risky criminal trial on a minor charge.

Once Dudley learned who the judge would be, however, he became as worried about the Crown's prospects as a despondent Bulloch turned cock-a-hoop. A distinguished former barrister and Conservative MP, Sir Frederick Pollock was widely known as a bewigged octogenarian of antediluvian views who could be counted on to adhere rigidly to the eternal letter of the law. Moreover, the defendants were being represented by Sir Hugh Cairns, a Conservative former solicitor general and a brilliant parliamentary orator. Advantage: Bulloch.

Still, Pollock could not rule arbitrarily. The verdict was subject to the decision of a jury, after all, comprising twelve Englishmen, honest and true. Dudley, moreover, could also call upon the glittering and mighty talents—and the endless resources—of a government roused to action. The Crown's lawyer, Sir Roundell Palmer, was a Liberal and a proven friend of the Union, who would take malicious delight in inflicting a crippling blow on the Confederacy. Best of all, Dudley had a stack of witnesses lined up. First among them was Yonge, whose damning testimony would make Bulloch's defeat a slam dunk. Advantage: Dudley.

Originally an obscure matter in an arcane court concerning a modest ship's forfeiture, the *Alexandra* case was shaping up to be a knockdown fight between the Liberal government and the Conservative opposition, between the Union and the Confederacy, between Dudley and Bulloch. On it hinged Britain's enforcement, or not, of the Foreign Enlistment Act—and as such, the future of the South's clandestine naval program.

V

God, it was a disaster. An utter catastrophe—for Dudley, that is, who watched the three-day trial with mounting horror. As he lamented to Seward, "I have never seen any suit of one half the importance or magnitude of this so poorly put to the court and jury." Sir Roundell Palmer possessed a brilliantly sharp legal mind, but it turned out that this was his first actual state trial, and it showed.

On June 22, the trial opened and rapidly went south (and South) when Pollock directed—many would later say, misdirected—the jurors to bear uppermost in their minds that the key issue was whether it was lawful for an individual or company, based in a neutral country, to build an unarmed ship that happened to later be used against a country with which Britain was at peace. To his mind, it was. It only became unlawful, he told them, if the defendants armed the ship within Her Majesty's dominions, exactly as the Foreign Enlistment Act stipulated.

According to Pollock, it was the jury's task to decide whether the defendants intended to arm the *Alexandra* in Liverpool for use against the North, or if they were simply businessmen fulfilling a contract. A cobbler could not be held responsible if a thief bought some shoes and then wore them when robbing houses, wouldn't you agree?

It was obvious which way Pollock leaned. For him, the law could not be massaged to fit the government's case. The law was precisely as the law read, not how Russell and his Liberal friends decided it *meant* to read for convenient political reasons. For the judge, the long-inscribed words of the Foreign Enlistment Act, compassed by long-dead men for a long-ago war, remained as sacred and as eternal as those engraved by the Lord upon the tablets atop Mount Sinai or enshrined in this Constitution the Americans kept talking about.

Only after the war ended would it emerge that Pollock wasn't quite the magisterial guardian of the Queen's commandments he affected to be. In a staggering conflict of interest, Pollock had not only been a long-time subscriber to Hotze's pro-Confederate *Index* newspaper, but he had invested a considerable amount in Erlanger cotton bonds. He had every reason to make sure Bulloch got the *Alexandra* out.

Yet even without Pollock stacking the deck for his own benefit, the trial was a fiery wreck for Dudley and the Union cause. When Clarence Yonge took the stand, Sir Hugh Cairns made mincemeat of him. Before an upright jury, Yonge was mercilessly exposed under cross-examination as a bigamist, a greasy deserter, a false friend, and a mercenary charlatan who gave no question a straight answer. Cairns made merry chasing him around hedges and through coverts, Yonge squirming pathetically as jurors noted his evasions even as he told the truth, which of course was heavily discounted as the word of a treacherous snake.

Against Yonge's unsalvageable testimony, Sir Roundell could make little headway. Cairns did not even bother calling his own witnesses. He simply demolished the claims and characters of those presented by the government. John De Costa, one of Dudley's witnesses, had been touted as a Liverpool "shipping agent and a steamboat-owner," which made him sound like a perfectly respectable citizen. Unfortunately, as Cairns pointed out, the Portuguese American De Costa, nicknamed "the Yank," was a well-known rogue who owned nothing but an old tug and a lengthy criminal record. That De Costa, despite his dubious background, had given a very full and sober deposition mattered not a jot when he was accused of being paid by Detective Maguire for his testimony. (To be fair, he probably was.)

On the last day of the trial, Cairns deployed the traditional English fair-play argument, alleging that the government's evidence had been supplied by dirty informants, disgruntled former employees, and dock-land felons to drum up a wild-eyed fantasy that such upstanding, decent-minded fellows as Bulloch and Prioleau, or the gentlemen of Fawcett Preston and Lairds, were part of a vast Confederate conspiracy. As for that pathetic "specimen of humanity" Clarence Yonge, Minister Adams should have driven "from his door the miscreant who must have polluted the very air he breathed" instead of handing him to the Crown "to be brought before a jury of Englishmen, in order that they might hear the tale which this unmitigated villain told."

Strong stuff. So strong, in fact, that the jury took less than thirty seconds to return a verdict for the defendants. They didn't even trouble themselves to leave the box.

Palmer immediately lodged an appeal to the Court of Error, claiming that Pollock had wrongly laid down the law. But the damage had already been done. On every one of the trial's ninety-eight counts, Bulloch had prevailed. The letter of the law stood triumphant. In Liverpool, the news was greeted gleefully. The *Liverpool Mercury* cheered that Dudley and Adams had justly suffered such "a signal defeat" that it was "impossible that any similar prosecution should be instituted in the future."

The *Alexandra* verdict was Dudley's lowest point. Moran noticed that he was "dejected about it," and understandably so. This had been Dudley's third successive defeat after the *Florida* and the *Alabama*, and arguably his greatest, since, thanks to the consul's own blunders, Bulloch now had legal carte blanche to commission any ship he wanted, so long as it was not armed in Britain. The Union cause was back at square one.

Dudley's sole comfort from the debacle was that, while the appeal was in process (a rehearing was set for November), the *Alexandra* had to remain in detention. It was an annoying caveat for Bulloch, and an expensive one for Prioleau, to be sure, but irrelevant in the grand scheme of things. The South had won another battle.

VI

A few days later, to celebrate the great victory, Prioleau invited the crème de la crème of the Confederacy's friends—including the former Fraser Trenholm clerk Bushby (now an independent shipowner), Klingender the front man, and Ashbridge, head of Liverpool's Southern Club—to a party aboard *The Southerner,* Fraser Trenholm's latest blockade-runner. Prioleau intended the affair to be an exercise in humiliation.

Dudley read about the shindig in the next day's paper, as Prioleau knew he would. In an arrogant speech, Prioleau had ridiculed him, a buffoon who, in his quest for "important information," had "spent large sums in the vain endeavour to acquire [it]—(Laughter)." Heaping on the mockery, Prioleau spoke of the consul's "system of espionage and surveillance which had been instituted against the [Confederates], which had been carried out with so much zeal and so much honesty"— you can hear the sarcasm—"and which had lately exploded with so little damage at Westminster Hall [in the Court of Exchequer]—(Laughter and cheers)." Finishing up, Prioleau made fun of "that scorned individual" Clarence Yonge and raised his glass to Frederick Hull, Bulloch's longtime solicitor and adviser. The latter got to his feet and sneered at Dudley and Maguire, the "gentlemen" who had led the charge against the *Alexandra.* Then he begged everyone's pardon—he meant to say "one or two blackguards in the dress of gentlemen."

Bulloch said nothing during the ritual degradation of his foe, but he laughed along with every word. Why shouldn't he? He was winning. As for Dudley, he tried to ignore the slings and arrows hurled in his direction, but there was no disguising the fact that he was losing.

ELEVEN

The Lucky Shoemaker

I

By any measure, Dudley had messed up—badly. From the moment that Lincoln proclaimed emancipation till the day he lost the *Alexandra* case, the Liverpool consul had been overconfident that Bulloch's time was up, the endgame a foregone conclusion. His cockiness had even led him to do little about an earlier warning from Maguire that Lairds was building two armed ironclads named *294* and *295*.

Dudley looked into the matter, but decided that they could not be for the Confederates. Bulloch, he assumed, would never have so blatantly violated the Foreign Enlistment Act—either in letter or in spirit. The likeliest client was actually the Emperor of China, who was then trying to suppress the bloody Taiping Rebellion. It was perfectly reasonable to suppose Lairds had picked up a plump contract from the seven-year-old Son of Heaven.

Assumptions, Dudley would soon discover, were dangerous things in his line of work.

II

Of all the ships that Bulloch ever built, he loved his twin "Laird Rams" the most. Almost identical, they shared the single aim of fulfilling the third and final phase of his master plan: "sweep away the entire blockading fleet of the enemy." Bulloch pledged to unleash his monsters upon Lincoln's "heavy, unwieldy tubs [and] drown them out at sea."

Bulloch had designed a 224-foot man-of-war equipped with a bulbous metal ram extending from the prow for shock attack, rotating gun turrets for long-range targeting, powerful engines for speed, and thick iron armor for protection. The result was a pair of war machines that could lay waste to the Union's motley collection of wooden frigates, sloops, and hastily commissioned gunboats. Nothing else like them existed in any navy—and possibly for good reason.

The Rams turned out to be much more difficult to build than Bulloch (or the Lairds, for that matter) had anticipated. As these were Lairds' first armored warships, problems were only to be expected, but they quickly mounted. Bulloch and the Lairds had agreed that they would start work on the first Ram (*294*) and fix issues as they arose; the second one (*295*), being a month or so behind, would then benefit from the lessons learned.

A sound plan, except that as it became clear that many of *294*'s problems weren't so easily ironed out, completion dates were repeatedly pushed back. As Bulloch explained to Mallory, the "whole character of work [is] new and builders cannot make close calculations; great labor and unexpected time required to bend armor plates, and the most important part of the work, the riveting, is far more tedious than anticipated." The rotating turrets, based on a novel design by the British engineer Captain Cowper Phipps Coles, were a particular headache. It took months of negotiation to arrange a licensing fee with him, and even then he pedantically barred Lairds from making any modifications without his approval. Only in mid-December 1862 had Coles finally signed a contract.

By that time, Bulloch had more pressing things to worry about than debating technical specifications.

III

Bulloch had known from the start that Stage Three was going to be the toughest. Armed ironclads were not civilian vessels by any definition.

"Wooden ships could evade the law," he judged, "but object of armored ships too evident to disguise."

When he had first commissioned the Rams back in the summer of 1862, Bulloch believed that he would be able to rely on his old trick of disguising his ships as private vessels. He had gotten the *Florida* out using a fake Sicilian firm as a front, after all, and he had camouflaged the *Alabama* as a Spanish merchantman. Since then, owing to the raiders' predations and Dudley's interference, the British government had begun turning a more skeptical eye toward these types of claims. These days, there would *definitely* be questions if an invented company claimed a pair of ironclads as its own.

But what if they belonged to a legitimate *government*? Just as Dudley had paid scarce attention to ships he believed were for China, if Bulloch could find a country willing to vouch for the Rams then they would avoid scrutiny and Lairds would have a perfect cover story. And with that, Bulloch had his new trick.

The Confederacy had a friend in Emperor Napoleon III of France. Perhaps he could claim the Rams were for his navy? In the new year of 1863, Bulloch began making regular visits across the Channel to essay an introduction but eventually heard that the emperor, while supportive of the South, was unwilling to entangle himself in a clandestine scheme.

Bulloch's luck turned during one such trip to Paris in March, when a friendly shipbuilder and politician named Jean-Lucien Arman said he knew some people who could help.

IV

The "people" in question were brothers. The younger, Adrien, was the managing partner of a small financial firm, Bravay & Co., based at 6 Rue de Londres in Paris's 9th Arrondissement. What Bravay & Co. actually financed was opaque, but it seems to have served as a kind of private business office for Adrien's elder brother, François. Now in his mid-fifties, portly, muttonchopped, jovial, a keen opportunist not unaverse to fast dealing, and a talented charlatan, he had raised himself (and Adrien) from the dust.

The lucky shoemaker

In the 1840s, tired of his family's poverty, young François had twirled his hat on the end of a stick, pledging himself to venture in whatever direction its buckle pointed. It turned out to be south, toward the French equivalent of the Wild West—Egypt. There he would seek his fortune.

François Bravay did not find it until Sa'id Pasha became *wāli* (governor) of Egypt in 1854. At the time, Egypt was a province of the Ottoman Empire, and the wāli was counted as a tribute-paying vassal of the Sublime Porte in Constantinople, though Sa'id proclaimed himself the higher rank of khedive (hereditary viceroy) in a bid for greater independence.

Sa'id, educated in Paris, was a fun-loving sort of ruler but very serious about bringing his country up to French standards, albeit with Egyptian characteristics. He was addressed as "Our Master Whose Abode Is the Paradise," and more than a thousand grandees attended his son's circumcision, but during his rule Egypt was otherwise thoroughly Gallicized. Every soldier was handed a thick copy of a biography of Napoleon, and French advisers oversaw the improvement of the country's railways and canals, the reformation of its import and export trade, the curbing of the Nile slave trade, and the modernization of its agriculture. For a young Frenchman in a hurry like Bravay, there were rich pickings to be had.

One day, at least according to Bravay, a stranger walked into his shoe shop bearing a torn embroidered slipper. Bravay repaired it beautifully, much to the stranger's delight. The next day, a messenger came and squired him to a palace whose owner, of course, was the stranger—who turned out to be Sa'id. "The lucky shoemaker," as the newspapers liked to say, found himself being handed a lucrative contract to supply thousands of shoes for the Egyptian army by his appreciative client.

Bravay was on excellent terms with Sa'id and became renowned, and denounced, as one of his chief flatterers and more assiduous toadies. Leaving behind shoes, he embarked on wine importing, then branched out into higher-margin arms dealing. Dismissed by his better-bred compatriots as a vulgar parvenu, Bravay quickly accumulated vast wealth and bought a château in France, which he filled with opulent furniture, and a mansion in Paris, which he filled with corpulent guests. As he winningly said of his own checkered life, he had spent half of it suffering from hunger, and the other, from indigestion.

In the summer of 1862, Sa'id stayed with Bravay during a tour of France to view ships for sale, as the nascent Egyptian navy was in need of some. Bravay's largesse paid off when he had a most profitable audience with Sa'id later that year. "The Viceroy positively wishes me to complete some commissions for him," he excitedly wrote to Adrien on December 28. "He has ordered me to have built for him in France two armored frigates, after the best and most perfect designs."

The brothers, alas, celebrated too soon. On January 17, a little less than three weeks later, Sa'id, too fun-loving, died at age forty, leaving Bravay adrift with a *verbal* order for two Egyptian ironclads. Luckily for the former shoemaker, two months later, following Monsieur Arman's introduction, Bulloch arrived at what he delicately called a "satisfactory arrangement" with the Bravays to assure the Rams' future.

The deal came just in time to save Bulloch's hide. His finances were in such parlous disrepair that he'd had to ask Lairds to stop work on the Rams. At the time, Fraser Trenholm had just £4,500 in the kitty—not even enough to arm one of the Rams—and no bank would extend any credit until the Confederates put up more collateral in the form of cotton. Unfortunately, there was precious little to be had.

Captains, scared off by rising capture-and-confiscation rates by the U.S. Navy, were making ever-fewer voyages with ever-emptier holds. In 1861, nearly 5,600 runs had been attempted to and from the Confederacy, but in 1863 that number had fallen to about 1,450 and would drop to 800 the following year. In Liverpool, Prioleau's cronies in the Southern Club suffered accordingly. William Grazebrook, an arms dealer and blockade-runner chieftain, went bankrupt, and he was by no means the only one.

If Bulloch didn't get the Rams out soon to sink the U.S. Navy so his raiders could ravage Union shipping with impunity and the runner fleet again freely convey cotton, the game was over.

V

His scheme was very simple and very clever.

First, Bulloch legally dissociated himself from the Rams. With the help of his slithery solicitor, Frederick Hull, he composed a formal letter to the Lairds "express[ing] the most cordial regrets" that the continuing interference of Her Majesty's Government in his private affairs (the *Alexandra*, for example) had become so aggravating that he felt himself unable to oversee the completion of the ships. He therefore asked Lairds "to sell the ships for such sum as would insure me a reasonable profit and to [then] release me from all further obligations under the contract."

Next, François Bravay appeared in Liverpool with miraculously good timing, made his way to the Lairds shipyard, boasted of his agreement with "His Serene Highness the Pasha of Egypt," and offered to buy the two Rams he could see sitting half finished in the drydock. The Lairds, of course, were keen to sell on favorable terms to such an estimable client and arranged with Bulloch to come in and sign the transfer papers on June 18, 1863.

Lairds then drew up a fresh contract to complete the Rams "precisely as they were to have been finished for me," crowed Bulloch. In return, Bravay agreed to fund the £55,000 balance owing on the two Rams, meaning that the fine firm of Bravay & Co. owned, after a painstakingly choreographed series of steps that would stand up to the most intense scrutiny in any British court, two first-class warships ostensibly destined for the Egyptian navy. In an exotic touch, Bulloch and Bravay named them *El Tousson* and *El Monassir*, Tousson being a royal Egyptian name and Monassir a reference to a Nile tribe.

As the legitimate property of a French citizen fulfilling an Egyptian government order, the Rams were off-limits to Dudley. Now paid for, work on them would progress quickly. According to Bulloch, the first Ram would be launched by Lairds on "the spring tides of the full moon" between July 4 and July 7, and be fully finished six weeks later with all her armaments and stores. The second was two months behind. To synchronize their completions, Bulloch planned to hold the first Ram in Liverpool until the other was done. Sometime in October, then, the twin sisters would head out to sea, free as could be.

Then, at some prearranged destination, probably at a French port or in international waters, Confederate officers would board and commission the ships into their navy as the *North Carolina* and the *Mississippi*. Once the Rams were safe, Bravay would have his £55,000 refunded by Bulloch with a very fat commission added on for his middleman services. As to getting that £55,000, Bulloch expected Fraser Trenholm's coffers to be filled by then. Mallory had promised that he would send a portion of the Erlanger Loan proceeds, enough to cover the debt.

"As you will readily perceive," Bulloch told Mallory, "the affair required a good deal of management and occupied far more time than if the transaction had been a real one."

VI

Bulloch left Liverpool after finalizing the Bravay deal. It was critical to vanish. To "keep up this illusion [of Bravay's ownership] I can no longer appear openly on board the ships or even in the yards of the Messrs. Laird," he wrote before slipping away to Paris, well away from Dudley's spies. From there he could "direct [the Rams'] further completion from behind the desk of the Messrs. Bravay & Co."

He could not, however, stay abroad permanently. Harriott and his children still lived in Liverpool, and Bulloch had a responsibility to help Prioleau at 10 Rumford Place. He traveled there occasionally, as incognito as possible. Hoping to throw off Maguire or any other lurking Union agents, Bulloch dispensed with his American-cut suits and wore in their place shabbier ones. He even shaved off his distinctive mutton-chop whiskers and mustache to be less recognizable.

The one time he was spotted was when he attended Prioleau's obnoxious party on *The Southerner*, on June 28, to celebrate the great *Alexandra* victory. But otherwise, he kept a prudently low profile, even staying away from the celebratory July 4 launch of the first Ram at the Lairds yard.

Once back in Paris, his main responsibility was to find crews for the Rams. Because their "grim aspect and formidable equipment clearly show that they are solely intended for the real danger and shock of battle," Bulloch felt that recruiting sailors seeking "the captivating excitement of adventure [and] the positive expectation of prize money" would be more difficult than it had been with the *Florida* and the *Alabama*.

But he wasn't worried, even so. Here in France, he and the newly arrived Samuel Barron—appointed captain of both vessels by Mallory—could surely dig up a suitable skeleton crew to take the Rams out of Liverpool come October, when they would be ready. After Bravay transferred them to their new Confederate officers, they would destroy blockaders for target practice as they raced to Wilmington, North Carolina, to pick up their full complement of men.

Bulloch's imagination soared as he savored the terror they would instill among the Union fleet. Initially, he predicted, they would "sweep the blockading fleet from the sea front of every harbor from the Capes of Virginia to Sabine Pass," thereby preventing "anything like permanent, systematic interruption of our foreign trade for the future." Once that was done, they could proceed up the Chesapeake to bombard Washington and set Lincoln's teeth a-chatter with fear.

Then they'd steam to Portsmouth, New Hampshire, "a city given over to hatred of our cause and country," as well as home to a large government dock and shipyards. The Rams would of course demolish the navy yard before sending the mayor a demand for $10 million in gold and $50 million in cash to replenish the Confederate treasury. If payment were not received within four hours, the Rams would raze the town before heading to Philadelphia to extort even more. New York would be next.

So entranced was he with these mad fantasies that Bulloch failed to notice that in breaking his own rule to steer clear of Liverpool he had made not a mistake but something far worse: a blunder. Until Prioleau's *Southerner* shindig, Dudley had written off the Rams as Chinese, but the long-absent Bulloch's appearance in Liverpool so close to the launching of the first Ram a week later, on July 4, set off alarm bells. There was no such thing as a coincidence when it came to the wily Bulloch.

From then on, Dudley believed the Rams were "obviously" for the Confederacy, but he knew he would need something huge to convince Russell to move on them after the *Alexandra* fiasco. Having no hard evidence, Dudley was not sanguine as to his chances. "I hope to stop them here, shall do all that can be done, but my efforts may fail, quite likely will fail," he mournfully reported.

The main problem was that his supply of intelligence had dried up. His usual methods of "persuasion or bribery," Dudley said, no longer worked in Liverpool. Bulloch had traditionally taken a relaxed attitude toward those working for his foe, mostly to avoid alerting Dudley that he knew their identities. Dudley's shipyard informants during the *Alabama* affair, for instance, had usually only been moved off sensitive projects or had their hours cut to teach them a lesson. But from around the time the first Ram was launched, Bulloch began insisting that the Lairds take harsher measures to choke off Dudley's pipeline.

For that reason, Austin Hand, an American immigrant employed as a ship caulker, was terminated after telling the consul that he had seen Bulloch at the yard a year earlier "superintending the laying of the keels of the two rams." William Brady, who had "furnished [Maguire] with evidence" regarding the Rams was likewise fired, as was a carpenter named Neil Black, who after being sacked was warned by three other shipbuilding firms that he, like the others, was permanently blacklisted. "The effect has been to intimidate those who are well disposed," wrote Dudley, "and caused many who were in my employ to refuse longer to serve me."

Dudley finally managed to scrape together four affidavits concerning the Rams for Adams and traveled to London on July 8 to brief the minister. Even the consul had to admit that the testimonies "are not as strong and conclusive as I would like, but they are all we have."

Nevertheless, on July 11, Adams, still smarting from the recent *Alexandra* loss and needing a win, vastly oversold the contents to the foreign secretary, who must have groaned at the sight of yet another sheaf of Dudleyiana sitting on his desk as he prepared to decamp to Scotland for the summer. According to Adams, these bombshell documents proved the existence "of a systematic plan of warfare" by the Confederates and their friends at Liverpool. Russell dutifully read the affidavits and was duly unimpressed.

One was from Clarence Yonge, a knave Russell had sincerely hoped he would never again encounter after his disastrous performance during the trial. In it, Yonge claimed that while he was working for Bulloch a year earlier, he'd seen the plans for the Rams at the Fraser Trenholm office. Why he had not mentioned this before was a good question, and it seemed awfully convenient to Dudley's case that he was doing so now, especially when he was short of money.

Another affidavit came from George Temple Chapman, regarded as one of Dudley's tamest informants. Anything he said was hardly likely to be taken seriously, especially when all he added was that he had once been to the Lairds yard and seen two partially built ships of "immense strength." This was chicken-feed intelligence by any definition.

The next was from Dudley himself, saying that the Rams were intended for the South. Well, he *would* say that, wouldn't he?

And the last was jointly deposed by William Russell and Joseph Ellis, the first an American sailing master now living in Liverpool and the second, a shipwright. They claimed they had been present at Lairds for the launching on July 4 and believed the Ram to be a ship of war—which nobody was denying, least of all the Lairds, who were proudly advertising the fact.

All in all, the thinnest of gruels, the weakest of teas, the smallest of beers. Against Dudley's affidavits, Russell had a letter from Collector Edwards in Liverpool. After inspecting the Rams, he was satisfied "that the two iron ships . . . were not built for the Confederates, but are for Frenchmen, who first contracted for them." The Lairds had told him this, and as proof positive he added that the French consul in Liverpool, M. Lenglet, had called upon his office to affirm that the ships were indeed French property.

Russell, of course, was familiar with Edwards's selective blindness when it came to Confederate chicanery. But this time, he was citing an accredited diplomat of a major European power as claiming the ships were on the up-and-up, not merely stating his own interpretation of the law. That lent significantly greater weight to his assessment.

When he heard Edwards's story, though, Dudley started digging deeper. In mid-July, he went to see Edwards to try to persuade him he was falling for another of Bulloch's cons, but the collector merely "gave full credence to what the Lairds said about them." To this Dudley sharply retorted that "the Lairds [had also claimed] that the *Alabama* was for the Spanish . . . when they and every body else knew as they do now in the case of these two Rams, that they are for the Confederate Government." The meeting then abruptly ended.

Finding Edwards unmovable, Dudley focused instead on the collector's claim that Consul Lenglet had vouched for the Rams. "Check every thing," ran Dudley's motto these days. He sent Henry Wilding, his vice-consul, to talk to his French counterpart while he did the same with Lenglet to confirm that their stories matched.

Apparently, a certain François Bravay and one of the Lairds had come to the consulate on the morning of July 4 to ask for details as to how to acquire French registry for the two Rams he was acquiring on behalf of the khedive of Egypt. Bravay then invited Lenglet to a luncheon arranged at the Lairds shipyard to celebrate the launch of the first Ram later that day, but the consul and vice-consul were busy.

A couple of days later, the same Laird returned and told Lenglet that Dudley was seeking to detain the Rams for spurious reasons. He asked the consul to do him the favor of paying a visit to the Customs Office to assure Edwards that the Rams were rightfully owned by Bravay, who had since left the country. Lenglet did as he was asked—it was part of a consul's job, after all, to aid commercial interests—and that was the end of the matter.

Dudley was convinced this proved the Lairds and Bravay, with Bulloch's sinister hand pulling the strings, were involved in "an artful contrivance" to conceal the Rams "under some such foreign papers."

From Russell's point of view, that was *perhaps* true. Or maybe it was just Dudley's overheated imagination at work. If a Frenchman owned a couple of Lairds-built ships, it made sense for him to inquire about how to navigate the registration process at the consulate and to keep the Customs Office informed.

Just in case there was something he had missed, Russell sent Dudley's affidavits to the law officers for their opinion. Once stoutly in Dudley's corner, they had been badly burned by the *Alexandra* debacle and were not so eager to try their hand again. In an understandable reaction, especially given the rubbish Dudley had submitted, on July 24 they recommended doing nothing about the Rams.

Even so, Bulloch had a history of finding cunning ways around the Foreign Enlistment Act, as Russell well knew. It seemed just a little *too* neat that a mysterious Frenchman armed with an Egyptian commission from a conveniently dead potentate had shown up at the exact moment

Lairds was building two ironclads and Bulloch had established an alibi with his disappearing act.

There was something . . . off about this whole affair, but equally it *could* all add up. Or maybe it was just meant to look as if it added up.

VII

Russell called up from the records department any recent material relating to Egypt and this Bravay character. There was nothing, aside from a brief dispatch sent back in February by Robert Colquhoun, the British consul in Alexandria. In it, Colquhoun had mentioned that a François Bravay "claims to execute a verbal order from the late Viceroy of Egypt for two steel-clad frigates."

Russell's eyebrows rose. A "verbal order"? This was the first he'd heard of it. Not having the terms of such a lavish deal on paper was certainly a departure from the norm in Europe. Still, Sa'id had often made off-the-books deals to avoid having to seek preapproval from Constantinople, which was always eager to put Egypt back in its vassalage. Whatever the reason, it was going to be difficult to disprove Bravay's claim that he'd approached Lairds on the viceroy's behalf, since the latter party, now reposing in eternal paradise, was in no state to contradict it.

Or perhaps he already had? Colquhoun also reported that, while the late Sa'id had briefly been interested in buying two ironclads, he had soon "decided against the principle of such ships" and dropped the order just before he'd died in early January 1863. Was that true? If so, it was surely a little odd, then, that his nephew and successor as khedive, Isma'il, was still moving ahead with the purchase, at least according to this François Bravay.

But maybe it wasn't odd at all. Isma'il had the financial wherewithal to buy ships, and he was in the midst of trying to Westernize his country. A metal navy might just be part and parcel of such a modernization program, much like Isma'il's ongoing construction of the French-financed Suez Canal and his building an opera house.

For that reason, the idiosyncratic nature of Egyptian politics had to be taken into account. It was well known among old Egyptian hands that Sa'id and Isma'il had loathed each other. Sa'id had always made sure to keep Isma'il well away from his court, dispatching him on any number of hopefully dangerous military expeditions. Upon becoming khedive a few days after Sa'id's death, Isma'il, in turn, had taken pleasure in ignoring his predecessor's instructions to bury him in his sumptuous mausoleum on the banks of the Nile. After that, he purged his uncle's retainers and trucklers, all barring one: François Bravay, who had made sure to switch loyalties from the setting to the rising sun as soon as Sa'id began to ail.

Bravay and Isma'il were of a piece. Many-chinned and endless-stomached, both enjoyed rich, splendid feasting and high living (Isma'il would later die midway through an impressive attempt to down two bottles of Champagne simultaneously, leaving behind fourteen grieving wives). Bravay knew that when it came to royalty you needed to lay on flattery with a trowel, and in return Isma'il loved spending money on his friend.

To Isma'il, then, two Rams would have been but a trifle, especially to help out a crony. So it was perfectly possible that he wanted them just to spite dearly departed Uncle Sa'id, who had apparently canceled the order on his deathbed. From that perspective, yes, the story added up, but the foreign secretary still had a few questions.

Russell instructed Colquhoun in Alexandria to see if he could gain a clearer picture of the situation. On August 31, Colquhoun reported back with a one-sentence telegram reading simply: "I understand that the viceroy [Isma'il] has positively refused to accept the iron ships, and they remain on M. Bravay's hands."

Now, being lumbered with a pair of pricey rust buckets was certainly an inconvenience for the Frenchman, but if that were the case, then Bulloch could not be behind the latest scheme: Bravay *had* had deals with Sa'id and Isma'il for the Egyptian navy, just as he claimed. Indeed, all the available evidence pointed *away* from Bulloch. Customs officials in Liverpool remained adamant that the Lairds' contract with Bravay was legitimate. Mr. Morgan, the senior surveyor of ships there and a close colleague of Edwards, informed London that he had recently discussed the "rumors" of Confederate involvement with the Lairds themselves, and they had begged innocent of any such dishonorable imputation. As the "word of Messrs. Laird is above suspicion," added Morgan piously, the Rams, too, must be aboveboard.

For Russell, that was the clincher. Surely, not even the mighty Lairds, as arrogant as they were, would dare to lie barefacedly to representatives of Her Majesty's Government? The Laird brothers themselves affirmed to Russell in writing that their firm was building the ships for "Bravay & Co., and that . . . our engagement is to deliver the vessels to them in the port of Liverpool."

Russell drew the only conclusion possible: Bravay owned the ships, and he was working—or had been working—for the Egyptians. Bulloch was in the clear and Dudley was pointing the finger at an innocent man (at least this time).

On September 1, a day after the Colquhoun telegram, Russell told Adams that he saw no reason to accede to American requests to detain the Rams. As the government would not "interfere in any way with these vessels" the imminent trial run of the first Ram would consequently be permitted to take place, and neither would Her Majesty's Government impede the completion of the second, which had been launched on August 29 with the French tricolor patriotically flying. Come their completion in October, they were free to leave.

VIII

Russell had done the right thing in rejecting Dudley's charges. Consider the findings that lay before the foreign secretary:

The Lairds had officially denied colluding with the Confederates.

The government's own lawyers believed the Foreign Enlistment Act had not been violated and that the foreign secretary had no legal standing to hold the ships.

Every customs official in Liverpool had sworn that the Rams were French.

The French consul himself said they were French.

Aside from his blamelessly attending a party aboard *The Southerner,* nothing had been seen of Bulloch for many months.

Bulloch's name did not appear on any document connecting himself to Bravay, and there was no known link between the two.

Bravay, a French banker, owned the Rams and had long ago made an agreement with the Egyptian government to acquire ironclads.

The current khedive of Egypt did not deny having had an agreement, even if he now did not want the Rams.

But most pertinently, despite months of effort, Dudley had failed to produce a single shred of evidence contrary to any of these facts.

If Russell nevertheless held the Rams without due cause, he would be assuming immediate and tangible risk, especially after the *Alexandra* case. Lairds and Bravay would inevitably launch a major suit for damages against the government. This would be an embarrassment not only to Russell but would place Palmerston's ministry in jeopardy. Russell could not afford to lose another major case in the courts. Letting the ironclads go, then, was the safer, smarter course. The worst that could happen was that the Yankees would huff and puff a bit *if* the Rams turned out to be trouble, but Lincoln would not be so foolish as to stir up another hornet's nest like the *Trent* Affair. Eventually, everything would settle down.

And yet, for the next two days, Russell noodled on the problem. He weighed the pros and cons, assessed the likelihoods and the probabilities.

And then he knew what he had to do.

IX

On September 3, Russell did the *wrong* thing—almost always a wiser, if harder, path. "I have made up my mind," he ruled, "that the vessels ought to be stopped."

Over the years, Dudley, annoying and pushy as he was, had provided a steady flow of sound intelligence—until recently, that is—by dint of diligence and fortitude. The *Alexandra* debacle could not be laid at his feet. It had been the government's mishandling of the case that had brought defeat, to be honest. Dudley's witnesses at the trial, flawed and wicked as they were, had been telling the truth, whereas Bulloch had done nothing but obfuscate and manipulate and dissemble since the moment he arrived in Britain. Now he would be undone by his own cunning.

Without any evidence of Bulloch's guilt in hand, Russell plumped for Dudley. He placed his faith and political future in the consul's judgment, his character, and his record. Unlike his Confederate counterpart, Russell trusted Dudley's motives, which meant he trusted the man.

Russell had never met Dudley, had not even corresponded directly with him. But on this subject, the diminutive foreign secretary—son of a duke, an earl in his own right, a former prime minister, an heir to one of the oldest political dynasties in England, a familiar of Napoleon and Wellington—found common ground with the tall, spare progeny of a humble Quaker farmer from New Jersey.

That September 3, Russell went around, above, behind, and beyond the law to formulate policy. In breaking his own long-standing rule to never act on suppositions and hearsay, that day Russell acted on nothing *but* suppositions and hearsay, backed up by a gut feeling that Dudley was right.

Without consulting the cabinet or even the prime minister, circumventing the law officers, and ignoring the objections of the Customs Office, Russell instructed Collector Edwards in Liverpool "to detain [the Rams] until further orders." He would take full responsibility for any legal or financial liability.

Then he crossed his fingers and hoped some evidence turned up to prove him right.

TWELVE

The Man with No Hands

I

Russell's horse soon came in, much to his relief. Two days later, on September 5, a delayed dispatch arrived from Colquhoun in Alexandria. In something of a coup, the consul had actually managed to talk to the elusive François Bravay himself. He was "a singular person, with a thorough knowledge of the country, from the rulers of which he has managed to extract an enormous fortune," reported Colquhoun, though "he is frequently in [financial] difficulties, his ready money going to create friends in high places, not in Egypt only."

To Colquhoun, Bravay insisted that he had had a verbal agreement with the late Sa'id for the ships, but he only now confirmed that Isma'il had been "firm in declining to have anything to do with the iron-clads." Rattled by the questioning, Bravay then added to his story, claiming that Isma'il had taken pity on him and invited him to "send me out the plans [for the Rams], and I will see if I can recommend them to the Turkish government, the Sultan being now anxious to increase his navy." So now he was hinting that they were to be Ottoman ships.

Where Bravay muddied the waters was in omitting to say *when* this had all occurred. He made it sound as if it happened in the last week or two, but Russell was sure that Isma'il had rejected the deal all the way back in January, when he became viceroy. So, why had Bravay been parading around Liverpool as late as July, just two months ago, claiming that the two Rams were for Egypt? Russell was now convinced that this whole story was a legend. The only questions that remained were, who had put Bravay up to it and who was he really working for?

In the matter of the Rams, some had dirty hands, others clean, and some, like the spectral Bulloch hovering faraway, no hands at all—which made him a prime suspect.

II

A few weeks later, Russell sent Captain Hore, the British naval attaché in Paris, to "interview" Adrien Bravay at the firm's offices. The latter was very, very worried, and justly so. Suspecting (correctly) that London had rumbled his brother and his dubious deal, Adrien was understandably more than willing to talk so long as he and François got a free pass. Russell offered him one: Britain would buy the Rams at a fair price but only in exchange for information.

Sensing that this was his only way out of the jam, Adrien scurried to his safe and extracted the crucial missing piece of the puzzle as proof he had something big to trade: the Deed of Release from Lairds to a certain Mr. James Bulloch.

Signed on June 18, 1863, just five days before the start of the *Alexandra* trial, when Bulloch had been taking extra precautions in case Dudley prevailed, the terms stated that Bulloch had originally contracted for the Rams and paid £150,000 as an initial deposit, but that they were being transferred to Bravay's ownership.

There it fatally was, a notarized agreement for two warships, signed by William, John Jr., and Henry Laird, and Bulloch himself—a definitive link among the Confederate agent, the Lairds, and Bravay & Co. Adrien then let Hore in on another secret. There was an unwritten addendum to the Deed of Release: François had "purchased" the Rams from Lairds on the understanding that Bulloch would buy them back (plus fee) once they had left Liverpool and were commissioned into Confederate service. Taken together, Russell now had irrefutable proof that Bulloch, the Lairds, and Bravay had knowingly conspired to evade the Foreign Enlistment Act.

Dudley, that assiduous Cassandra of a consul, had been proven right after all. He had long warned of Bulloch's cunning machinations, and now to witness his nemesis hoist by his own petard, trapped by his own hand, and tangled in knots of his own devilish devising—it surely gave even him, the dourest of Quakers, an excuse to laugh.

Nothing could save Bulloch now. All at once his strategic plan to break the blockade by sinking the U.S. Navy had unraveled, leaving the Confederacy reliant on a vulnerable fleet of runners and just two prowling raiders. Outright victory, either at sea or on land, was no longer a realistic outcome.

III

For the first time, Bulloch lost his head. His letters turned increasingly conspiratorial and lost their usual urbane irony and tone of omniscient superiority. "Through his spies," Dudley "was swearing to my constant presence [in Liverpool] and superintendence of the ships," he raged. The injustice of it all rankled deeply.

Once he discovered that Adrien had talked, Bulloch's fantasia that the Rams were Egyptian by commission had collapsed. Still, Russell feared that he might chance sneaking a skeleton crew aboard to spirit the Rams out to sea under guise of undertaking a local trial run. Just in case he was right, he sent Rear Admiral Dacres in mid-September to caution the Lairds against even thinking of abetting any such exploit.

The admiral was very polite about it. Just as a precaution (of course) against an attempted "forcible abduction" of the Rams, Dacres told the shipbuilders, a small and hardly noticeable detachment of Royal Marines would be placed on board "in a friendly spirit" (obviously). They were there only to "see that the ship returns to port the same day" if Messrs. Laird decided to send a Ram out for a trial. Should they not feel able to "accept the protection thus offered to them" then, he gently suggested, it would perhaps be rash of them to allow the trial to proceed, owing to the adverse consequences that would surely follow. In the same "friendly spirit," Dacres went on, Captain Inglefield of HMS *Majestic*, an 80-gun ship of the line, would anchor nearby with three gunboats for company.

Until then, the Lairds had been trying to brazen it through, but now they were scared. Terrified of being criminally indicted for violating the Foreign Enlistment Act if a Ram did escape, they quickly caved. In a panic, the brothers announced they were indefinitely postponing any scheduled trials.

The curtain was coming down.

IV

The first to take his bow was Edwards, the Liverpool customs collector. In early October, he was asked to take a leave of absence from his post. Two months later, once a respectable interval had passed, he was "removed from office owing to some difficulties with the London authorities," as Bulloch circumspectly put it. Only then, and for the first time, did Edwards finally meet the Confederate operative. The defenestrated bureaucrat professed to be "indifferent" to Dudley's long-standing accusations that he had been in Bulloch's pocket, but in fact "he had been deeply pained [and] never wholly recovered from the feeling of mortification produced by such an unfounded and gratuitous aspersion upon his official integrity." So said Bulloch. On the other hand, Squarey, Dudley's solicitor, was less sympathetic, saying that Edwards had shown "so much partisanship for the rebels and been so thoroughly caught in connivance with them, that the Gov't ha[d] lost all confidence in him."

Then the lights went out for the Lairds. After Dudley arranged to supply Inglefield with intelligence on an anonymous basis, he told the *Majestic*'s captain that the Lairds had quietly loaded 120 tons of coal on board the first Ram and that the shadowy villain Bulloch had apparently hired a "number of men [who] are ready for secret service" to steal her.

Dudley was no longer the naïf he had been when he first arrived in Britain. He had learned the Liverpool way and had dispensed with playing by the rules in order to win the game. These particular scraps of intelligence, for instance, had come from a questionable pair of sources, both courtesy of Detective Maguire: a "Mr. Murphy" and John De Costa, the crimp known around the docks as "the Yank" who had testified on Dudley's behalf during the *Alexandra* trial.

De Costa had been mocked and humiliated by Bulloch's lawyers and was now only too delighted to put the boot in. The identity of Murphy is lost to us, but the very fact that Maguire cited him alongside De Costa would seem to indicate that he was not numbered among Liverpool's more law-abiding citizenry. Indeed, he was probably the head of the Murphy family, a local clan notorious for its street-fighting prowess and criminal activities. Together, De Costa and Murphy supplied men to watch the goings-on around Lairds.

Before feeding these wispy claims to the unwitting Inglefield, Dudley spun them in such a way as to give them more texture and weight. By such means, the likes of De Costa and Murphy magically turned into first-class inside sources of sterling credibility. It was an underhanded method of making fake "intelligence" sound real—but it worked. Until then, the government had still been pretending to be concerned with protecting the Lairds from "any attempt at the forcible abduction of your property" by unnamed miscreants. Thanks to Dudley's calculating interference, this fig leaf was now thrown away, and the Rams officially seized.

Inglefield, much to the vexation of the Lairds, permanently stationed Royal Marines on each ship. There they were hooted and jeered at by the workmen. At one point, a marine guarding the second Ram was "set upon by 3 or 4 men, struck several times and only escaped a severe thrashing by running away," reported Inglefield, who was received with cold and snobbish disdain by the Laird brothers during his visits on-shore. When the captain complained about the violent behavior of their employees, the Lairds shrugged their shoulders and said they couldn't possibly be responsible for their workers' extracurricular activities. This attitude did not, to put it mildly, endear them to the authorities, allowing Dudley to chortle to his superiors, "I think I can now say to you with every assurance of truth that the two Rams are stopped."

V

Next, it was Bulloch's turn to leave the stage. For a time he had had his hopes pinned on the favorable *Alexandra* verdict against the government being upheld in the appeal, due in November. In that instance not only would the *Alexandra* be released from temporary detention, but Bulloch could launch a counterattack on the government, claiming that the Rams, too, had been seized illegally and that Russell had had no right to occupy the Lairds shipyard.

As a strategy, this wasn't a bad one. Indeed, come November Justice Pollock's original verdict supporting Bulloch was predictably upheld. But instead of surrendering the ship to avoid further litigation, Russell simply *re*-appealed the case to the House of Lords, which scheduled a hearing for six months later. Until that time, of course, the *Alexandra* would remain in government hands.

Bulloch had not yet grasped the hard reality that every time Russell lost, he actually won. The foreign secretary had realized that bloody-minded legal obstructionism, as a kind of lawfare, was more devastating than any court verdict. Why should he take the risk of rushing before a judge and jury, as he had (disastrously) with the *Alexandra,* when it was much easier to detain the Rams for an indeterminate length of time, prevaricate and delay, hinder the Lairds by using Royal Marines to scare off potential customers, and force the offenders to endure endless legal troubles until they exhausted both their money and their will to fight?

For Russell, then, the coming struggle for the Rams was to be a slow war of attrition, not a decisive battle at sea—the clash of arms Bulloch still thought he was fighting. The Southerner, like the South, was being blockaded.

Legally speaking, now that he'd seized the Rams, Russell would have to progress to a new trial in the Court of Exchequer. Bulloch believed the judge—Pollock, if he were lucky—would find in the Bravays' favor, but Russell kept postponing going to court. The foreign secretary came up with ever-more-fanciful reasons to explain the delays. One, for instance, was that he needed to look into sending a commission to Egypt to interview Viceroy Isma'il, who would in turn be requested to come to Britain and testify in court (Russell professed to be very concerned about the etiquette of allowing him to swear an oath on the Koran). All of this, of course, would eat up months of time, and Russell knew perfectly well that such a dignified eminence as the khedive of Egypt would never consent to be cross-examined by vulgar lawyers in some jumped-up foreign court—but none of these theatrics were real in the first place.

On January 6, 1864, by which time Russell still had made no effort to bring the Rams case to the Court of Exchequer, Bulloch finally caught onto the plan: "Object seems simply to be prevention of their getting to sea," he curtly wrote. His solicitors could not elicit any information from the government as to when the case would be tried nor even the precise nature of the charges.

By February, the truth could no longer be avoided. Owing to Dudley and his "numerous, active, and unscrupulous" spies in Liverpool, wrote Bulloch, "the conjoint efforts of Lord Russell and Mr. Adams have proved irresistible, and it is now settled beyond a doubt that no vessel constructed with a view to offensive warfare can be built and got out of England for the service of the Confederate States." It was clear that any even mildly questionable ship would from now on be detained indefinitely. Even if he succeeded in getting a vessel freed—as happened when the House of Lords eventually ordered the liberation of the *Alexandra*—the government had other means to hand. In the benighted *Alexandra*'s case, she would next be spuriously detained in Nassau until December 1864, too late to be of use to the Confederates.

"English operations have failed," Bulloch dispiritingly concluded. He had no other choice than to sell his treasured Rams to the British government. To Mallory he wrote that the decision was "an act which I assure you, sir, caused me greater pain and regret than I ever conceived it possible to feel."

The only piece of good news for Bulloch that dire winter of early 1864 was that Russell was willing to spend more than Bulloch's £150,000 investment, so long as he surrendered quietly. Indeed, because the assessed value of the Rams in their current unfinished state was

£182,000, the Confederate stood to make a profit on them—certainly a welcome development given that his debts had risen to more than a million pounds, which he had no way of ever repaying. Recently, Prioleau had managed to sneak in seven hundred bales of cotton, which, if sold, might possibly make a minuscule dent in Bulloch's interest charges.

In May, following prolonged negotiations, Bulloch accepted £220,000, which seems impressive at first glance. But that figure came attached to conditions. It was, for instance, payable *only* if Lairds fully completed and armed the Rams by a fast-approaching deadline; if they did not, the price would drop to £195,000 and keep on falling the more overdue they were. The Lairds, servilely pleading to "be liberally dealt with," settled, fearing being lumbered with two giant iron albatrosses if they held out for better terms. When all was said and done, the brothers received a bare-bones £29,000 to finish the ships, while the Bravays and Bulloch each emerged from their ordeal just £4,500 richer. Perhaps not so impressive, after all.

Dudley was pleased to witness the humbling of this haughty ship-building dynasty. Likewise, the fall of the Bravays was, he thought, thoroughly deserved. Not only were difficult questions being raised in France regarding their activities, Isma'il, unamused at François's dragging his good name into a scandal, afterward barred him from the palace. Bravay died, blind and destitute, in 1874.

Yet while Dudley had decisively won the battle for the Rams, his personal war with Bulloch was far from over.

THIRTEEN

The Great Red God

I

On June 14, 1864, three weeks after Bulloch had reluctantly agreed to sell the Laird Rams, Captain Raphael Semmes was bottled up in the French port of Cherbourg. He had been at sea for nearly two years, and the *Alabama* desperately needed a refit. Her engines were worn out, her boiler required major repairs, her sails were patched, and her hull was barnacled. Even the men's once snappy uniforms had been bleached by the salt of the sea. Most alarming was the rotten state of the *Alabama*'s gunpowder, old and damp, as Semmes had recently discovered during a recent capture, when numerous shells had failed to explode.

Now, he trained his spyglass on USS *Kearsarge* roaming three miles offshore. She was under the command of Captain John Winslow—as it happened, a former comrade of Semmes's during the Mexican-American War—who had long been hunting the *Alabama*. Now he had found her.

Semmes had two choices: the bold or the boring.

If he stayed in Cherbourg, he would be safe. Eventually, the *Kearsarge* would have to leave for reprovisioning, or a storm would sweep in and he could escape. That is what most commanders would have done.

Semmes was not most commanders. He attacked.

He fancied his chances. While the *Kearsarge*'s guns could throw a broadside of 430 pounds' worth of metal, compared with *Alabama*'s 360, Semmes knew his men were better trained. What's more, he knew he could sink a warship. He had already done so back in January 1863, besting USS *Hatteras* off Galveston, Texas. He would do the same to the *Kearsarge*.

Semmes's boundless confidence made him overlook one crucial thing that the *Kearsarge* had and he didn't. A few weeks earlier, Winslow had protected his hull with makeshift chain-mail armor consisting of vertically hung anchor chains bolted to the wood amidships and covered by boards.

Like some medieval baron, Semmes issued a formal declaration that he would deign to duel with the *Kearsarge* in five days' time, on June 19, a Sunday, which he considered his lucky day. (He'd sunk the *Hatteras* on a Sunday, as well as taken his first prize then.) On the morning in question, the *Alabama*, escorted by the French frigate *Couronne* to make sure the battle occurred outside of territorial waters, steamed out for the showdown. If Semmes won, he would earn immortality as the Nelson of the Confederate Navy. If he lost, which he wouldn't, the *Alabama* would have the honor of going down in a blaze of glory. Mars, the great red god, would decide the matter.

It was a fine day for sightseeing. The coming battle was no secret and thousands of people, many all the way from Paris, had come to watch the fight. Churches were deserted that Sabbath in Cherbourg. Anyone who owned or could rent a boat was on the water. One such was a wealthy Englishman named John Lancaster, who brought his family across the Channel on his yacht, *Deerhound*. After all, it wasn't every day that one got to watch a mini Trafalgar in real time.

As Winslow dutifully held a Sunday service, his lookout spotted Semmes. When the *Alabama* was a mile distant, Winslow ordered *Kearsarge* turned starboard to the enemy. Semmes came on fast and loosed a few shots too high, met by a broadside at nine hundred yards, which did no damage. Now with the *Alabama*'s own starboard facing the

Kearsarge, the two ships embarked on one of the strangest spectacles in naval history.

At between half and three-quarters of a mile, the ships circled each other like wary boxers, seven times in all, firing constantly. Semmes intended to catch up to Winslow so he could send his expert boarding parties to fight on deck, but the *Kearsarge,* slightly nimbler than her antagonist, kept out of his reach.

Semmes's only hope, then, lay in a lucky hit to slow her down. He soon got one when a shot smashed into the *Kearsarge*'s sternpost. The blow might otherwise have crippled her but for the *Alabama*'s damp powder not exploding. Several other hits by the *Alabama* failed to inflict damage, owing to Winslow's armor, and Semmes was forced to switch to solid shot. At the same time, the *Kearsarge*'s gunners had knocked out Semmes's rudder early on, and now they focused on sweeping his deck. Blood seeped into the sand covering the *Alabama*'s planks, and lethally sharp splinters flew all about. Two shots blew through a gunport, killing and wounding several men.

Semmes demanded more steam, but the old boilers threatened to blow if pushed any harder. *Alabama* was clearly having the worst of it, but the shell that ended her crashed through the hull at the waterline and drove into the engine room, maiming and trapping those inside.

Water flooded the *Alabama.* Lieutenant Kell, the second in command, informed Semmes he estimated she had ten minutes of life left in her. Stunned into reality, and forced to concede that these were no longer the days of the Elizabethan seadogs of yore and lore, Semmes ordered his men to "cease firing, shorten sail, and haul down the colors. It will never do in this nineteenth century for us to go down and the decks covered with our gallant wounded."

Winslow's reaction was odd. Five more shots screamed toward the stricken *Alabama* after Semmes had lined the crew on the deck to stand at attention in an admirable display of grace under pressure as he raised the white flag. Winslow later claimed that he had believed

The end of the line for the Alabama

the "surrender" was yet another of Semmes's ruses—understandable, given his history of dirty tricks.

Semmes then told Kell to get the men into whatever boats were still serviceable. There wasn't enough room, so men leaped into the water and clutched whatever bits of wood they could grasp to escape the coming vortex as the *Alabama* sank.

As Lancaster rushed the *Deerhound* toward the wreck to pick up survivors, and the *Alabama*'s rowboats headed for the *Kearsarge*, Semmes and Kell stood on the listing deck. Traditionally, a losing captain surrendered his sword to his vanquisher, but Semmes would never. He and Kell both threw theirs into the gray Norman fathoms before themselves leaping overboard.

Kearsarge would rescue seventy of the *Alabama* men, some French boats another fifteen, and the *Deerhound* forty-two, including an almost lifeless Semmes and Kell, before rushing for home. Twenty-six were killed during the fight or drowned, compared with just one death on the *Kearsarge*.

Semmes was incredibly lucky in being hauled in by Lancaster. A stiff prison sentence, or hanging, would have otherwise been his lot if Winslow had got to him first and taken him to America. As it was, he was landed in Southampton safe and sound.

II

Following the loss of the Rams and the *Alabama*, Prioleau and Bulloch's importance had greatly declined. Richmond recognized their contributions to the cause, but their usefulness was now limited.

In March 1864, the Confederate government had finally done what it probably should have done at the war's outbreak: nationalize the blockade-running industry and place it under the supervision of the war department. So much effort had been wasted bringing in non-military luxuries, like Prioleau's furs, antiques, and liqueurs, that to many Southerners the trade no longer seemed romantic. If anything, the likes of profiteers like Prioleau and his friends came across as unpatriotic. Henceforth, Richmond strictly limited imports to "articles of necessity," and the central and state governments had first call on cargo space for their military needs.

That spring, the government commissioned, too, its own fleet of blockade-runners, twenty-seven all told, while Bulloch was relegated to acquiring eleven small and medium-size runners. He set about the task with his usual energy, using the money from the sale of the Rams.

The effects were immediate. Under the military mandate and the end of the embargo, both Caleb Huse's arms exports and cotton imports rose dramatically, causing Dudley no little alarm. As he summarized, over the course of 1864, forty-two runners used Liverpool to bring in about 124,000 bales, of which roughly 22,000 were handled by Fraser Trenholm. That was an average of 1,800 bales monthly for the firm, itself way up from the previous year, when Prioleau and Bulloch had struggled to import between 300 and 500 bales a month. The Confederacy, Dudley worried, still had a lot of kick to it.

Despite the improvement, it was nowhere near enough to stave off the slow-motion implosion of the Confederate economy. Ultimately, the losses, both of materiel and manpower, were unsustainable. Even as Liverpool hosted those forty-two blockade-runners, no fewer than forty-three were lost or captured heading into or out of Bermuda alone. The fates of Bulloch's eleven new blockade-runners amply illustrate the collapse of blockade-running in the closing stage of the war. By 1865, less than a year after they had been acquired, just three were active. Of the rest, two had arrived in Nassau but would never run the blockade, one was never finished, one had run aground after a chase, three had been captured, and one had been sunk carrying six hundred cotton bales and $50,000 in irreplaceable Confederate gold.

III

Meanwhile, Bulloch had not yet given up. The American whaling fleet in the far North Pacific and Arctic Sea, far away from Lincoln's blockaders, made for a soft target. In September, he purchased the *Sea King*, a Glasgow ship that had been working the India tea route. Bulloch intended to convert her into an ad hoc raider to replace the *Alabama*.

These days, though, Bulloch had to contend with constricting conditions. Not only had he to evade Dudley's surveillance, but he could no longer build a vessel bearing the remotest resemblance to a warship—even if he could afford to *and* could find a shipyard willing to risk the wrath of the government. Nevertheless, he still had his bag of tricks, diminished as it was. In Liverpool, he arranged for the *Laurel*, a small steamer, to convey the *Sea King*'s armaments to a rendezvous off the Madeira Islands, much to Dudley's confusion. The consul was aware of the *Laurel*'s existence, of course, but because there was no other obvious raider anywhere in Britain that needed arming, Dudley naturally assumed she was a run-of-the-mill runner—which was exactly what Bulloch wanted him to think.

What Dudley also didn't know was that Bulloch had sneaked several Confederate naval officers into Liverpool, scattered them around various boardinghouses under aliases, and told them to steer clear of one another and to keep their telltale uniforms packed away.

When the *Sea King* and the *Laurel* met to transfer the armaments in mid-October in the lee of the well-named Las Desertas, a rocky island off Madeira, it was clear that pro-Southernism in Britain had nearly run its course. Earlier, Semmes and Maffitt had found British sailors more than eager to sign on for bounty and adventure. Now, however, forty-two of them refused to join a Confederate warship even after being offered as much as £17 as an inducement. At one point, an officer produced a bucket of glittering gold sovereigns as proof that he could pay cash up front, but it was to little avail. Just twenty-three stayed.

Lieutenant James Iredell Waddell had been selected to command the Confederate Navy's next *Alabama*, which he christened *Shenandoah*. Despite having only 46 officers and men on a ship intended for 150, he immediately embarked on his mission to the Pacific.

IV

Visitors to Liverpool's St. George's Hall that same month were in for a splendid time. Prioleau had organized the grand event of the year: the Southern Bazaar.

True, the *Alabama* had been lost, but there was much to celebrate nevertheless. A couple of weeks earlier, on October 3, that Scarlet Pimpernel of the Seas, Captain Semmes, had escaped the Union's clutches and would by Christmas be home enjoying his promotion to rear admiral and a vote of thanks by the Confederate Congress.

The spectacular surroundings of St. George's matched the excitement. Opened a decade earlier, it formed a monumental Greco-Roman edifice of the most austere proportions. After entering its giant bronze doors—resembling those that once guarded King Agamemnon's palace and into which were carved the hallowed initials SPQL: *Senatus Populusque Liverpoliensis,* "the Senate and People of Liverpool"—the visitor would find himself enveloped by the Great Hall, nearly sixty yards long, twenty-five wide, and six stories high. The space was illuminated by ten colossal brass and bronze chandeliers, each fittingly decorated with ships' prows, heads of Neptune, and liver birds (a kind of mythical cormorant, the symbol of Liverpool). Some thirty thousand ceramic tiles arranged in geometric patterns paved the floor, overseen by a glorious blue-and-gold vaulted ceiling. Upon arches, spandrels, and cofferings were painted the allegorical angels of Fortitude, Science, Art, Justice, and all the rest, as well as the city's coat of arms. Reddish marble columns lined either side of the hall with statues of the Great and the Good interspersed between.

Prioleau had rented the hall for a four-day charity extravaganza. All the money raised by the event would be donated to the Southern Prisoners' Relief Fund, which was devoted to aiding Confederates held captive in the North. That was, at least, its ostensible intent. The true motivating spirit behind the bazaar was to serve a higher propagandistic purpose: undercutting President Lincoln's reelection campaign.

Prioleau and the Confederates were placing their last hopes in the candidacy of General George McClellan, a Northern Democrat who favored continuing the war but was open to seeking an armistice with the South to avoid needless rack and ruin. In mid-1864, the fighting had bogged down into a stalemate, and the North was tiring of war almost as much as the South was exhausting its manpower and resources.

If Lincoln won on November 8, however, the conflict would go on until the Confederacy surrendered unconditionally. But if Lincoln lost, McClellan would be willing to discuss terms. Confederate leaders expected to extract from him an agreement to grant the South autonomy and to approve a "slow" emancipation—liberation in decades-long stages, continually postponed—as the price for ending the war early and reconciling their warring countrymen. Again allied in friendship, the once-rivals could cooperate to expand a new American empire across the continent and abroad based on the Monroe Doctrine. For the greedy Yankees (as the Southern plantation class regarded them), such an offer would surely be too tempting to turn down. They'd probably even accept the creation of Confederate slave colonies in Cuba, Mexico, and Brazil in the interests of a peace settlement at home.

Prioleau was understandably bullish. For the first time in ages, the Confederacy's chances looked quite rosy. Despite *The Economist*'s warning that the Erlanger bonds were "unfitted for investors," in

September their price had recovered from a disastrous £35 a year earlier to £84, the highest they had been since before the battle of Gettysburg in July 1863. A lot of people were obviously gambling heavily that a McClellan armistice would include a provision to honor bondholders' cotton claims.

On October 18, the same day, as it happened, that the *Laurel* rendezvoused with the *Sea King* at Las Desertas, the bazaar opened its doors. Prioleau termed it "a grand fancy fair" and charged accordingly for tickets to keep out the riffraff. Likewise, in order to dissuade dockside slatterns from applying as help, Prioleau had also primly insisted that every young lady he interviewed to serve refreshments must be "good looking and very neatly dressed."

Henry Hotze, of course, sent a "special correspondent" from *The Index* to Liverpool to report on the fairy-tale affair. The hack was beside himself with rapture, describing the exhibition as being "like a scene out of the opera, or an illustration of the *Arabian Nights*." From the "pomp of architecture in the noble room itself" to the "masses of colour in banners and canopies, fabrics of all gorgeous tints, the loveliest women" dressed in a "weltering sea of crinoline," the eye "was bewildered with the multiform beauty that it surveyed."

Arranged in the Great Hall were a range of tented stalls, each representing a Confederate state. Designed by the Liverpool firm of Anderson & Sons, they alternated between rectangles and octagons, and all were of cloth striped red, white, and blue. Arising from each octagonal stall's cupola was an arrangement of intertwined Confederate and British flags, and outside the rectangular ones was a banneret embroidered with the South's motto, *Deo Vindice* ("Under God, Our Vindicator").

The Southern-minded belles of Liverpool volunteered their services to man the stalls. Everything was for sale or being raffled to raise money and—this was unspoken, for obvious reasons—the competition was mercilessly fierce. "Georgia," for instance, was the domain of Mrs. Bulloch and her friend, Mrs. Trapmann, whose husband was a French cotton-financier crony of Prioleau's. Inside, they proudly showed off a handsome clock, surrounded by playful bacchanalian cherubs, and exhibited several specimens of fine needlework. Mrs. Prioleau and Lady Wharn-cliffe, meanwhile, stood sentinel over at "South Carolina," which presented several autographs of Robert E. Lee, Jefferson Davis, and General Beauregard. At "Virginia," for reasons known only to herself, Mrs. Klingender (the wife of Prioleau's longtime front man) decided that a large, scary statue of Mephistopheles would attract admirers. In the "Arkansas" stall, Mrs. Sillem and Mrs. Willink (both wives of blockade-runner owners) got more into the spirit of the thing with a model of the *Florida,* wheels of American cheese, and several live American rabbits. So too did "Kentucky" and "Tennessee," which shared a tent, where the Kentucky contingent presented rings and brooches fashioned by Southern prisoners out of old combs and what-not, and the Tennesseeans (including Mrs. Hull—the wife of Bulloch's oleaginous solicitor) exhibited a collection of Jefferson Davis busts. "Louisiana," meanwhile, embarrassed everyone by presenting a trio of monkeys who were being taught to sing. More embarrassingly still, the Louisiana stall would bring in more money than any other.

Mr. Bliss and Mr. Burward, the steward and chef, respectively, of the Southern Club, served turtle soup and roast mutton between raf-fles. Dozens of these were held every day, the Southern ladies handing out gold watches, pipes (including one of Lee's), revolvers, inspirational paintings, and teapots. The one that raised the most (£125) was for a little Shetland pony (named Varina Davis, after the South's First Lady), which was won, and then generously re-donated back to the committee for another round, by Henry Brewer, an Alabama merchant who served as a covert go-between for Hotze and Erlanger, the Paris banker. There was not quite as much interest in "a tailless Manx cat, ugly enough and black enough to have convicted any old Lancashire woman of witch-craft two or three centuries ago."

Throughout the day and into the evening, music was supplied by several pianists and a band playing light pieces specially composed by a Mr. Streather for the wonderful event. There was a "Eulogy on Stone-wall Jackson," a soulful "Farewell to Freedom," and to cheer everyone up, a rousing ditty called "Down Among De Cotton" performed by a minstrel playing a banjo and whose lyrics formed a perfect cauldron of Confederate racist stereotyping, King Cottonism, and self-pity. A few of the slightly less offensive samples might include, "Dey's makin' war agin de South, and calls it 'mancipation / Down among de cotton / But 'taint a fact—and now I'll tell you what's de situation / Dey only wants de cotton."

The bazaar was enormously popular. On some days, more than five thousand people attended. Even Dudley, obviously barred from the event, had to admit to Seward that Prioleau had pulled off a coup. "Every thing in and about it was South," he added contemptuously. "Nothing [was] omitted to show or express a desire for the success of the Insurgents."

After the bazaar closed its doors, Prioleau tallied the takings: a total of more than £20,000 that he could send to Confederate prisoners. After two Southern sympathizers in New York named Tobias and Atkinson promised to "keep the whole thing as secret and as quiet as possible," Prioleau sent them the bulk of the money, with agents in Baltimore, Philadelphia, and New Orleans handling smaller amounts.

Then he sprung the trap. As Prioleau wrote to a friend, he had publicly advertised his intention to donate the proceeds. Now, Washington was faced with a dilemma. Seward would either have to approve the charitable donation, in which case Lincoln would be humiliated by the Union's poor treatment of its prisoners, or he would reject it, thus casting upon the government "the odium of refusing relief to helpless, unarmed, and starving human beings." McClellan would benefit from the fallout in the upcoming election.

Prioleau considered himself awfully clever. But little did he, or anyone else, know that the bazaar marked the end of the line for the Confederacy in Britain.

V

The collapse came quickly. On November 2, two weeks later, a one-line telegram arrived in British newsrooms with the disturbing revelation that the cruiser *Florida* had been captured by an American warship, the *Wachusett,* in the port of Bahia in Brazil.

After a busy run that summer, in early October Captain Morris (Maffitt had resigned owing to ill-health) had brought the *Florida* into port for re-coaling. By happenstance, the *Wachusett*, under Commander Napoleon Collins, was also anchored there. Her captain had long been fruitlessly searching for the elusive raider, and the opportunity was too good to miss. It seems that after Morris and many of his crew went ashore, having been assured by the Brazilian authorities that their ship was under their protection, the *Wachusett* launched a surprise attack at 3:00 A.M. on October 7. After ramming the *Florida* on the starboard quarter, the *Wachusett* fired two shots across her deck and demanded her immediate surrender. Many men who leaped overboard to try to swim for shore were shot or drowned. The rest were taken prisoner.

By any definition, this unauthorized hostile act was a major breach of Brazilian neutrality. But Collins had known it was now or never. In a day or two, the *Florida* would have flown away to continue her rampage. Accordingly, Collins refused to allow the Brazilian authorities to intervene and instead towed the *Florida* into international waters.

The *Wachusett* arrived at Hampton Roads with her prize on November 12. The Brazilians were furious, as might be expected, and demanded the release of the *Florida,* giving Seward a painful diplomatic migraine. On November 28, once $13,000 in gold had been removed from the *Florida*'s safe by the navy, a United States Army transport ship somehow collided with her. Soon afterward, the *Florida* sank, miraculously relieving Seward's headache.

Seward could afford to be high-handed. On November 8, Lincoln had smashed McClellan in the presidential election. After Lincoln's victory, the price of Erlanger bonds plummeted as the chances of an armistice receded with each mile the Union armies advanced. By March 1865, they would be trading at around £7 or £8, the province only of pitiful, besotted loyalists and bottom-feeding speculators. A month later, following Lee's surrender at Appomattox, they were worthless.

One month after the election, armed with Lincoln's overwhelming mandate, Seward derived enormous satisfaction from rejecting Prioleau's request to distribute the bazaar funds among the North's prisoners. The money, he wrote to Adams (who was instructed to make it public), was "insidiously tendered in the name of humanity" and composed just a minute fraction of the profits Prioleau and his Confederate friends in Liverpool had raked in from commerce raiding, arms dealing, and blockade-running during a war, Seward waspishly added, "promoted and protracted by British subjects." Dudley considered this a "most excellent letter."

By refusing the money, and as a result being portrayed as a heartless monster in the press, Seward had indeed been caught in Prioleau's trap. But Prioleau was caught in a more lethal one. He had been depending on Seward caring about how he, and the Union, would come across if he said no to the prisoner fund. With Lincoln's place in the White House secured, however, Seward was happy to see the contents of his letter published in every newspaper in the land. To him, a couple of days' worth of slings and arrows in some foreign rags meant nothing when he was protected by an electoral majority. This kerfuffle would soon be forgotten, but the war would grind on remorselessly.

In attaching themselves to Prioleau's cynical scheme to boost McClellan, the bazaar's cheerleaders had in fact only proved themselves gauzy sentimentalists pathetically hankering for a world lost to the past and deludedly convinced that the Confederacy had a future. That glorious moment in the Great Hall was preserved forever, like a sepia snapshot, and they hardly suspected the end was nigh. But then, neither had the bemedaled archdukes and tiaraed princesses dancing at the Winter Palace in November 1917 dreamed that the Russian Revolution would sweep them all away just weeks later. Nor had the Byzantine emperor Constantine XI Palaeologus, staring at the Ottoman armies of Mehmet II from the ramparts of Constantinople in 1453, known that within a couple of months his last remnant of the Roman Empire would be forever extinguished.

During those four magnificent days in Liverpool, the Confederate States of America had blared a high note. But the trumpet's silver sound would soon fall into silence.

VI

In February 1865, far beyond news of the war, Waddell's *Shenandoah* was wreaking havoc on American whalers in the Bering Sea, capturing nearly forty in total. It was an impressive tally, but *Shenandoah* did nothing to lift the blockade.

Yankee whalers were easy targets, but they were easily replaceable and, in any case, hardly treasure ships. For instance, from the *Edward* Waddell took 50 barrels of beef, 49 of pork, 600 pounds of coffee, and 400 of butter. The loss of these delicious provisions, we can be sure, had no effect on the war's outcome. In short, by this stage in the conflict, the $1.4 million in damages inflicted by the *Shenandoah* was almost meaningless. Not even Dudley was particularly exercised by her predations.

It was only on June 22, 1865, that Waddell learned from one Captain Smith of the captured *William Thompson* that Lincoln had been assassinated two months earlier, and that Charleston, Savannah, and Richmond had long since fallen. Nobody believed it. Waddell's own lieutenant Whittle was "certain that [Lincoln's murder] was not done by anyone from our side" and that Smith's contention that Lee had surrendered at Appomattox was false.

It simply could not be. Whittle had been in the habit of throwing *Uncle Tom's Cabin* overboard whenever he found a copy in a ship's library, and neither he, Waddell, or any of his fellow officers accepted the reality that the South was now ruled by Yankees, "a race of cruel, fanatical Scoundrels, lost alike to honor, decency, honesty & christianity." The raiding must continue.

It was only at 4:15 P.M. on August 2, "the darkest day of my life," according to Whittle, when the crew boarded a ship bound for Liverpool, the *Barracouta,* that the truth could no longer be denied. The *Barracouta* was an English-flagged vessel, and her captain could be trusted when he said "our dear country has been overrun; our President [Davis] captured [on May 10]; our armies & navy surrendered; our people subjugated." At this unpleasant revelation, Waddell finally ordered a halt to all raids on American vessels.

The question now was what to do. Heading for an American port was out of the question. Not only was there a risk of being charged with piracy, but handing over the pride of the Confederate Navy to the enemy was unconscionable. Waddell decided to go to Liverpool. He knew Bulloch would make sure the *Shenandoah* was treated honorably.

Nine thousand miles and three months later, the *Shenandoah*, which many assumed had been lost, appeared in the Mersey on Monday, November 6, 1865. Crowds gathered along the wharves to witness for themselves the incredible sight. According to the *Liverpool Mercury*, she was flying the "Palmetto flag"—the reporter probably meant the Confederate naval ensign—and moored alongside HMS *Donegal*, a ship of the line commanded by Captain Paynter. It was to him that Waddell surrendered, announcing that he was entrusting his ship to the care of Her Majesty's Government and handing over a letter to that effect to be forwarded to Russell. Summoning the crew to the deck, Waddell, in his dress uniform, ordered the flag lowered at 10:00 A.M.—the last time this would officially happen. The war had finally ended—and in Liverpool, no less.

Two days later, the government promised to parole the officers and men, unless they were British and subject to punishment for violating the Foreign Enlistment Act. Captain Paynter went on board to separate the Britons from the others, but he didn't take his job too seriously. Upon being asked his nationality, not a single man admitted to being a British subject, instead claiming to be a citizen of the Confederacy. A reporter present noticed that several "had an unmistakably Scotch accent, and seemed more likely to have 'hailed' from the banks of the Clyde than the Mississippi." All were free to go.

The crew packed their belongings and were taken to the docks, where onlookers stared at the "swarthy-complexioned, weather-beaten men, dressed in gray uniforms, and wearing eccentric-looking hats and caps." Bulloch was almost certainly present, though he would have kept in the background for the sake of discretion. When things had quieted down, he visited Waddell at a hotel near his house and arranged for the crew's wages to be paid.

Dudley, to his bitter disappointment, had missed the great moment of the *Shenandoah*'s arrival. By happenstance, he had returned from a brief trip to New Jersey just two days after the spectacle, on November 8. Seeing Bulloch's last raider, the mysterious *Sea King*, docked in the Mersey must have come as a wonderful surprise. At 2:00 P.M. on Friday, November 10, Dudley boarded the *Shenandoah*, formally took possession of her in the name of the United States government, and raised the American ensign.

Eleven days later, Captain Thomas Freeman, an American merchant captain, and a small crew of riggers steered her out of the Mersey. Dudley was there, bittersweetly enjoying for the first time the experience of steaming on one of Bulloch's ships. Before she headed out to sea, destination New York, Dudley bade the aptly named Freeman farewell at the Bell-Buoy and returned to Liverpool. He had unfinished business.

The *Shenandoah* never made it to America. Encountering high winds, she lost some spars and came back to Liverpool, where she was sold to a merchant and eventually passed to the sultan of Zanzibar.

FOURTEEN

Retribution

I

Dudley had long prayed that divine retribution would come for Prioleau's sins. That it did, if helped along by the Liverpool consul himself.

When the war was over, the U.S. government sued Fraser Trenholm's sister firm, John Fraser & Co., to extract the import duties it owed on every good smuggled through the blockade. Prioleau's rich old mentor, George Trenholm, was left with nothing but a suitcase of money he'd managed to hide. Terrified of suffering the same fate, Prioleau destroyed virtually every single piece of correspondence relating to the Confederate naval program.

But Washington came for him nevertheless. In late 1865, the government brought suit against Fraser Trenholm to recover cash and Erlanger Loan proceeds, and to expropriate any blockade-runners the company still owned.

Dudley had long been agitating for a strike against Prioleau, which would form the basis for a fresh offensive against Bulloch, the consul's primary target. Dudley was therefore greatly disappointed that Seward assigned the task to his consular counterpart in London, Freeman Morse, an inoffensive political appointee from Maine.

Dudley, wise to Prioleau's knavery, insisted that he be closely consulted by Morse, but the latter considered Dudley too radical for his tastes. There was a fundamental difference between their two approaches. Reflecting President Andrew Johnson's call for reconciliation between the warring nations, Morse was willing to cut deals with former Confederates, providing they made a full accounting of their affairs. Dudley was the more unforgiving sort. Treating the former enemy as honorable, if errant, gentlemen, and to absolve them for what he saw as their criminal, wicked treachery, was wrongheaded. They needed to be exposed, shamed, and punished.

Dudley urged Morse to stand strong and not let Prioleau wriggle free, but the London consul ignored the advice. In early November 1866, Morse informed Seward that he had arrived at a settlement with the fallen cotton broker. Prioleau would hand over a list of Confederate assets controlled by Fraser Trenholm in return for a large portion of the profits earned from their sale on the open market. As a bonus, Prioleau agreed to provide information regarding his transactions with the Confederacy during the war. The well-meaning Morse, unaware that Prioleau had already burned anything incriminating, was pleased to report that the Southerner's assistance would be invaluable. And that was it: no restitution, no revenge, not even an apology.

Dudley was livid. For the final agreement, Morse had come to Liverpool for a six-hour talk with Prioleau and his (and Bulloch's) solicitor Frederick Hull, without notifying Dudley. Despite knowing more about Fraser Trenholm's activities than anyone else, the Liverpool consul had been deliberately kept in the dark. Morse's blindsiding of him Dudley found "most discourteous, if not ungentlemanly," but making matters worse was that Morse had fallen hook, line, and sinker for Prioleau's pandering charm. He had offered him, and by extension Bulloch, a sweetheart deal. As Morse naively boasted, Prioleau and Hull had "met me cordially and frankly, showed no backwardness in making a full exposé, and remarked on parting that they much regretted they had not met me a year ago, as it would have been much better for them and for the United States."

Dudley remarked that he wasn't surprised at their solicitude. After all, once the ships and other assets were sold, Morse had guaranteed Prioleau a minimum £150,000 payoff from the proceeds. Dudley, trying to keep his temper, argued that Morse had been bamboozled into obliging the U.S. government to pay a large sum to a firm that "had been [more] active in aiding the rebellion and fitting out piratical expeditions" than any other. It should have been Fraser Trenholm paying the money to the treasury, not the other way around. As it was, this backstairs arrangement "looks to me like giving Fraser, Trenholm & Co. a million of dollars and getting nothing in return."

Morse retorted that Dudley's undiplomatic reaction was exactly why he had been cut out. Prioleau had had only one condition: He "would not under any circumstances negotiate with Mr. Dudley." If the consul were brought in, Prioleau threatened, he would take his chances in court, which the emollient Morse was desperate to avoid.

Morse argued that, with the settlement he had negotiated with Prioleau, the cotton broker's fair treatment would "[induce] others in similar circumstances to pursue a like course." Indeed, before Morse had left Liverpool, "it was intimated to me [by Hull] that Captain Bullock would be the next to seek terms," he wrote. But again, that would only happen if Dudley were excluded from the arrangements.

To Morse, as to Dudley, Bulloch was the big fish. Only Bulloch knew all the details of the commerce-raiding and ironclad schemes, on that the two consuls agreed, but Dudley believed the price of Bulloch's information—letting him off, as if he were just a naïf who happened to be involved peripherally with a few ships—was too high. Morse should have called the Confederates' bluff and proceeded remorselessly to litigation.

Yes, it would have taken years to bring Bulloch and Prioleau to trial. But imagine the rewards, exclaimed Dudley. Inexorably rising legal bills and forcing the pair of them to swear oaths under pain of perjury would have extracted a disclosure of "all the property of every kind, sort, and description. Their books, papers, and letters would have been open to us; not such as they choose to produce, as is the case now, but all of them.

The parties would be subject to cross-examination; a full, complete, and perfect discovery could not have been avoided." Their names would have been exposed, and those, too, of every blockade-runner owner. The Lairds and other shipbuilders would have been summoned to testify and to answer for their transgressions. Liverpool itself would be put on trial.

Morse, for his part, could not comprehend why Dudley cared so much. Had Morse not ensured a windfall for the treasury by getting Prioleau to agree to sell Fraser Trenholm's assets? Had he not saved the government a fortune in legal costs? Morse simply failed to grasp that, for Dudley, his long duel with Bulloch was never about the money. It was about justice being done and damn the diplomatic solutions. In Dudley's eyes, pursuing the wicked to the very ends of the earth was not far enough.

Dudley and Morse presented their cases to Adams and Seward. Adams weighed their arguments and found Morse had exceeded his authority in not consulting Dudley. Seward agreed. On November 29, 1866, he sent a terse message by the new Atlantic cable, ordering Adams to "disavow and reject, in the name of the United States, the whole arrangement made by Consul Morse." The following January, he handed total responsibility over the matter to Thomas Dudley.

Prioleau's world collapsed. The immense weight of Fraser Trenholm's accumulated debts, totaling many millions of dollars and the result of a combination of the failure of blockade-running, losses on cotton speculation, sour Erlanger Loans, and financing Bulloch's ships on credit, destroyed the firm. As partner, Prioleau had invested all his capital in Fraser Trenholm and accordingly came within a whisker of personal bankruptcy—a shameful fate in Victorian Britain. What letters survive from this period make for a depressing litany of writs, warrants, legal notices, subpoenas, demands for payment, bills, and rejected applications to ease his loan terms.

Faced with years of lawsuits from Dudley and a host of aggrieved creditors, Prioleau sold his beloved 19 Abercromby Square and fled with his family to Bruges in Belgium. There, he established a minor banking firm, but returned to London some years later. His humiliating fall from the heights of society, his vaporized fortune, and the ceaseless legal battles exacted a heavy toll on his health and he would die in 1887, aged sixty.

<h1 style="text-align:center">II</h1>

Prioleau's fate was an unenviable one, if satisfying for Dudley, but it looked likely that he would be Dudley's last victim. The consul had been given a mandate to pursue and destroy Bulloch, but as time went on there was a diminishing appetite in Washington for hunting down former Confederates and bringing them to account. Reconstruction, not retribution, had become the spirit of the age.

To Dudley, it was almost as if the war had never happened. Forgiving and forgetting made for an easier life for everyone, as he complained in his talks with his friend Benjamin Moran at the Legation. Like Dudley, Moran, too, wanted a reckoning, but his great white whale was Bulloch's spy in the Foreign Office.

He'd given up hope of finding him until one Saturday afternoon, July 22, 1865, to be precise, "a little dark-haired fellow with a long bullet head" visited Moran in his dreary basement office. His name was Henry Hudson of Bridge Street, Hammersmith, the man said, and until recently he had been a lowly subeditor at Hotze's *Index*. Now out of a job and near-destitute, he wanted to sell information. As Hotze's subscriber list had always been kept secret, Moran was interested in buying. "The fellow may be useful," he wrote, "but he is clearly a rogue and a needy one at that. Still, I think we should keep him and pay for his evidence if need be."

"Little Hudson," as Moran called him, was still trusted by the Confederate network, which enabled him to elicit intelligence from otherwise closed sources. In mid-November, Hudson went to Liverpool to sniff around. Who he talked to is unknown, but it was probably Matthew Butcher, the former captain of the *Enrica/Alabama*. Butcher had also been present at the shipyard meeting with Bulloch and one of the Lairds on July 26, 1862, just after Hotze's telegram warning of the ship's detention had been sent. During a boozy chat with Hudson, Butcher mentioned a certain Victor Buckley as Bulloch's mole.

The name was vaguely familiar to Moran. Minister Adams had met Buckley several times at various functions, and he recalled that the charming young man had been "quite cordial" to Mrs. Adams and her daughters. He checked the Foreign Office List and discovered that this Buckley was the clerk in "charge of the correspondence with the U.S." Hudson also confirmed that Buckley was an *Index* subscriber, while a *New York Times* exposé in early December of the list of investors in the Erlanger Loan resolved any doubts that Buckley was the long-sought mole: His name was among those who had speculated in cotton bonds.

And not just as a fun flutter on the side. Rather unwisely, Buckley had put in the huge amount of £2,000, more than ten years' his then salary, a figure that put him in the same league as the marquess of Bath and John Laird, MP. The difference was the noble lord and the ship-building magnate could afford to lose the money. At the end of the war, when the bonds were rendered worthless, Buckley must have been driven to near-bankruptcy, perhaps explaining why he and his patient fiancée, Mary, would not get married until 1866, when Buckley's salary had risen to a more respectable £425 a year. How had a junior clerk like Buckley raised £2,000 in the first place? Almost certainly from his cut of Fraser Trenholm's blockade-running profits.

Hudson, realizing that he'd hooked a client—one who regularly paid him £10—could find no more information on Buckley in Liverpool. So he traveled to Paris to see Henry Brewer, an arms dealer who'd handled Erlanger funds (he'd also won that pony raffle at the Southern Bazaar). Brewer was at the time looking after Hotze's files in his absence—the Swiss lived a peripatetic existence between hovels in London and garrets in Paris—and he showed Hudson the original warning note Buckley had sent to Hotze carelessly using his real name. Hudson then made a copy from memory and brought it back to Moran.

Moran directed Hudson to get the original by any means necessary, no matter the cost. A copy was worthless as evidence—they were easy to forge—but the real thing was a smoking gun. "If I can get the proof,"

Moran bragged to his diary, "I am made at once." Hudson accordingly returned to Paris a few more times but despite diligently invoicing Moran for his escalating receipts, he was never able to steal the original, which later disappeared. It would not be until November 1866, a year later, that Moran, annoyed at being reeled in, terminated his dealings with Hudson. Any hope of unmasking Buckley had vanished. He had gotten away with it.

Even if Moran had succeeded in acquiring the signed note, it was unlikely that much would have resulted. Since the war's end, Buckley had made his way back into the Foreign Office's good graces, his transgressions forgotten. By 1882, he would be second to the senior assistant clerk but contracted rheumatic fever and died in his mid-forties. That same year, Moran, who had been serving as charge d'affaires in Portugal, retired and returned to Britain. An invalid, he died four years later at Bocking Hall in Essex, finally closing the book on Victor Buckley.

III

Dudley's sole motive in remaining in Liverpool, a city he hated in a country he disliked, was to bag Bulloch. Always a step or two ahead of others, Bulloch had taken the precaution in December 1865 of baptizing his children into the Church of England—the first step toward becoming a British subject and insulating himself against American legal action. Afterward, he leased an office at 13 Rumford Place, just a door or two down from his old haunt at Fraser Trenholm, and set himself up as a cotton broker.

Though Bulloch could be seen casually walking around Liverpool, much to Dudley's irritation, the Southerner was more worried than he let on. On Christmas Day 1868, President Johnson had issued a "full pardon and amnesty to all persons engaged in the late rebellion" in the interests of promoting "fraternal feeling among the whole people" of the United States. Importantly, though, it applied only to "the offence of treason." The proclamation said nothing about not pursuing former Confederates for financial compensation or trying to extradite them home. To cover himself, Bulloch completed his British naturalization within a month of its appearance.

A wise move, for Dudley had not rested since the Morse imbroglio. The problem had always been pinning a crime on Bulloch. Unlike Prioleau, Bulloch had never been a rich man and he had owned almost nothing in his own name. He had worked as a confidential agent of the Confederate government, dutifully serving its interests and acting under official orders. Neither had he ever done anything illegal, at least according to the British courts.

Sticking in Dudley's craw was his belief that, while Bulloch had acted legally, he had done many things wrong. He was guilty in a moral, if not legal, sense. But ever fewer people seemed to care about morality. Dudley was determined to make them care.

Working alone, he assiduously, obsessively, collected and hoarded every piece of paper relating to Bulloch's activities during the war. His cabinets bulged and overflowed with thousands upon thousands of handwritten letters, affidavits, legal documents, receipts, newspaper clippings, observations, and official memoranda, all meticulously cataloged and filed in preparation for a final showdown.

Dudley's efforts would have been in vain had it not been, ironically, for the desire of Britain and the United States to bury the hatchet after their wartime rancor. There were new challenges to face for the glorious Greece and rising Rome, and it was better to work together, not against each other, to regulate the world.

Britain was the first to offer an olive branch when Parliament passed the amended Foreign Enlistment Act of 1870, which sealed the loophole in its 1819 predecessor, so ably exploited by Bulloch. Henceforth, it would be a criminal offense to *build*, not just arm, fit out, or equip, any ship that one had reasonable cause to believe would be militarily employed by any foreign state at war with a state friendly to Britain.

If the 1870 Act were applied retroactively, Bulloch, now a British subject, would have been caught bang to rights. But of course it couldn't be. Bulloch was in no danger of prosecution. Even so, the passing of the act and the tacit admission that Britain had been wrong in not pursuing Bulloch more actively meant that the temper of the times had shifted.

The British government was signaling that it was willing to make a deal with the Americans. At the time, there were a large number of outstanding issues putting the two great powers at loggerheads, among them the Canadian border, territorial fishing rights, the status of Alaska, and Irish terrorists sheltering in America. The most divisive of them, however, concerned compensation for the predations of Bulloch's *Alabama, Florida,* and *Shenandoah* on American merchant ships.

Dudley devoted himself to extracting as much as possible from the British. If he could not put Bulloch in jail or bankruptcy court, then at least he could expose him by proving that his raiders had been not Robin Hoods but piratical reivers.

The Americans made two types of claims in their bid for compensation. The first was of a "direct" nature: They assessed the monetary value of the lost ships and property at $15 million, or about 5 percent of the British national budget—so nothing to sneeze at. Then there was the "collateral" claim, which added in things like the loss of expected economic growth, extortionate insurance rates, and the diminution of the American merchant fleet. This figure came to another $110 million. And, finally, not to forget the cost of the raiders' allegedly prolonging the war for two years: Tack on another $2 billion for that, though the Americans, trying to pull off another Louisiana Purchase, helpfully offered to accept Canada in lieu of cash.

Aside from the direct claim, these were clearly made-up numbers, and Canada was not up for sale. There was no way the British would agree to these demands—declaring war on the United States would actually be a much cheaper option. Nevertheless, Britain *was* willing to discuss the specific issue of the $15 million to make the problem go away.

Hence the process later known as the Alabama Claims, in which both sides agreed to refer the case to a "tribunal of arbitration," a first in international diplomacy. Five arbitrators would convene in Geneva to read the evidence and hear the arguments presented by the American and British representatives, then decide the victor by majority vote.

Though he did not attend, this was to be Dudley's finest performance. The American arbitrator was none other than Adams, whose entire case would stand or fall according to Dudley's assiduous record keeping.

On December 15, 1871, in an elegant, red-paneled room (now called La Salle de l'Alabama) furnished with plush velvet chairs and long wooden tables in Geneva's five-hundred-year-old town hall, the legal teams convened to hash out a settlement. It would take some time. The initial "British Case" alone took up 168 dense pages, with four giant volumes of supporting documents on the side. Thanks to Dudley, however, the Americans had amassed a devastating broadside in retort: a highly adversarial *480-page* case, buttressed by no fewer than seven even more-giant volumes. In them, the name Bulloch came up many, many hundreds of times, linking him inextricably to the raider campaign. At the same time, Adams found room to include a fulsome tribute to the Liverpool consul's hard work over so many years.

Four months later, there was an exchange of counter-cases, which added another two thousand closely printed pages to the pile. And then, finally, on Saturday, September 14, 1872, the decision was formally read out as the Swiss gunners outside fired their guns in celebration. The tribunal ruled that $15.5 million in gold was appropriate compensation for the damage caused by Bulloch's navy and must be paid within one year. For the sake of British amour propre, the sum was balanced by an award of nearly $2 million to London for losses suffered by Britons during the blockade. It seemed a fair exchange for Anglo-American amity.

IV

Dudley stayed not a moment longer in Liverpool than he needed. He was exhausted from his long labor collecting evidence for the Alabama Claims arbitration. "The strain has been very great upon me, so much so as to affect my health," he wrote, "and I fear continuance in office, with the like strain, will seriously undermine my constitution."

On October 7, 1872, three weeks after the tribunal announced its decision, Dudley submitted his resignation as consul. It was only then, after a decade of service unstinting, that the Lord, His work complete, let His servant depart in peace. Looking back, Dudley could at least reflect that, quite apart from defeating Bulloch, he had performed good works. He had saved, among others, Clarence Yonge—well, to the best that Yonge could be saved.

Without telling anyone, Dudley had aided Yonge in immigrating to the United States in 1864, where for a time he was stationed with the army on Hart Island near New York, then used as a training base for the 31st Infantry Regiment of the United States Colored Troops. After his discharge, again thanks to Dudley's help, Yonge obtained a position in the General Land Office of the Department of the Interior in Washington.

He told Dudley he was happy there, despite having suffered a "temporary depression of spirits [because] there was no good left in the country" after his rough treatment at the hands of Bulloch's barrister Sir Hugh Cairns during the *Alexandra* trial. He felt "very differently now," and though he regretted he hadn't taken Dudley's advice "about going to the West"—"in truth I lacked confidence in myself"—he had taken up studying law, hoping to follow in Dudley's footsteps. Helping to sustain him was that he had reconciled with (the first) Mrs. Yonge.

Despite his many flaws, Yonge was still human. Touchingly, he asked Dudley to send him four ambrotypes (a type of photograph) of his young daughter and son, the children he'd left behind in Savannah to go gallivanting. He'd forgotten to bring the pictures from the safe house in Holmfirth, near Manchester, where he'd holed up after being recruited by Dudley. He "value[d] them very highly," especially the one of his little girl, who'd since died. By the time Dudley was working on the Alabama Claims case, Yonge seems to have abandoned his legal career and moved to the small town of Opelika in Alabama to become a contractor and painter, thereafter disappearing from history.

Dudley himself returned to Camden, New Jersey, to reestablish his law practice and participate in state Republican politics. He did well for himself, serving as president or director of several railroads, a gaslight company, and a mining firm, allowing him the wherewithal to purchase The Grange, a country estate. He wrote dozens of articles and pamphlets on various subjects but remained remarkably silent on his wartime secret service. The closest he ever came to revealing what had happened in Liverpool was a piece printed in the *Pennsylvania Magazine of History and Biography* entitled "Three Critical Periods in Our Diplomatic Relations with England During the Late War," which circumspectly laid out his role in the *Alabama* and Laird Rams episodes.

And there his story stopped. On the morning of April 15, 1893, the same month as the article appeared, the seventy-three-year-old Dudley disembarked from a train at Philadelphia's Broad Street Station and collapsed almost instantly from a massive heart attack. He was buried next to his late wife, who'd died nine years earlier, in Colestown Cemetery near Cherry Hill, New Jersey. Soon afterward, the Grand Army of the Republic, the fraternal organization for Union veterans, requested permission to lay the flag and flowers at his grave, saying that he had served his country as faithfully as a soldier.

V

After the Alabama Claims, Bulloch did the best he could to ignore the regular mentions of his name in the newspapers. He did not have to worry about the police knocking on his door, yet the decisive strike against him in Geneva, combined with the insinuations that he was dishonorable and had acted criminally, certainly hurt business for many years. The financial panic of 1873 made life tougher still.

He was not bankrupted, but his debts were mounting. In an example of life coming round full circle, he was considerably aided by a decision in Washington that he was owed $8,510.62 by, of all things, the U.S. Navy. In 1861, the *Bienville*, the mail ship he had been commanding at New Orleans when he was recruited into the secret world, had been purchased by the navy for military service. Since Bulloch had owned some shares in its holding company, he was to be compensated. Payment had been delayed owing to the late unpleasantness.

All this time, Bulloch said nothing about the Alabama Claims and gave no interviews. Instead, he worked hard, and by the early 1880s his reputation and fortunes in Liverpool had recovered sufficiently for him to retire at age fifty-seven.

Now a gentleman of leisure, Bulloch had time to set the record straight. He drafted a manuscript, *The Secret Service of the Confederate States in Europe; or, How the Confederate Cruisers Were Equipped*, whose title was more exciting than its contents. It was a long justificatory slog, a prolix exercise in Lost Cause romanticism occasionally enlivened by passages on his *Fingal* voyage in 1861 and the true-ish story of the *Alabama* and *Florida* escapes. No publisher could be found for the manuscript, so he paid for a few hundred copies to be printed in Britain, though G.P. Putnam's Sons in New York eventually took it on as a favor to a rising young man in American affairs: Teddy Roosevelt.

Roosevelt, born in 1858, was the son of the New York socialite Mittie Bulloch, one of Bulloch's younger half sisters. Teddy had heard all the stories about the man he fondly called "Uncle Jimmie" and was fascinated by him. Even if their politics diverged, Roosevelt was enchanted by the affable old gent's rousing sea tales. They shared, too, an interest in naval strategy and talked for many hours on the subject when Bulloch visited the Roosevelts' estate on Long Island in the summer of 1877.

It was a discreet visit, for Bulloch remained forever cagey about traveling to the United States, especially after the Alabama Claims. Chary of some vengeful, still-aggrieved litigant whose ships had been sunk by one of his raiders popping up and dragging him into court, Bulloch always made sure to brandish a British passport on the few times he crossed the Atlantic.

Unwilling to make Uncle Jimmie uncomfortable, in 1881 Teddy made a special trip to Liverpool to show Bulloch the draft manuscript of what would become the bestselling book that would make his name, *The Naval War of 1812*. In his preface, Roosevelt gave due credit to "Captain James D. Bulloch, formerly of the United States Navy . . . without whose advice and sympathy this work would probably never have been written or even begun." If Dudley ever read it, he would certainly have been surprised by Roosevelt's evasive locution that curiously omitted Bulloch's secret service with the Confederate States of America.

It was on the back of the *Naval War*'s success that Roosevelt persuaded Putnam's to publish Uncle Jimmie's interminable book as a favor—helped along by a $20,000 investment in the company. It sold poorly, but Bulloch shrugged it off. He had told the world the truth, as he saw it, and with that he vanished into the background. For the rest of his life, he never wrote another book or article, not even a letter to the editor, about the war.

Only once would he emerge from the shadows. In 1884, he asked Jefferson Davis to see if he could put in a good word for him with the incoming president, Grover Cleveland, a Democrat who might be open to employing former Confederates in "Federal offices of trust."

"I wish to obtain," Bulloch wrote in one last, insulting blow to Dudley, "the office of United States Consul at Liverpool." As he explained in this bizarre supplication, he enjoyed a "very special familiarity with the Maritime Laws of Great Britain and the local usages of this particular port." His suit found no favor: Too many in Washington recalled his role in destroying American commerce and prolonging a murderous war by abetting blockade-running.

In 1897, Bulloch's wife, Harriott, died of a stomach ailment two months after he heard, to his delight, that Teddy had been appointed assistant secretary of the navy. Bulloch's influence would live on, even if physically he was weakening. After moving into his daughter's house, he survived long enough to see his nephew win election as the Republican vice president in November 1900.

Two months later, in early January 1901, at age seventy-seven, James Bulloch died of cardiac arrest and was buried in Toxteth Park Cemetery, Liverpool.

Twenty years later, in 1921, the twenty-ninth volume of *Official Records of the Union and Confederate Navies in the War of the Rebellion* appeared. Unthrillingly titled *Navy Department Correspondence, 1861–1865, with Agents Abroad*, its 821 pages finally revealed Bulloch's clandestine letters hitherto hidden from the public. Two years afterward, Thomas Dudley's grandson sold his ancestor's papers to the Huntington Library in San Marino, California, where they currently reside.

And with that, the ghosts of the antagonists in this secret war, whose duel had defined the struggle at sea, were finally laid to rest.

ACKNOWLEDGMENTS

Writing a book may remain a solitary pursuit, but it is rarely achieved without the assistance of others. To that end, I wish to thank Brigitte Stephenson, curator of the Sanford Museum, Sanford, Florida, for her kind assistance procuring correspondence from the Henry Shelton Sanford Papers; the staff of the Huntington Library, San Marino, California, for providing copies of notes and letters from the Thomas Haines Dudley Papers; Distinguished Professor Joseph Fry of the University of Nevada, Las Vegas, for sending me a copy of his hard-to-find book on Henry Sanford many years ago; the staff of the National Archives, College Park, Maryland, for digitizing for me the *Despatches from United States Consuls in Liverpool*, whose volumes contain Dudley's enormous official and confidential correspondence; and Bill Barker, archivist of Mariners' Museum and Park, Newport News, Virginia, for sending Matthew Maguire's report in the James Dunwoody Bulloch Papers. Invaluably, Canon Walter King sent me his unpublished biography of his great-grandfather and helpfully answered my (numerous) inquiries.

My agent and wise counsel, Eric Lupfer, helped untwist and straighten an inordinately complex story into a catchily alliterative and coherent structure ("Runners, Raiders, Rams"). I'd been sitting on this idea for years, musing how to make it work, but he provided the key to unlocking it.

I must also express my gratitude to the John Simon Guggenheim Memorial Foundation for kindly awarding me a Guggenheim Fellowship, the receipt of which allowed this book to be written. I owe a particular debt (and lunch) to André Bernard.

At Mariner Books, I've been fortunate to enjoy the talents of a crack team. My executive editor, Alexander Littlefield, skillfully piloted the manuscript from beginning to end and set me right where I had erred; associate editor Zach Phillips insisted on a livelier way to meet our protagonists and made any number of sensible contributions; and assistant editor Jessica Vestuto diplomatically negotiated with various vendors and made sure everyone always was on the same page. I must also mention the excellent design work of Chloe Foster, as well as the helpful suggestions of Karen Richardson, the copyeditor.

Of course, family comes first (though traditionally last in the acknowledgments, for reasons that escape me). I'd like to thank my brother, Ari, and sister, Zoë, as well as my extended family (Craig, Liz and Chad, Ben and Jaime, Erna, and David and Carolyn), for their support. In permanent pole position is my wife, Rebecca, beloved of beloveds, and son, Edmund, who at thirteen is both a lion and a fox.

NOTES

Prologue

I

Dudley and Liverpool: Letters to Seward, October 26 and November 23, 1861, in *Despatches from United States Consuls in Liverpool, 1790–1906*, Reels 19, 20, microfilm in the National Archives. Hereafter *LCD*, for Liverpool Consular Despatches. Liverpool: Herman Melville's quasi-autobiographical account of his visit in *Redburn*, in G. T. Tanselle (ed.), *Redburn, White-Jacket, Moby-Dick* (New York: Library of America, 1983), pp. 165–230; M. Macilwee, *The Liverpool Underworld: Crime in the City, 1750–1900* (Liverpool: Liverpool University Press, 2011). Other sources on crime include: F. Bell, *Midnight Scenes in the Slums of New York: Or, Lights and Shadows* (London: W. Kent and Co., 1881), pp. 230–31; T. Lane, *Liverpool: Gateway of Empire* (London: Lawrence and Wishart, 1987), pp. 23–25, 34, 38–39, 77–96, 117–18; H. Shimmin, *Liverpool Sketches, Chiefly Reprinted from the* Porcupine (London: W. Tweedie, 1863), pp. 1, 91; R. Muir, *A History of Liverpool* (Liverpool: University Press of Liverpool, 1907), p. 301; C. Dickens, "Poor Mercantile Jack," in Dickens, *The Uncommercial Traveller and A Child's History of England* (London: Macmillan & Co., 1922), pp. 34–43; and N. Hawthorne, *Passages from the English Note-Books* (Boston: James R. Osgood and Co., 1875), diary entries of August 9, p. 10; September 1, pp. 28–29; October 19, 1853, p. 51. Women fighting: Hawthorne, *Our Old Home: A Series of English Sketches* (Edinburgh: William Paterson, 1884), p. 238. Murders in 1858: A. Hume, *Condition of Liverpool, Religious and Social; Including Notices of the State of Education, Morals, Pauperism, and Crime* (Liverpool: T. Brakell, 1888), p. 26.

II

B. Dyer, "Thomas H. Dudley," *Civil War History*, 1 (1955), no. 4, pp. 401–13; W. J. Potts, "Biographical Sketch of the Hon. Thomas H. Dudley, of Camden, N.J., Who Died April 15, 1893," *Proceedings of the American Philosophical Society*, 35 (1895), pp. 102–28; "Thomas H. Dudley," in A. C. Rogers (ed.), *Our Representatives Abroad: Biographical Sketches of Ambassadors, Ministers, Consuls-General, and Consuls of the United States in Foreign Countries* (New York: Atlantic Publishing Company, 1874), pp. 257–68; T. H. Dudley, "The Inside Facts of Lincoln's Nomination," *The Century*, 40 (1890), pp. 477–79; D. H. Maynard, "Dudley of New Jersey and the Nomination of Lincoln," *Pennsylvania Magazine of History and Biography*, 82 (1958), no. 1, pp. 100–8. Dudley tells his own story in "Appointment & Initial Experiences as Liverpool Consul," Thomas Haines Dudley Papers DU-1275, probably written in 1884.

Chapter One: On Secret Service

I–II

J. D. Bulloch, *The Secret Service of the Confederate States in Europe; or, How the Confederate Cruisers Were Equipped* (New York: Modern Library, 2001 ed.; 1883 orig.), pp. 24–27; V. Bullock-Willis, "James Dunwoody Bulloch," *The Sewanee Review*, 34 (1926), 4, pp. 386–401; E. A. Ford, "The Bullochs of Georgia," *The Georgia Review*, 6 (1952), 3, pp. 318–31; J. G. B. Bulloch, *A Biographical Sketch of Hon. Archibald Bulloch, President of Georgia, 1776–77* (privately printed, 1907); S. C. Kinnaman, *Captain Bulloch: The Life of James Dunwoody Bulloch, Naval Agent of the Confederacy* (Indianapolis, IN: Dog Ear Publishing, 2013), pp. 20–198; W. E. Wilson and G. L. McKay, *James D. Bulloch: Secret Agent and Mastermind of the Confederate Navy* (Jefferson, NC: McFarland & Co., 2012), pp. 11–35; G. P. Shine, "'A Gallant Little Schooner': The U.S. Schooner *Shark* and the Oregon Country, 1846," *Oregon Historical Quarterly*, 109 (2008), no. 4, pp. 536–65; R. H. Dana, *To Cuba and Back: A Vacation Voyage* (Boston: Ticknor and Fields, 1859), pp. 11–23, 278. On his politics, see Bulloch, *Secret Service*, pp. 22, 24, 27. The Murray Street address is given in a classified advertisement in the *New York Herald*, March 27, 1861. Regarding the Benjamin letter, its full contents are mysterious as Bulloch destroyed it, though he quoted (from memory) its purportedly only line in his memoirs ("The Secretary of the Navy desires you to come to Montgomery without delay."). Bulloch later claimed, however, that he was first asked to go to Britain during his meeting with Mallory in Montgomery. Yet Bulloch purchased a ticket to Liverpool while he was *still* in New York via a roundabout route from Montreal. How, if he only first heard the proposal *later* in Montgomery, did he know he was going to be traveling there? Put another way, there was more to the Benjamin letter than Bulloch later pretended, probably in an attempt to disguise, for legal reasons, his early involvement in the clandestine naval scheme. It is possible that while still in New Orleans on April 23 he was tipped off that he was to be sent to Britain, though there is no evidence of this. The New York letter therefore remains the strongest indication of Bulloch's recruitment. On transferring his assets: Hiram Barney (Customs House official) to Seward, July 10, 1861, *The War of the Rebellion: A Compilation of the Official Records of the Union and Confederate Armies* (Washington, DC: Government Printing Office, 70 vols., 1880–1901), 2, 2, p. 18. Hereafter *Official Records (Army)*.

III–V

Montgomery: *Journal of the Congress of the Confederate States of America, 1861–1865* (Washington, DC: Government Printing Office, 1904), 1, p. 50, February 13, 1861; W. H. Russell, *My Diary North and South* (Boston: T.O.H.P. Burnham, 1863), pp. 165–80. Mallory's background: P. Melvin, "Stephen Russell Mallory, Southern Naval Statesman," *Journal of Southern History*, 10 (1944), 2, pp. 137–60. On the Mallory-Bulloch discussions: Bulloch, *Secret Service*, pp. 30–35; Kinnaman, *Captain Bulloch*, pp. 238–42; Mallory to Bulloch, May 9, 1861, *Official Records of the Union and Confederate Navies in the War of the Rebellion* (Washington, DC: Government Printing Office, 30 vols., 1894–1927), 2, 2, pp. 64–65. Hereafter *Official Records (Navy)*. Lincoln's ships: J. T. Scharf, *History of the Confederate States Navy from Its Organization to the Surrender of Its Last Vessel* (New York: Rogers and Sherwood, 1887), p. 433. South's relative lack of industry: Table 3, "Value of Manufacturing Production," in D. G. Surdam, "The Union Navy's Blockade Reconsidered," *Naval War College Review*, 51 (1998), no. 4, pp. 93–94; Surdam, "The Confederate Naval Buildup: Could More Have Been Accomplished?" *Naval War College Review*, 54 (2001), no. 1, p. 110; and W. N. Still Jr., "Facilities for the Construction of War Vessels in the Confederacy," *Journal of Southern History*, 31 (1965), no. 3, pp. 285–89. An initial $1 million appropriation for Bulloch was approved on May 10, *Official Records (Navy)*, 2, 2, p. 66. Mallory on acquiring ironclads: Memorandum to C. M. Conrad, May 10, *Official Records (Navy)*, 2, 2, pp. 67–69. I've relied on the detective work of Wilson and McKay, *James D. Bulloch*, pp. 37–38, 43, regarding Hollis White. White's appointment to the Treasury: "Our Washington Dispatches," *New York Times*, March 26, 1861. Bulloch was annoyed that he had been exposed (see his August 13, 1861, report from London, *Official Records (Navy)*, 2, 2, p. 84). The *Newbern Daily Progress* of North Carolina, May 23, 1861, reprints the original *Richmond Dispatch* article.

Chapter Two: The White Gold

I

Moran's background: "In Memoriam," *Trübner's American, European & Oriental Literary Record*, 5 (1884), p. 48. On his political views: R. Fulton, "The *Spectator* in Alien Hands," *Victorian Periodicals Review*, 24 (1991), no. 4, pp. 187–96; S. A. Wallace and F. E. Gillespie (eds.), *The Journal of Benjamin Moran, 1857–1865* (Chicago: University of Chicago Press, 2 vols., 1948–49). Views of Dallas and on Adams's dress: May 16 and June 15, 1861, 1, pp. 811–12, 829; Hobbies: July 15, 1861, November 14, 1862, February 2, 1864, 2, pp. 945, 1,090, 1,258. Amusingly, in his own diary, Adams agreed that he indeed had looked like a butler: May 15, at http://www .masshist.org/publications/cfa-civil-war/view?id=DCA61d135. Queen Victoria's comment is mentioned in Moran, November 18, 1861, 2, p. 907. Adams's background: N. B. Ferris, "Tempestuous Mission, 1861–1862: The Early Diplomatic Career of Charles Francis Adams," unpublished Ph.D. dissertation (Emory University, 1962). Neutrality: R. J. M. Blackett, *Divided Hearts: Britain and the American Civil War* (Baton Rouge: Louisiana State University Press, 2001), pp. 6–47; F. L. Owsley Sr., *King Cotton Diplomacy: Foreign Relations of the Confederate States of America* (Tuscaloosa: University of Alabama Press, 2nd ed., 1959), pp. 179–96. Russell quoted in D. H. Doyle, *The Cause of All Nations: An International History of the American Civil War* (New York: Basic Books, 2015), p. 42. For definitions of legal status: J. R. Soley, *The Blockade and the Cruisers* (New York: Charles Scribner's Sons, 1883), p. 30; F. J. Merli, *Great Britain and the Confederate Navy, 1861–1865* (Bloomington: Indiana University Press, 1970), p. 42. Seward's instructions to keep Britain neutral: Seward to Adams, April 10 and May 21, 1861, in *Papers Relating to Foreign Affairs, 1861–1865* (Washington, DC: Government Printing Office, 1861–65), pp. 71–80, 87–90.

II

S. R. Wise, *Lifeline of the Confederacy: Blockade Running During the Civil War* (Columbia: University of South Carolina Press, 1988), pp. 12–13; J. M. McPherson, *War on the Waters: The Union and Confederate Navies, 1861–1865* (Chapel Hill: University of North Carolina Press, 2012), pp. 46–47; E. D. Adams, *Great Britain and the American Civil War* (London: Longmans, Green and Co., 2 vols., 1925), 1, p. 140; K. J. Weddle, "The Blockade Board of 1861 and Union Naval Strategy," *Civil War History*, 48 (2002), no. 2, pp. 123–42; W. N. Still Jr., "A Naval Sieve: The Union Blockade in the Civil War," *Naval War College Review* 36 (1983), no. 3, pp. 38–45. Lincoln's blockade proclamation: M. Bernard, *A Historical Account of the Neutrality of Great Britain During the American Civil War* (London: Longmans, Green, Reader, and Dyer, 1870), p. 80. Navy buildup: Soley, *Blockade and the Cruisers*, p. 17. Hunt for Bulloch: Henry Wilding to Seward, July 5, 1861, *LCD*, 19. Wilding to C. F. Adams, September 12, quoted in D. H. Milton, *Lincoln's Spymaster: Thomas Haines Dudley and the Liverpool Network* (Lanham, MD: Stackpole Books, 2003), p. 29.

III–IV

Liverpool waterfront: Melville (ed. Tanselle), *Redburn*, pp. 165–230. Rumford Place: W. Loy, "10 Rumford Place: Doing Confederate Business in Liverpool," *South Caro-*

lina Historical Magazine 98 (1997), no. 4, pp. 349–74. Prioleau: R. Wilson, "Historical Sketch of the Prioleau Family in Europe and America," *Transactions of the Huguenot Society of South Carolina*, 6 (1899), pp. 5–37. Trenholm: E. S. Nepveux, *George Alfred Trenholm and the Company That Went to War, 1861–1865* (Charleston, SC: Ethel S. Nepveux, 1973); M. F. Farley, "'The Manners of a Prince': Confederate Financier George Trenholm," *Civil War Times Illustrated*, 21 (1982), no. 8, pp. 18–25. Prioleau's flag habit: Anderson's diary entry, August 4, 1861, in W. S. Hoole (ed.), *Confederate Foreign Agent: The European Diary of Major Edward C. Anderson* (University, AL: Confederate Publishing Company, 1976), p. 42. See also F. Hughes, "Liverpool and the Confederate States: Fraser, Trenholm and Company Operations During the American Civil War," unpublished Ph.D. dissertation (University of Keele, 1996), pp. 57–59. Confederate finances and financing: S. B. Thompson, *Confederate Purchasing Operations Abroad* (Chapel Hill: University of North Carolina Press, 1935), p. 9; R. Lester, *Confederate Finance and Purchasing in Great Britain* (Charlottesville: University Press of Virginia, 1975), pp. 4–17; E. K. Cooper, "Printing Presses Financed the Southern War Effort," *Civil War Times Illustrated*, 2 (1963), no. 5, pp. 14–16. For Prioleau's statement that no funds had arrived, Bulloch, *Secret Service*, p. 38. Bulloch noted his need to make cash deposits and the dire state of his finances in his report to Mallory, *Official Records (Navy)*, 2, 2, August 11, 1861, pp. 83, 86. Mallory had already admitted the lack of money to Jefferson Davis, July 18, ibid., p. 79. On rough costs of ships, report by Mallory, August 16, p. 91, and for the cost of a new ironclad, James North to Mallory, August 16, p. 87.

V–VI

S. Beckert, *Empire of Cotton: A Global History* (New York: Vintage, 2014), pp. 242–64; Owsley Sr., *King Cotton Diplomacy*, pp. 2–42; N. Hall, "The Liverpool Cotton Market and the American Civil War," *Northern History*, 34 (1998), no. 1, pp. 149–69; D. G. Surdam, "King Cotton: Monarch or Pretender? The State of the Market for Raw Cotton on the Eve of the American Civil War," *Economic History Review*, 51 (1998), no. 1, pp. 113–32. Hammond: C. Bleser (ed.), *Secret and Sacred: The Diaries of James Henry Hammond, a Southern Slaveholder* (New York: Oxford University Press, 1989); Nepveux, *George Alfred Trenholm*, p. 23; Wise, *Lifeline of the Confederacy*, pp. 50–52; G. P. Watts, "Phantoms of Anglo-Confederate Commerce: An Historical and Archaeological Investigation of American Civil War Blockade Running," unpublished Ph.D. thesis (University of St. Andrews, 1997), pp. 101–9; W. W. Hassler, "How the Confederates Controlled Blockade Running," *Civil War Times Illustrated*, 2 (1963), no. 6, p. 44.

Chapter Three: The Black Crow

I

J. A. Fry, *Henry S. Sanford: Diplomacy and Business in Nineteenth-Century America* (Reno: University of Nevada Press, 1982), pp. 3–38; R. J. Amundsun, "The American

Life of Henry Shelton Sanford," unpublished Ph.D. dissertation (Florida State University, 1963), pp. 1–78. Instructions: Seward to Sanford, March 26, 1861, *Papers Relating to Foreign Affairs* (1861), pp. 53–54. "Pretty mistress," quoted in N. F. Sanders, "Henry Shelton Sanford in England, April–November 1861: A Reappraisal," *Lincoln Herald*, 77 (1975), p. 89. Moran on Sanford, in Wallace and Gillespie (eds.), *Journal of Benjamin Moran*, 1, p. 803; on Pollaky, January 28, 1862, 2, p. 946.

II

B. Kesselman, *"Paddington" Pollaky, Private Detective: The Mysterious Life and Times of the Real Sherlock Holmes* (Stroud, Gloucestershire [U.K.]: History Press, 2015), pp. 11–40. Freeman Morse (London consul) conducted Pollaky's interview for Sanford (letter, Morse to Sanford, June 29, 1861, Henry Shelton Sanford Papers 139/12/1, as well as July 12, 139/12/2). Bulloch's being found: Morse to Seward, July 19, 1861, *Official Records (Army)*, 3, 1, pp. 445–46. The "Casemate" and the Confederates: Anderson's diary entries of July 16 and August 5, 1861, in Hoole (ed.), *Confederate Foreign Agent*, pp. 31, 43; Anon., "A Rebel Diplomatist—Sketch of Capt. Caleb Huse," *New York Times*, April 10, 1864, and Huse's recollections, *The Supplies for the Confederate Army: How They Were Obtained in Europe and How Paid For* (Boston: T. R. Marvin & Son, 1904), pp. 5–9. Southern arsenal: A. Rose, *American Rifle: A Biography* (New York: Delacorte, 2008), pp. 138–39. Theater, Hamilton, the "English way," Holborn Casino: Anderson diary, August 13 and 24, September 15, 26, 29, and October 1, in Hoole (ed.), *Confederate Foreign Agent*, pp. 47, 49, 58, 63, 67–68. Isaac, Campbell & Co.: J. D. Bennett, *The London Confederates: The Officials, Clergy, Businessmen, and Journalists Who Backed the American South During the Civil War* (Jefferson, NC: McFarland & Co., 2008), p. 52; D. Burt, *Major Caleb Huse C.S.A & S. Isaac Campbell & Co.: The Arms, Clothing, and Equipment Supplied to the Confederate States of America, 1861–64* (Milton Keynes [U.K.]: AuthorHouse, 2009), pp. 18–21; Huse, *Supplies for the Confederate Army*, pp. 3–12, 18–19. On the firm's financial shenanigans: W. G. Crenshaw to J. A. Seddon, May 5, 1863, in *Official Records (Army)*, 4, 2, pp. 543–47. Bond: R. E. Long, *In the Shadow of the* Alabama*: The British Foreign Office and the American Civil War* (Annapolis, MD: Naval Institute Press, 2015), pp. 12–18; Huse, *Supplies for the Confederate Army*, pp. 19–20.

III

Pollaky to Sanford, undated but July/August 1861, Sanford Papers 139/13/12 and 139/13/14; see H. C. Owsley, "Henry Shelton Sanford and Federal Surveillance Abroad, 1861–1865," *Mississippi Valley Historical Review*, 48 (1961), no. 2, pp. 211–28, for an overview. From mid-July, Sanford and Pollaky began keeping a more watchful eye on Bulloch (Morse to Sanford, July 12 and 18, Sanford Papers 139/12/2 and 4), and by August he was regarded as the top man.

IV

Mephisto: Pollaky to Sanford, September 23 and 25, 1861, Sanford Papers 139/14/11 and 139/7/3. Sanford's plan to arrest Bulloch, quoted in Owsley, "Henry Shelton Sanford and Federal Surveillance Abroad," p. 214. Sanford's comment on accidents, quoted in Sanders, "Henry Shelton Sanford in England, p. 90; N. R. Sanders, "Lincoln's Consuls in the British Isles, 1861–1865," unpublished Ph.D. dissertation (University of Missouri, 1971), p. 37. For mention of his postal arrangements: Pollaky's letters to Sanford, August 18, September 24, 28, and 29, October 1, Sanford Papers 139/14/4, 139/13/19, 139/14/12, 139/14/14, 139/14/17, 139/14/18. Privacy of the mail: R. Porter, *Plots and Paranoia: A History of Political Espionage in Britain 1790–1988* (London: Unwin Hyman, 1989), pp. 77–78. Tailing Bulloch: see Pollaky to Sanford, September 24 (139/14/14), September 27 (139/14/15), October 1 (139/14/18). Anderson's noting the countrified detective and an encounter with Brett (another inept tail): September 26, October 2, Hoole (ed.), *Confederate Foreign Agent*, pp. 64, 68–70. Bulloch's articles, "Political Espionage in Liverpool" and "The Political Spy System in Liverpool," are enclosed with letter, Pollaky to Sanford, 139/14/32. Adams's irritation at Sanford: Charles Francis Adams Diary, June 13, October 28 and 30, 1861, at http://www.masshist.org/publications/cfa-civil-war/view?id=DCA61d164, http://www.masshist.org/publications/cfa-civil-war/view?id=DCA61d301, and http://www.masshist.org/publications/cfa-civil-war/view?id=DCA61d302. Bulloch's vanishing: Pollaky to Sanford, September 28, September 29–30, October 1, and October 7, list correspondence received by Huse, Anderson, and others but none for or to Bulloch, in Sanford Papers 139/14/17, 139/14/19, 139/14/18, and 139/14/21.

V

Meeting and *Fingal*: Wilson and McKay, *James D. Bulloch*, pp. 51–52; Kinnaman, *Captain Bulloch*, p. 267; Bulloch, *Secret Service*, pp. 76–78. Anderson, September 2, in Hoole (ed.), *Confederate Foreign Agent*, pp. 53–54, has the fullest description of the meeting. Bulloch's payment arrangements are described in his letter to Mallory, December 5, 1861, *Official Records (Navy)*, 2, 2, pp. 114–15. John Low: W. S. Hoole (ed.), *Four Years in the Confederate Navy: The Career of Captain John Low on the CSS Fingal, Florida, Alabama, Tuscaloosa, and Ajax* (Athens: University of Georgia Press, 1964), pp. 1–8.

VI

Clerk informant: Pollaky to Sanford, October 11, 1861, Sanford Papers, 139/14/24, and see "Official List of Cargo for *Fingal*," 139/7/16. Pollaky's attempts to find the *Fingal*: letters to Sanford, October 15 and 18, 139/13/10, 139/14/28. Brennan's reports: letters to Pollaky/Sanford, October 8, 1861, Sanford Papers 139/7/12, and 13 (the second was urgently sent at 8:00 P.M.); October 9 (139/7/17); October 10 at 2:00 P.M., noting the 8:00 A.M. departure (139/7/18). Another Brennan October 10 report to Pollaky is enclosed with letter to Seward, October 11 (including Brennan's sketch of the ship), forwarded to Welles, October 28, *Official Records (Navy)*, 1, 6, p. 368. Low's movements and title transfer: Anderson entry, October 10, in Hoole (ed.), *Confederate Foreign Agent*, pp. 77–78. Agent X: Anderson, September 26, 1861, in Hoole (ed.), *Confederate Foreign Agent*, pp. 65–66. Anderson confirms (October 10, p. 77) that "our friend in the Foreign Office" had tipped them off. For Moran's suspicions, December 2, 1861, in Wallace and Gillespie (eds.), *Journal of Benjamin Moran*, 2, pp. 915–16. A minor chronological conflict is between Anderson's and Brennan's notes. The major has much of the action seemingly happening on October 10, but he seems to have merged two days (October 9 and 10). Brennan's reports, in contrast, are more precisely dated.

VII

Major Anderson commented on Captain Anderson's drinking benders in Hoole (ed.), *Confederate Foreign Agent*, p. 105, and his idea of kidnapping a detective is in his entry of October 2, p. 70.

VIII

Moran on Sanford: October 18, August 9, November 19, 1861, in Wallace and Gillespie (eds.), *Journal of Benjamin Moran*, 2, pp. 894, 860, 907–8. Hostile discussion with Sanford: Adams Diary, November 2, http://www.masshist.org/publications /cfa-civil-war/view?id=DCA61d306, and November 4, http://www.masshist.org /publications/cfa-civil-war/view?id=DCA61d308. *Gladiator* operation: Sanders, "Henry Shelton Sanford in England," pp. 92–93; Sanders, "Lincoln's Consuls," pp. 41–42; Ferris, "Tempestuous Mission," pp. 343–51; Eastman visit, Adams Diary, November 5, at http://www.masshist.org/publications/cfa-civil-war/view?id=DCA61d309; Moran on Marchand, November 7, in Wallace and Gillespie (eds.), 2, p. 902; J. B. Marchand (ed. C. Symonds), *Charleston Blockade: The Journals of John B. Marchand, U.S. Navy, 1861–1862* (Newport, RI: U.S. Naval War College, 1976), pp. 36–47. Cambridge House: Sir George Trevelyan, quoted in A. Foreman, *A World on Fire: Britain's Crucial Role in the American Civil War* (New York: Random House, 2010), p. 170n. Garibaldi: R. J. Amundson, "Sanford and Garibaldi," *Civil War History*, 14 (1968), no. 1, pp. 40–45.

IX

Fingal voyage: Bulloch, *Secret Service*, pp. 78–88; and for Major Anderson's version, Hoole (ed.), *Confederate Foreign Agent*, pp. 81–99. Detective Brennan had sent a sketch of the *Fingal* to Pollaky, which was distributed to ships' captains (the drawing is enclosed in Brennan's letter to Pollaky, October 10, 1861, *Official Records (Navy)*, 1, 6, p. 369. For warnings to keep a lookout for her, see Welles to Flag-Officer Goldsborough, October 24, 1861, and Goldsborough to Lieutenant Cavendy of USS *Gemsbok*, November 3, pp. 335, 391.

Chapter Four: The Crowning City

I

Mrs. Blodgett's boardinghouse: J. Hawthorne, *Hawthorne and His Circle* (New York: Harper & Brothers, 1903), pp. 173–85. Consul's office: *Hawthorne and His Circle*, p. 87; N. Hawthorne, "Consular Experiences," *Our Old Home*, pp. 5–33; "Inventory of Archives of the U.S. Consulate," November 23, 1861, *LCD*, 20. Paradise Street: *Gore's Directory for Liverpool and Its Environs* (Liverpool: J. Mawdsley & Son, 1860); Lane, *Liverpool: Gateway of Empire*, p. 116. On Dudley's "nervousness" and admirable competence: T. C. Pease and J. G. Randall (eds.), *The Diary of Orville Hickman Browning* (Springfield: Trustees of the Illinois State Historical Library, 2 vols., 1925–1933), 2, p. 110, where William Seward speaks of Dudley being "really a good officer"; and G. Welles, *Diary of Gideon Welles, Secretary of the Navy Under Lincoln and Johnson* (Boston and New York: Houghton Mifflin, 3 vols., 1911), 1, July 17, 1863, p. 374, in which Welles refers to Dudley's being an "excellent consul" though "somewhat, and excusably, nervous." Also, entries of September 18, 1863 (p. 1,210); January 15 (p. 1,255), May 4, 1864 (p. 1,294); February 8 (p. 1,375); March 13, 1865 (p. 1,391), in Wallace and Gillespie (eds.), *Journal of Benjamin Moran*, 2, which reference Minister Adams's haughtiness toward Dudley. For Moran's (low) estimates of American consuls, entries of September 17, 1861 (p. 880); October 2, 7, and 11, 1861 (pp. 887–89); January 27, 1862 (p. 946); March 11 and 12, 1862 (pp. 964–65). Moran's positive appraisal of Dudley: June 24, 1861, pp. 832–33. Hawthorne talks about a typically friendly welcome from the Chamber of Commerce in his diary for August 5, 1853, in *Passages from the English Note-Books*, p. 3, but for Dudley's recollection, "Appointment & Initial Experiences," Dudley Papers DU-1275. The contentious meeting was on November 27, according to his letter of November 29 to Seward, *LCD*, 20. (Dudley makes a slight error in saying that Melly was secretary.) Chamber of Commerce: W. O. Henderson, "The American Chamber of Commerce for the Port of Liverpool, 1801–1908," *Transactions of the Historic Society of Lancashire and Cheshire*, 85 (1933), pp. 1–61.

II

Appointment as consul: Dudley to Seward, December 2, 1861, *LCD*, 20. Wilding: Dudley to Seward, October 31, 1861, *LCD*, 19; M. F. Sweeney, "An Annotated Edition of Nathaniel Hawthorne's Official Dispatches to the State Department, 1853–1857," unpublished Ph.D. dissertation (Bowling Green State University, 1975), p. 19; Hawthorne, "Consular Experiences," *Our Old Home*, p. 30; letters, September 26 and October 9, 1857, in J. C. Dana (ed.), *Letters of Hawthorne to William D. Ticknor, 1851–1864* (Newark, NJ: Carteret Book Club, 2 vols., 1910), 2, pp. 62–64. *Trent*: N. B. Ferris,

The Trent *Affair: A Diplomatic Crisis* (Knoxville: University of Tennessee Press, 1977); Foreman, *A World on Fire*, pp. 172–98; T. L. Harris, *The* Trent *Affair: Including a Review of English and American Relations at the Beginning of the Civil War* (Indianapolis, IN: Bobbs-Merrill Company, 1896), pp. 137–62. Dudley relates the story of Albert's intervention as he heard it, in Dudley, "Three Critical Periods in Our Diplomatic Relations with England During the Late War," *Pennsylvania Magazine of History and Biography*, 17 (1893), no. 1, pp. 39, 43–44. Yancey: Doyle, *Cause of All Nations*, p. 48. Parliament: T. E. Sebrell, *Persuading John Bull: Union and Confederate Propaganda in Britain, 1860–1865* (Lanham, MD: Lexington Books, 2014), Appendices 1 and 2, pp. 209–11. Exports: "Prohibition of the Export of Saltpetre, etc.," *Letter of the Secretary of State, Transmitting a Report of the Commercial Relations of the United States with Foreign Nations* (Washington, DC: Government Printing Office, 1862), p. 17; H. B. Hancock and N. B. Wilkinson, "'The Devil to Pay!': Saltpeter and the *Trent* Affair," *Civil War History*, 10 (1964), no. 1, pp. 20–32. Dudley's address: Sanders, "Lincoln's Consuls," p. 200n13.

III–V

Huse's purchases: J. Gorgas, "Abstract of Summary Statement Showing Quantity and Value of Army Supplies Purchased and Shipped by Maj. C. Huse," February 3, 1863, *Official Records (Army)*, 4, 2, pp. 382–84. Steamers: K. J. Foster, "Builders vs. Blockaders: The Evolution of the Blockade-Running Steamship," in C. G. Reynolds (ed.), *Global Crossroads and the American Seas* (Missoula, MT: Pictorial Histories Publishing Co., 1988), pp. 85–90; A. C. Wardle, "Mersey-Built Blockade Runners of the American Civil War," *Mariner's Mirror*, 28 (1942), pp. 179–88; Scharf, *History of the Confederate Navy*, p. 466; S. Negus, "A Notorious Nest of Offence: Neutrals, Belligerents, and Union Jails in Civil War Blockade Running," *Civil War History*, 56 (2010), no. 4, p. 357. Blockade-running stratagems: Soley, *Blockade and the Cruisers*, pp. 153–67; T. E. Taylor, *Running the Blockade: A Personal Narrative of Adventure, Risks, and Escapes During the American Civil War* (New York: Charles Scribner's Sons, 1896), pp. 22–24, 47–54, 73–75, 86–87. Nassau: Wise, *Lifeline of the Confederacy*, pp. 63–71; Taylor, *Running the Blockade*, pp. 22–24, 86–87; R. Semmes, *My Adventures Afloat: A Personal Memoir of My Cruises and Services on the* Sumter *and* Alabama (London: Richard Bentley, 1869), pp. 35–51; Scharf, *History of the Confederate Navy*, pp. 472–74, 478–80; A. C. Hobart-Hampden, *Sketches from My Life* (New York: D. Appleton & Co., 1887), pp. 87–102; "Captain Roberts" (pseud.), *Never Caught: Personal Adventures Connected with Twelve Successful Trips in Blockade-Running During the American Civil War, 1863–64* (London: John Camden Hotten, 1867), pp. 14–15, 24–25. Profits: L. W. Skelton, "The Importing and Exporting Company of South Carolina (1862–1876)," *South Carolina Historical Magazine*, 75 (1974), no. 1, pp. 24–32; Taylor, *Running the Blockade*, pp. 41, 69, 85. Cotton certificates: Lester, *Confederate Finance and Purchasing*, pp. 15–22; M. W. Price, "Blockade Running as a Business in

South Carolina During the War Between the States, 1861–1865," *American Neptune*, 9 (1949), p. 32. On the fees exacted by Huse's creditors for arms, see complaint by Crenshaw to Mason, July 4, 1863, in *Official Records (Army)*, 4, 2, pp. 628–30.

Chapter Five: A River in Sicily

I

Bushby, who seems to have had fingers in a lot of pies, also served as vice-consul for the Grand Duchy of Oldenburg. See J. Hussey, *Cruisers, Cotton and Confederates: Liverpool Waterfront in the Days of the Confederacy* (Merseyside [U.K.]: Countyvise Ltd., 2009 ed.), p. 135. Bushby is mentioned by Dudley in a June 18, 1862, letter to Seward, where he alleges he owns ships "as a blind or cover" (*LCD*). *Prince Albert*: Wise, *Lifeline of the Confederacy*, p. 317. Klingender: Moran's entries of December 22, 1862, and February 7 and March 4, 1863, in Wallace and Gillespie (eds.), *Journal of Benjamin Moran*, 2, pp. 1,099, 1,118, 1,127. Prioleau quoted and Anderson's suitcase mentioned in Dudley, December 6, 1861; *Journal of Commerce* advertisement enclosed with December 28 dispatch; December 20 for frequent mentions of Fraser Trenholm. Consulate staff: Table, "Names of Persons Employed at United States Consulate at Liverpool," December 31, 1861, all *LCD*, 20. Wilding's earlier hiring of Maguire: For much of 1861, between April and December, the Liverpool consulate had been run by him on an acting basis, and Wilding had paid Maguire out of his own pocket to keep an eye on Confederate activities in the town. See Wilding to Seward, December 30, 1864, enclosing statement and receipts for cash paid to Maguire, all dated 1861, *LCD*, 29. Maguire: Dudley refers to Maguire in December 11, 1861, letter, *LCD*, 19. For the 6 Dorans Lane address, Maguire's invoice, April 24, 1862, Dudley Papers DU-2131. Details of the other businesses are taken from the "Doran-Lane" entry in *Gore's Directory for Liverpool*. On Maguire's past, "Wreck of the *Queen Victoria*," *Morning Chronicle*, March 24, 1853; "Wreck of the Dublin Steamer, *Queen Victoria*," *Preston Chronicle and Lancashire Advertiser*, February 19, 1853; "Wreck of the *Queen Victoria*," *Chelmsford Chronicle*, February 25, 1853, which contains a note on Maguire's previous employment in Hull. "Concealment of Birth," *Bradford Observer*, July 23, 1846, mentions that he was a superintendent. On Maguire's exploits, see "Arrest of a Fugitive" and "The Capture of Jeremiah Winks," January 1 and 28, 1861; the *Newcastle Daily Journal*, January 25, carries the fullest story. Other cases, "The Revelations in the Chancery Court," May 16, 1860; "The Habana Cigar Company—Revelations for Smokers," *Liverpool Mercury*, April 2, 1859.

II

Slavery: D. Richardson, "Liverpool and the English Slave Trade," pp. 67–72; A. Tibbles, "Oil Not Slaves: Liverpool and West Africa After 1807," pp. 73–77, in Tibbles (ed.), *Transatlantic Slavery: Against Human Dignity* (Liverpool: Liverpool University

Press, 2005); A. Tibbles, *Liverpool and the Slave Trade* (Liverpool: Liverpool University Press, 2018); M. Lynn, "Liverpool and Africa in the Nineteenth Century: The Continuing Connection," *Transactions of the Historic Society of Lancashire and Cheshire*, 147 (1997), pp. 29–31. Lairds and Birkenhead: Anon., "A Visit to Birkenhead," *Littell's Living Age*, 6 (1845), no. 60, pp. 25–26; Anon., "Mr. John Laird—The Birkenhead Ironworks and Docks," *Liverpool Daily Post*, July 29, 1861; "Iron Shipbuilding at Birkenhead," *Illustrated London News*, October 25, 1856, p. 416; K. Warren, *Steel, Ships and Men: Cammell Laird, 1824–1993* (Liverpool: Liverpool University Press, 1998); D. Hollett, *Men of Iron: The Story of Cammell Laird Shipbuilders, 1828–1991* (Birkenhead, Merseyside [U.K.]: Countyvise Ltd., 1992), pp. 1–12; F. Neal, "Shipbuilding in the Northwest of England in the Nineteenth Century," in S. Ville (ed.), *Shipbuilding in the United Kingdom in the Nineteenth Century: A Regional Approach* (St. John's, Newfoundland: International Maritime Economic History Association/Trustees of the National Museums and Galleries on Merseyside, 1993), pp. 111–45. The Square: C. Williams, J. Powell, and J. Kelly, "Liverpool's Abercromby Square and the Confederacy During the U.S. Civil War," a guide to the Lowcountry Digital History Initiative hosted by College of Charleston (2015), at http://ldhi.library.cofc.edu/exhibits/show/liverpools-abercromby-square.

III

Ella: Dudley to Seward, January 11, 1862, *LCD*, 20. The earliest invoice from Maguire for "money expended to parties from whom information was received" is January 4, 1862, Dudley Papers DU-2720. Multiple invoices note his newspaper subscriptions and travel expenses. Mr. Bullen: September 5, 1862, Dudley Papers DU-2750. Maguire's invoices, Dudley Papers: "Treating Money" (August 1, DU-2745); the rigger (February 24–March 1, DU-2724, February 21–March 7, 1862, DU-2768); see also, July 25 (DU-2744); February 21–March 7 (DU-2768); June 13, 1862 (DU-2738). Haigh: Dudley to Seward, February 15, 1862. *Bermuda*'s cargo: February 14, 1862, enclosing Brady/Brody employment note, February 13, *LCD*, 20. Tower Building: From early 1862 onward, Dudley's notepaper is engraved with the new address. Earliest date is his dispatch to Seward, January 30, 1862, *LCD*, 20.

IV

Fawcett Preston: H. White, *Fossets: A Record of Two Centuries of Engineering* (Bromborough, Cheshire [U.K.]: Fawcett Preston & Co., 1958), pp. 46–48. Dudley and the *Oreto*: January 24; February 4, 12, 19; March 5, 12, 22, 1862, *LCD*, 20. Miller & Sons: R. Thorp, *Mersey Built: The Role of Merseyside in the American Civil War* (Wilmington, DE: Vernon Press, 2018), pp. 54–73; Hussey, *Cruisers, Cotton and Confederates*, pp. 150–51. Sanctity of contracts: Quoted in A. English, "The Laird Rams: Warships in Transition, 1862–1885," unpublished Ph.D. dissertation (University of Exeter, 2016), p. 45. Agent Federal: Parry to Wilding, February 24, 1862, Dudley Papers

DU-3362, and Maguire invoice, DU-2768, February 21 to March 7, 1862; the Fawcett Preston note is mentioned by Dudley on March 5. Parry says he was the pilot in statement of August 23, 1862, printed in *Papers Relating to the Treaty of Washington* (Washington, DC: Government Printing Office, 6 vols., 1872), 1, p. 281. Hereafter *Treaty of Washington*. Abolitionism in Liverpool: D. M. George, "John Baxter Langley: Radicalism, Espionage and the Confederate Navy in mid-Victorian Britain," *Journal for Maritime Research*, 19 (2017), no. 2, p. 121–42. Customs inspections: Dudley to Adams, February 17, 1862, enclosed with Adams to Russell, February 18; E. Hammond (undersecretary of state to Russell) to secretary of the treasury, February 19; Morgan (inspector) to Edwards, February 21; Edwards to commissioners of customs, same date, *Treaty of Washington*, 1, pp. 274–76. Mudie: Board of Customs to Lords Commissioners of Her Majesty's Treasury, April 6, attaching the *Oreto*'s Victualling Bill, March 4, in *Papers Relating to Foreign Affairs* (1861–1862), pp. 66–67. John Henry Thomas: *Treaty of Washington*, 1, pp. 277–78.

V

N. Arielli, G. A. Frei, and I. Van Hulle, "The Foreign Enlistment Act, International Law, and British Politics, 1819–2014," *International History Review*, 38 (2016), no. 4, pp. 636–56; "Declaration of the British Government," declaration of May 13, 1861, reprinted in the *New York Times*, May 29. Bulloch, *Secret Service*, pp. 47–48.

VI

Letters, Dudley to Seward, March 1, 12, 15, 19, 22, 1862, *LCD*, 20. Bulloch had not disembarked with the other four, though Dudley's informant swore he had been on board. To avoid any connection, Bulloch had in fact parted company with the *Annie Childs* at a stop in Queenstown, Ireland, then made his way to Liverpool via ferry and train, arriving on March 10 at 4:00 P.M., shortly after his compatriots. Bulloch, *Secret Service*, p. 103.

Chapter Six: The First Raider
I–II

Shipbuilders: *Gore's Directory for Liverpool*, p. 335; Thorp, *Mersey Built*, p. 37. *Oreto*'s construction: Bulloch to Mallory, August 13, 1861, *Official Records (Navy)*, 2, 2, pp. 84–85; Bulloch, *Secret Service*, pp. 41–42; Thorp, *Mersey Built*, p. 73. Instructions: Bulloch, *Secret Service*, p. 104. In his letter to Mallory, December 5, 1861, *Official Records (Navy)*, 2, 2, pp. 114–15, Bulloch says they "are on file in Messrs. Fraser, Trenholm & Co.'s safe in Liverpool, with all my other papers, which it would not have been safe to bring over." Yonge and Low: Bulloch to Mallory, January 3 and 16, 1862, and June 30, 1863, *Official Records (Navy)*, 2, 2, pp. 123–24, 132, 448. Anderson: W. S. Hoole (ed.), "Letters from a Georgia Midshipman on the CSS *Alabama*," *Georgia Historical*

Society, 59 (1975), no. 4, p. 416. Maffitt and Bulloch in the Coast Survey: Kinnaman, *Captain Bulloch*, p. 138. Departure: Bulloch to Mallory, January 27, 1862, *Official Records (Navy)*, 2, 2, pp. 138–39. Agent X: Prioleau wrote to Bulloch associate James North on February 20 (*Official Records (Navy)*, 2, 2, p. 147) saying that he wanted the *Oreto* to depart immediately "for [the] most urgent [of] reasons," a hint that he had been alerted by Agent X that day. The role of X is not conclusively known, as no documents have been preserved, understandably. However, the procession of events (Dudley's letter of February 17, Adams's February 18 note to Russell—which would have passed through Agent X's hands—Russell's forwarding of that note to the treasury on the nineteenth, Prioleau's suddenly urgent warning on February 20, and the customs inspection of February 21) was surely not coincidental. Preparing to leave: Bulloch, *Secret Service*, pp. 104–5. Duguid: Hussey, *Cruisers, Cotton and Confederates*, p. 151; Dudley to Seward, March 5, 1862, *LCD*, 20, claims he was "captain"; Thorp, *Mersey Built*, pp. 89–102. Low's and Maffitt's instructions: Bulloch to Low, and Bulloch to Maffitt, March 21, 1862, in Bulloch, *Secret Service*, pp. 107–10. Heyliger: Memminger to Heyliger, April 18, 1864, and Memminger to Prioleau, same date, in *Correspondence Concerning Claims Against Great Britain* (Washington, DC: Government Printing Office, 1871), 6, p. 160. Second gunboat: Dudley to Seward, March 1, 1862, *LCD*, 20.

III–IV

Maffitt's arrival: "Extracts from the Journal of Lieutenant J.N. Maffitt," in *Official Records (Navy)*, 1, 1, p. 763. Anderson's political views, Adderley & Co., Harris: *Treaty of Washington*, 3, pp. 68–69. Consul's query: Whiting to Bayley, May 9, *Treaty of Washington*, 1, p. 284. Bayley's views, *Treaty of Washington*, 3, p. 66. *Bahama's* arrival and movements: *Treaty of Washington*, 3, p. 70; Thorp, *Mersey Built*, pp. 106–8. Anderson's caution, ca. late May 1862; McKillop's surprise visit (McKillop to Bayley, May 28); Jones's statement, June 4; McKillop's report, June 6, in *Treaty of Washington*, 1, pp. 284–86. Anderson argues against seizure (June 7): *Treaty of Washington*, 3, p. 72. Low's admonition to Duguid: Hussey, *Cruisers, Cotton and Confederates*, p. 106. Liverpool's sailors: A. H. Clark, *The Clipper Ship Era: An Epitome of Famous American and British Clipper Ships, Their Owners, Builders, Commanders, and Crews, 1843–1869* (New York: G.P. Putnam's Sons, 1911), pp. 120–21. Maffitt's derision for Jones: E. M. Maffitt, *The Life and Services of John Newland Maffitt* (New York and Washington: Neale Publishing Company, 1906), p. 239. Hickley's June 13 letter to Bayley, in *Treaty of Washington*, 1, p. 287. See the testimonies quoted regarding the crew mutiny, in *Treaty of Washington*, 1, p. 289; and for Hickley's seizure and its countermanding, p. 287. Hickey's letter: *Treaty of Washington*, 3, p. 72. Lee's verdict: *Treaty of Washington*, 3, p. 74, and 1, p. 290. *Oreto* manifest: August 7, 1862, in *Treaty of Washington*, 1, p. 291. Maffitt controlling Duguid: Maffitt to Mallory, August 1, 1862, in Maffitt, *Life and Service*, p. 242. Nassau departure and *Prince Alfred*: *Treaty of*

Washington, 3, pp. 75–76. Arms transfer: "Journal of Maffitt," *Official Records (Navy)*, 1, 1, pp. 764–65.

Chapter Seven: The War Rules

I–II

Relative size of Lairds: P. Barry, *Dockyard Economy and Naval Power* (London: Sampson Low, Son, & Co., 1863), pp. 301–12. Hamilton and Bond: Long, *In the Shadow of the* Alabama, p. 77. "Sympathetic" rumor: Semmes, *My Adventures Afloat*, p. 400. Plans: "Contract and Specification of Screw Steam Vessel and Her Machinery," printed in C. G. Summersell, *CSS* Alabama*: Builder, Captain, and Plans* (Tuscaloosa: University of Alabama Press, 1985), pp. 105–14. The stated length was to be 210 feet, but would actually be 220. Delays: Bulloch to Mallory, April 19, 1862, *Official Records (Navy)*, 2, 2, pp. 185–86. Launch ceremony: Bulloch, *Secret Service*, p. 162; Kinnaman, *Captain Bulloch*, p. 292; Maguire Spy Report, May 6 (misdated, May 16), MS 0283, James Dunwoody Bulloch Papers.

III

Enrica: Dudley to Seward, March 1, April 23 (Beauford and Cuddy), April 26, May 16, 1862, in *LCD*, 20. Maguire's visit to Lairds: Maguire Spy Report, March 28, 1862, Bulloch Papers. Subscription and blockade-runner activity: Dudley to Seward, March 26 and 29, April 4, 9, 11, 16, 19, 23, 25, and 30, May 7, 14, 16, and 30, *LCD*, 20. The *Journal of Commerce* on September 6 printed a full list of ships arriving in Nassau, which was sent to Seward by Dudley, same date, *LCD*, 22. Loan scheme: Dudley to Seward, May 2 and June 9, *LCD*, 20. Figure of £750,000: Dudley to Seward, December 8. Intelligence-gathering costs: Note to Seward of July 17, 1862, covering the quarter up to June 30, *LCD*, 22, where it eats up a third. Mutual dependence: Dudley's to Seward, December 6, 1862.

IV

Hotze: J. V. Trahan III, "Henry Hotze: Propaganda Voice of the Confederacy," in P. G. McNeely, D. R. Van Tuyll, and H. H. Schulte (eds.), *Knights of the Quill: Confederate Correspondents and the Civil War Reporting* (West Lafayette, IN: Purdue University Press, 2010), pp. 216–37; S. B. Oates, "Henry Hotze: Confederate Agent Abroad," *The Historian*, 27 (1965), no. 2, pp. 131–54; L. A. Burnett (ed.), *Henry Hotze, Confederate Propagandist: Selected Writings on Revolution, Recognition, and Race* (Tuscaloosa: University of Alabama Press, 2008). Hotze's propaganda successes and contributors: Hotze to Hunter, March 11, 1862, Hotze to Benjamin, September 26, 1862, *Official Records (Navy)*, 2, 3, pp. 360–62, 535. Subscribers: See Sebrell's exhaustive compilation in *Persuading John Bull*, pp. 126–36, and Appendix 3, p. 212. Agent X's subscription: Long, *In the Shadow of the* Alabama, p. 71. Hotze's meeting with Anderson: Entry, October 4, 1861, in Hoole (ed.), *Confederate Foreign Agent*, p. 71. Intelligence work: Hotze's financial registers are printed in J. F. Jameson, "The London Expenditures of the Confederate Secret Service," *American Historical Review*, 35 (1930), no. 4, esp. pp. 812, 814.

V

Dudley's list: Enclosed with report to Seward, June 9, 1862, *LCD*, 20. Grazebrook: Hoole (ed.), *Confederate Foreign Agent*, July 29 and 31, August 1 and 5, pp. 37, 38–39, 43. Edwin Haigh's participation in Prioleau's cover scheme is mentioned by Dudley in a letter to Seward, June 18, 1862, *LCD*, 20. Amended list: Hughes, "Liverpool and the Confederate States," Appendix D, pp. 341–51. Southern Club: Blackett, *Divided Hearts*, pp. 63–64, and see Dudley's letters to Seward, September 19 and October 1, 1862, *LCD*, 22. American Chamber of Commerce connection: Dudley to Seward, October 14, *LCD*, 22.

VI

Maguire and making fun of Dudley: Bulloch, *Secret Service*, pp. 161–62. *Agrippina*: Bulloch, *Secret Service*, p. 168; Bulloch to Mallory, April 11, 1862, *Official Records (Navy)*, 2, 2, pp. 183–84. Hamilton registry: Kinnaman, *Captain Bulloch*, p. 295. Semmes to command: Mallory to Bulloch, May 3, 1862; Bulloch to Mallory, July 21, *Official Records (Navy)*, 2, 2, pp. 190, 222–26. Crewmen: M. Rigby, "Britons on the *Alabama*," in Anon. (ed.), *Crossfire: A Civil War Anthology [American Civil War Round Table]* (Milton Keynes [U.K.]: Military Press, 2003), pp. 55–59. Butcher: F. J. Merli and R. Eley Long (eds.), "Captain Butcher's Memoir of the *Alabama*'s Escape," in Merli (ed. D. M. Fahey), *The* Alabama, *British Neutrality, and the American Civil War* (Bloomington: Indiana University Press, 2004), pp. 126–30; Bulloch, *Secret Service*, p. 164. Butcher's time with Cunard: Dudley to Seward, July 12, 1862, *LCD*, 20.

VII–VIII

Security arrangements: Dudley to Seward, June 18, 1862, *LCD*, 20. William Passmore confirmed the *Enrica*'s location in the Great Float (affidavit included in A. T. Squarey's affidavit, August 28, 1871, Dudley Papers, Box 47, DU-3808). Robinson: Dudley to Edwards, July 9, and Dudley to Seward, July 25, 1862, *LCD*, 20. Dudley putting the pieces together: Letter to Adams, June 21, *Treaty of Washington*, 4, p. 448. Dudley's stay in London: Moran, June 21, 1862, Wallace and Gillespie (eds.), *Journal of Benjamin Moran*, 2, p. 1,024; and Dudley to Seward, June 27, *LCD*, 20. "Stop the expedition": Adams to Russell, June 23, *Papers Relating to Foreign Affairs* (1862), pp. 128–29; and see also, Adams to Seward, July 9, p. 128. Chain of events in Whitehall: Thomas Fremantle and Grenville Berkeley (lords commissioners of the treasury) to Russell, July 1, 1862, *Papers Relating to Foreign Affairs* (1862), pp. 130–31;

Morgan's inspection report, June 28, *Treaty of Washington*, 4, p. 449, and see also the commissioners of customs report to the lords, p. 450; Russell to Adams, July 4, *Papers Relating to Foreign Affairs* (1862), pp. 129–30. Dudley's exchange with Edwards: Dudley to Edwards, July 9, 1862, *LCD*, 20; Instructions to Edwards by the commissioners of the customs, *Treaty of Washington*, 4, p. 452. Dudley's belief that opinion was entirely for the South: Letters to Seward, April 26, and Adams, July 11, *LCD*, 20. Adams's view of Edwards: C. F. Adams, *Charles Francis Adams, By His Son Charles Francis Adams* (Boston and New York: Houghton Mifflin and Co., 1900), p. 312, and for the description (probable) of him as "staid and somewhat obese," "Liverpool News," *Glasgow Herald*, April 13, 1863. Bulloch defends Edwards in *Secret Service*, pp. 185–86. Hiring Squarey and going to Edwards's office: Dudley to Seward, July 18, *LCD*, 20; affidavit by Squarey, August 28, 1871, Dudley Papers, Box 47, DU-3808. Copies of the six affidavits, July 21, are included with Squarey's. Brogan and Passmore: Maguire invoice to Dudley listing Passmore, July 25, 1862, DU-4744, and invoice for Brogan, July 18, DU-2743, in Dudley Papers, Box 5. On July 21, Edwards wrote to the commissioners of customs to forward the affidavits, adding that "the only evidence of importance, as appears to me, is that of William Passmore, who had engaged himself as a sailor to serve in the vessel" (Letter, July 21, 1862, printed in *The Official Correspondence on the Claims of the United States in Respect to the* Alabama [London: Longmans, Green, and Co., 1867], p. 11). Dudley's activities in London: Dudley to Seward, July 22 and 25 (*LCD*), and Squarey to Dudley, July 23, Dudley Papers, Box 6, DU-3789; Affidavit by Squarey, August 28, 1871. Affidavits of Roberts, Taylor, and Redden: Cited or printed in *Treaty of Washington*, 4, pp. 456–58. Harding's "malady," ibid., p. 459; and for Palmer's recollection of the Harding delay, p. 459. Atherton's neutralism: "The Durham Election," *The Times*, July 9, 1861. J. B. Moore (ed.), *History and Digest of the International Arbitrations to Which the United States Has Been a Party* (Washington, DC: Government Printing Office, 6 vols., 1898), 1, pp. 678–82, discusses several theories as to what happened during Harding's incapacitation. Foreign Office: Long, *Shadow of the* Alabama, pp. 98–99, and for the fullest look at Sir John's career, pp. 100–101. Clerks, desks, and hours at Foreign Office: E. Hertslet (ed.), *The Foreign Office List, Forming a Complete British Diplomatic and Consular Handbook* (London: Harrison, 1865), pp. 9, 11. Palmer's and Atherton's Opinion of July 29: *Treaty of Washington*, 4, p. 458. Edwards's instruction to seize: "Copy of Reply, July 31, 1862, by Telegram—Sent at 11.35am," *Official Correspondence on the Claims of the United States in Respect to the* Alabama, p. 20.

Chapter Eight: The Magician

I

Paid clerk: Maguire Spy Report, Bulloch Papers. Broderick/Brogan: Among the Maguire receipts in the Dudley Papers, there are records of payments to Broderick as late as December 19, 1862 (DU-2766), and see that of October 24, 1862 (DU-2758), as well as Wilson and McKay, *James D. Bulloch*, p. 76.

II

Regarding the text of the note he passed to Hotze, Long, *In the Shadow of the Alabama*, p. 159, quotes a diary entry by Moran, who later transcribed a copy of the original, of December 20, 1865. Hotze's home address: Advertisement for "H.O. Brewer & Co., General Shipping and Commission Merchants," *The Index*, January 21, 1864, p. 47. *Index* offices: Mentioned in advertisement, same page, for "Bust of Jefferson Davis." According to a ciphered letter (Bulloch to Mallory, January 7, 1863, *Official Records (Navy)*, 2, 2, p. 331), Bulloch refers to being privy to "correspondence between Federal minister [Adams] and Secretary of Foreign Affairs [Russell] in reference to building and dispatch of 290." The only possible source for such intelligence was Buckley. Buckley's background: Long, *In the Shadow of the Alabama*, pp. 3–11, 22–24, 161, 164, and Walter King's unpublished essay, "Victor Buckley (1838–1882)," which he kindly sent me. Ranks and annual pay: Hertslet (ed.), *Foreign Office List*, pp. 9, 11, 168–173.

III

Bulloch, *Secret Service*, p. 168. Bulloch was extraordinarily circumspect about how he knew about the Foreign Office's decision. In his memoirs, all he says is, "on Saturday, July 26th, 1862, I received information from a private and most reliable source, that it would not be safe to leave the ship in Liverpool another forty-eight hours [*i.e.*, Monday morning]." In a ciphered letter to Mallory, January 7, 1863, *Official Records (Navy)*, 2, 2, p. 331), he unilluminatingly adds that "I learned that something of the kind [*i.e.*, detention] was going on and hurried off the ship." Bulloch very rarely resorted to cipher, yet he did in this instance—clearly owing to its sensitivity. Lairds' involvement: Merli and Long (eds.), "Captain Butcher's Memoir of the *Alabama*'s Escape," p. 130. Passmore's intelligence: July 26, in Maguire Spy Report, Bulloch Papers. Yonge: Affidavit, April 2, 1863, in C. C. Beaman Jr., *The National and Private "Alabama Claims" and their "Final and Amicable Settlement"* (Washington, DC: W. H. Moore, 1871), pp. 93–95; Low: Hoole (ed.), *Four Years in the Confederate Navy*, pp. 47–48. Written orders: Bulloch to Yonge, July 28; Bulloch to Butcher, July 30; Bulloch to McQueen, July 28, in Bulloch, *Secret Service*, pp. 173–77.

IV

Enrica's escape: Bulloch, *Secret Service*, pp. 168–72; Yonge affidavit, in Beaman, *National and Private*, p. 94; Moran, August 1, 1862, Wallace and Gillespie (eds.), *Journal of Benjamin Moran*, 2, p. 1,048; Merli and Long (eds.), "Captain Butcher's Memoir," pp. 129–33; D. H. Maynard, "Plotting the Escape of the *Alabama*," *Journal of Southern History* 20 (1954), no. 2, pp. 197–209; "Union Efforts to Prevent the Escape of the *Alabama*," *Mississippi Valley Historical Review* 41 (1954), no. 1, pp. 41–60. Description of Bulloch: Entry of September 12, 1862, Maguire Spy Report, Bulloch Papers. Craven: Bulloch to Mallory, September 10, 1862, *Official Records (Navy)*, 2, 2, p. 264.

Chapter Nine: The Dead Letter

I

"Shameless false witnesses": Bulloch to Mallory, August 11, 1862, *Official Records (Navy)*, 2, 2, p. 236. Early departure: Yonge affidavit, in Beaman, *National and Private*, p. 94. Semmes in Liverpool: Bulloch to Mallory, August 11, 1862, *Official Records (Navy)*, 2, 2, p. 235; Semmes, *My Adventures Afloat*, p. 413. Butcher's recollections: Merli and Long (eds.), "Captain Butcher's Memoir," pp. 134–35. Semmes, *My Adventures Afloat*, pp. 404–13, contains the fullest version of events on board, but see also George King's affidavit, September 27, in *LCD*, 22. Alternative version of speech: Henry Redden's affidavit, September 3, 1862, enclosed with letter, Dudley to Adams, same date, *Official Correspondence on the Claims*, pp. 24–27. Estimates of the number of men who refused to sign on vary: Semmes says ten, King thinks "I and about 8 others," but Redden claims forty-eight—an exaggeration. Officers: Summersell, *CSS Alabama*, pp. 28–34. Bulloch's thoughts on departure: Mallory, September 10, *Official Records (Navy)*, 2, 2, pp. 263–64.

II

Moran, August 1, 1862, in Wallace and Gillespie (eds.), *Journal of Benjamin Moran*, 2, pp. 1,047–48. Discussions: Adams to Russell, September 4; Russell to Adams, September 22; Adams to Russell, September 30; Russell to Adams, October 4; Adams to Russell, October 9; Russell to Adams, October 16; Russell to Adams, December 19, 1862, and January 24, 1863, *Official Correspondence on the Claims*, pp. 24, 27–33, 45, 58.

III

British responses: Sebrell, *Persuading John Bull*, pp. 91–103; C. Ewan, "The Emancipation Proclamation and British Public Opinion," *The Historian*, 67 (2005), no. 1, pp. 1–19; D. A. Lorimer, "The Role of Anti-Slavery Sentiment in English Reactions to the American Civil War," *Historical Journal*, 19 (1976), no. 2, pp. 405–20; J. M. Hernon Jr., "British Sympathies in the American Civil War: A Reconsideration," *Journal of Southern History*, 33 (1967), no. 3, pp. 356–67. "Mad dogs": Russell to Lyons, November 1, 1862, in T. Newton, *Lord Lyons: A Record of British Diplomacy* (London: Edward Arnold, 2 vols., 1913), 1, p. 92. Palmerston's comment: Letter to Russell, October 22, 1862, in G. P. Gooch (ed.), *The Later Correspondence of Lord John Russell, 1840–1878* (London: Longmans, Green, and Co., 2 vols., 1925), 2, p. 328.

IV

Semmes, *My Adventures Afloat*, pp. 171, 189, 405, 412, 523–24, 717; A. Sinclair, *Two Years on the* Alabama (Boston: Lee and Shepard, 1896), pp. 22–25, 27–28, 110; Summersell, *CSS* Alabama, p. 35.

V

Summersell, *CSS* Alabama, pp. 36–46; Sinclair, *Two Years on the* Alabama, pp. 25–26; Hoole (ed.), "Letters from a Georgia Midshipman," pp. 416–24. Black sailors: "Description by Capt. Lawrence W. Brown of the Capture of the Ship *Sonora* by the *Alabama*," printed in L. Brown and I. Colby, "The *Sonora* and the *Alabama*," *Civil War Times Illustrated*, 10 (1971), no. 6, p. 35. Semmes and books: R. R. Newell, "Capture and Burning of the Ship *Anna F. Schmidt* by *Alabama*," *American Neptune*, 25 (1965), p. 20. Yonge's dismissal: Sinclair, *Two Years*, p. 78. Bulloch, in his letter to Mallory, June 30, 1863, *Official Records (Navy)*, 2, 2, p. 449, adds to Sinclair's version by mentioning the £400 and Low's presence.

VI

Maffitt to Bulloch, August 20, 1862, p. 760; "Extracts from the Journal of Lieutenant J.N. Maffitt," *Official Records (Navy)*, 1, 1, pp. 764–69; J. M. Taylor, "Shark Hunt," *Civil War Times Illustrated*, 38 (1999), no. 6, pp. 66–74. *Jacob Bell*: "Abstract Log of the CSS *Florida*," February 12, 1863, and "Extracts from the Journal," *Official Records (Navy)*, 1, 2, pp. 675, 670. The cost of the *Alabama*, for comparison's sake, was $250,305.44. See "Extracts from the Journal of Commander Semmes," *Official Records (Navy)*, 1, 1, p. 783.

VII

V. J. Laas, "'Sleepless Sentinels': The North Atlantic Blocking Squadron, 1862–1864," *Civil War History*, 31 (1985), no. 1, pp. 24–38; Watts, "Phantoms of Anglo-Confederate Commerce," Ch. 3; Hughes, "Liverpool and the Confederate States," Table, p. 65. Prices: Hall, "Liverpool Cotton Market and the American Civil War," pp. 154–55, 159; N. Hall, "The Liverpool Cotton Market and Cotton Re-Exports, c. 1815–1914," *Northern History*, 43 (2006), Fig. 5, p. 269. Capture rates: Owsley, *King Cotton*, p. 261; S. Lebergott, "Through the Blockade: The Profitability and Extent of Cotton Smuggling, 1861–1865," *Journal of Economic History*, 41 (1981), no. 4, Table 6, p. 879. Fraser Trenholm's exports: Wise, *Lifeline of the Confederacy*, p. 115. Scharf, *History of the Confederate Navy*, p. 488, notes the attritional losses.

VIII–IX

It was never clarified who Yonge's second wife was or her race. Semmes, who loathed Yonge so intensely he refused to mention his name in his memoirs, heard that she was a "mulatto woman" (*My Adventures Afloat*, p. 417) while Moran claimed that she was "a negro." Bulloch says she was "a mulatto with two negro children" (letter to Mallory, June 30, 1863, *Official Records (Navy)*, 2, 2, p. 448–49). Many years later, Dudley recalled that she was "a quadroon girl, a native of the West Indies." By this he meant that she was one-quarter black (Dudley, "Three Critical Periods," p. 51). Yonge himself later said in a weaselly way that she was not mixed race, thereby hoping to induce people into assuming that she was white, but also perhaps indicating that she was black. It is impossible to say at this stage, though the point may turn on differing nineteenth-century racial classifications. The balance of the evidence seems to point to her being biracial. As for Mrs. Yonge's relationship to the boy, that is another mystery. It's probable the lad was either her (illegitimate?) son, a nephew, a ward, or kin of some sort. The relevant portion of the transcript of Yonge's testimony on the subject is printed in *Report of the Trial Before the Right Honorable the Lord Chief Baron and a Special Jury in the Court of Exchequer at Westminster, Trinity Term, 26th Victoria* (London: George E. Eyre and William Spottiswoode, 1863), pp. 114–34. Yonge Affair: Moran, April 1, 1863, in Wallace and Gillespie (eds.), *Journal of Benjamin Moran*, 2, pp. 1,140–41, provides the fullest picture, and can be supplemented by Adams's diary (Adams calls him "Samuel R. Yonge"), April 1 and 2, at http://www.masshist.org/publications/cfa-civil-war/view?id=DCA63d091 and http://www.masshist.org/publications/cfa-civil-war/view?id=DCA63d092. Documents passed to Dudley: *Report of the Trial*, Appendix, pp. ix–xi; enclosures in two Dudley letters to Seward, March 28, 1863, *LCD*, 23. Dudley's assessment of and relationship with Yonge: Letters to Seward, April 3 and 8, 1863, *LCD*, 23. Yonge's letter to Dudley mentioning his stay in Holmfirth, November 20, 1864, DU-4505, Dudley Papers. This letter is signed "J. Edwards Davies" but is in Yonge's handwriting. Sheffield: Yonge to Dudley, April 11, 1863, DU-4483. Yonge's contact for mail was located at 198 Brook Hill, in the city center.

Chapter Ten: Traitor to His Benefactor

I

Alexandra: Dudley to Seward, March 11 and 13, 1863, *LCD*, 23. Maguire notes in an affidavit (March 28) his employment of workers at the Miller yard and records those attending the *Alexandra*'s launch (enclosed with Dudley to Seward, April 3, *LCD*, 23). In his postwar memoirs, Bulloch was cryptic as to the *Alexandra*'s true character, saying that she was merely "a small wooden screw-steamer" (Bulloch, *Secret Service*, p. 230), but his letters to Mallory, November 7 and 24, 1862, *Official Records (Navy)*, 2, 2, pp. 294, 302, belie that assertion of innocence. *Alexandra* as mail boat or yacht: W. D. Jones, *The Confederate Rams at Birkenhead: A Chapter in Anglo-American Relations* (Tuscaloosa, AL: Confederate Publishing Co., 1961), p. 46. Inglefield: *Treaty of Washington*, 1, p. 105n9. Erlanger Loan: Dudley connected this loan with its Liverpool predecessor, saying it was "an extension or increase of the same," in letter to Seward, January 6, 1863, *LCD*, 23; Moran, March 26, Wallace and Gillespie (eds.), *Journal of Benjamin Moran*, 2, p. 1,138. Amount raised: J. F. Gentry, "A Confederate Success in Europe: The Erlanger Loan," *Journal of Southern History*, 36 (1970), no. 2, p. 173. Bond prices and impact of fighting: M. D. Weidenmier, "The Market for Confederate Cotton Bonds," *Explorations in Economic History*, 37 (2000), no. 1, esp. Fig. 2, p. 82; W. O. Brown Jr., and R. C. K. Burdekin, "Turning Points in the U.S. Civil War: A British Perspective," *Journal of Economic History*, 60 (2000), no. 1, pp. 216–31. Dudley acquired and sent a copy of the original bond terms to Seward on March 19, 1863 (*LCD*, 23). Edwin De Leon: See his memoirs (ed. W. C. Davis), *Secret History of Confederate Diplomacy Abroad* (Lawrence: University Press of Kansas, 2005), pp. 171–79. Emancipation: Dudley to Seward, January 6, *LCD*, 23; Moran, January 2, 8, 12, and 14, February 10, Wallace and Gillespie (eds.), 2, pp. 1,102, 1,104, 1,106, 1,119. Manchester: F. Hourani, *Manchester and Abraham Lincoln: A Side-Light on an Earlier Fight for Freedom* (Manchester: R. Aikman & Sons, 1900). The number of anti-slavery rallies is cited, with reservations, by D. A. Campbell, *English Public Opinion and the American Civil War* (Woodbridge, Suffolk [U.K.]: Boydell Press, 2003), p. 215, based on Adams, *Great Britain and the American Civil War*, 2, p. 223. Exeter Hall: "Great Emancipation Demonstration at Exeter Hall," *New York Times*, February 16, 1863; Campbell, *English Public Opinion*, p. 222. Dudley and Liverpool meetings: letters to Seward, February 17 and 20, *LCD*, 23; enclosure from John Croppen, February 19, included in Adams to Seward, March 5, *Papers Relating to Foreign Affairs* (1862–63), pp. 135–36.

II

Moran, March 30 and 31, April 6, Wallace and Gillespie (eds.), *Journal of Benjamin Moran*, 2, pp. 1,139–40, 1,142–43; correspondence between Adams and Russell, March 30 and 31, April 2, 3, 5, 6, 8, and 23, *Papers Relating to Foreign Affairs* (1862–63), pp. 188–89, 202–5, 209, 222. The affidavits, all dated March 28, were sworn by Dudley, John De Costa ("shipping agent and steam tug owner"), Oliver Mumford (a ship's captain), Neil Black (a veteran shipbuilder), Thomas Hutson (a former Royal Navy seaman), and Detective Maguire, and are enclosed in a letter from Dudley to Seward, April 3, 1863, *LCD*, 23. "Southern proclivities": Newspaper cutting, April 6(?), enclosed with note from Adams to Seward, April 7, in *Papers Relating to Foreign Affairs*, p. 198. Bulloch's articles: among others, Letter to the Editor, "Yankee Espionage in England," *Newcastle Journal*, April 24, 1863. The letter was widely reprinted.

III

March 27, 1863, letter from Russell to Palmerston, quoted in Adams, *Great Britain and the American Civil War*, 2, p. 131; see Beaman, *National and Private*, p. 91, paraphrasing Russell's letter to Lyons. A summary of Bulloch's April 20 letter to Prioleau assessing Yonge's knowledge is in Anon. (ed.), *Civil War and the Confeder-*

acy: The Business Records of Fraser, Trenholm & Company of Liverpool and Charleston, South Carolina, 1860–1877, from the Merseyside Maritime Museum, Liverpool (Marlborough, Wiltshire [U.K.]: Adam Matthew Publications, 1999), and is quoted more fully in Foreman, *A World on Fire*, p. 456. Detective Constable: Dudley to Seward, May 2, 1863, *LCD*, 23; Squarey's letter of complaint to the town clerk, a Mr. Shuttleworth, April 25, same source. Yonge's character: Bulloch to Mallory, June 30, 1863, *Official Records (Navy)*, 2, 2, pp. 448–49.

IV

Russell's changing the rules: Letters to Lyons, April 7 and December 20, 1863, quoted in Jones, *Confederate Rams at Birkenhead*, pp. 52, 56–57. Legal fees: Bulloch to Mallory, June 30, 1863, *Official Records (Navy)*, 2, 2, p. 448. Feeling a "little uneasiness at the prospect of a jury trial" in Liverpool, Adams discussed moving the trial to London with the Queen's Advocate on April 22 (Adams to Seward, April 23, *Papers Relating to Foreign Affairs* (1862–63), p. 222). Dudley agreed to this in his letter to Seward, May 2, *LCD*, 23. Criminal prosecution versus forfeiture: Dudley to Seward, April 8 and 14, *LCD*, 23; Squarey to F. J. Hamel (solicitor to the Board of Customs), April 20, *Papers Relating to Foreign Affairs* (1862–63), pp. 231–32. "Southern proclivities": Quoted in Jones, *Confederate Rams at Birkenhead*, p. 47. Pollock: http://www.historyofparliamentonline.org/volume/1820-1832/member/pollock -jonathan-1783-1870; obituary, *The Times*, August 24, 1870. In general, see F. J. Merli, "Crown Versus Cruiser: The Curious Case of the *Alexandra*," *Civil War History*, 9 (1963), no. 2, pp. 167–77.

V–VI

Dudley's reaction: Moran, June 22, Wallace and Gillespie (eds.), *Journal of Benjamin Moran*, 2, p. 1,176; Dudley to Seward, June 26, *LCD*, 23, expressing exasperation with Palmer. Court proceedings: *The Times*, June 23, 24, and 25, 1863; transcript published in *Report of the Trial*; R. Palmer, *Memoirs* (New York: Macmillan & Co., 2 vols., 1896), 2, pp. 440–47. Pollock's Erlanger speculation and Hotze connection: List of bond owners, "The Rebel Loan," *New York Times*, December 9, 1865. The *Liverpool Mercury* (June 25) noted the jury's not "hesitating for more than a half a minute," and see next day's paper for "signal defeat." Yonge's disastrous appearance: Bulloch to Mallory (June 30, 1863, *Official Records (Navy)*, 2, 2, p. 449) said that "in face of the handling he got from Sir Hugh Cairns . . . I do not think he will venture to present himself before a jury again." De Costa: Macilwee, *Liverpool Underworld*, pp. 145–47; Bulloch, *Secret Service*, p. 236. The *Southerner*: "Dejeúner On Board the *Southerner*," *Liverpool Mercury*, June 29. A word on the "98 counts": This seems an extraordinary number, but Bulloch explained that "the 97th and 98th counts were abandoned by the Crown. The remaining 96 counts consisted of the first eight counts repeated twelve times, merely varying the offence charged. Thus, the first eight counts charge that the defendants did *equip* the vessel, the next eight counts that they did *furnish* the vessel . . . The first eight counts therefore represented the rest." Bulloch, *Secret Service*, p. 231.

Chapter Eleven: The Lucky Shoemaker

I–II

Dudley on the Rams: Occasional letters to Seward, August 8, September 3, October 4, December 30, 1862, *LCD*, 22. China: F. J. Merli, "A Missing Chapter in American Civil War Diplomacy: The Confederacy's Chinese Fleet, 1861–1867," in C. G. Reynolds (ed.), *Global Crossroads and the American Seas* (Missoula, MT: Pictorial Histories Publishing Co., 1988), pp. 181–96. Bulloch's intentions: Letter to Mallory, December 18, 1862, *Official Records (Navy)*, 2, 2, pp. 309–11. Construction: Bulloch to Mallory, February 3, 1863, *Official Records (Navy)*, 2, 2, pp. 351–52. The most detailed analysis of the Rams design is English, "The Laird Rams," and see R. Lester, "Construction of Confederate Ironclad Rams in Great Britain," *Military Collector & Historian*, 26 (1974), pp. 73–76.

III

Ships and the law: Bulloch to Mallory, February 3 and October 20, 1863, *Official Records (Navy)*, 2, 2, pp. 351–52, 507–11. France and Napoleon: Mallory to Bulloch, March 19, 1863, *Official Records (Navy)*, 2, 2, pp. 375–76.

IV

As early as 1858, the *Liverpool Mercury* was calling François "a rich parvenu, who is supposed to have made a very large fortune in the last seven years in Egypt" ("Egypt," *Liverpool Mercury*, March 23, 1858). Bravay himself liked to tell the story of twirling his hat ("The Returned," *Morning Chronicle*, October 4, 1858). Shoe story: "The Lucky Shoemaker," *Morning Post*, December 2, 1863. Hunger and indigestion: "Le Nabab," *The Examiner*, February 9, 1878. The *Gazette du Midi* (reprinted in the *Daily News*, August 26, 1862) noted Sa'id's staying with Bravay in France. A colorful account of life in Egypt that contains interesting material on Sa'id is Anon., "Ismail Pacha of Egypt," *Harper's New Monthly Magazine*, 39 (1869), pp. 739–50. English, "Laird Rams," p. 140n520, notes that the *Harper's* article was written by Edwin De Leon, the Confederate diplomat who in the 1850s had served as the American consul in Alexandria. Sa'id's Egypt: A. Mestyan, *Arab Patriotism: The Ideology and Culture of Power in Late Ottoman Egypt* (Princeton, NJ: Princeton University Press, 2017), pp. 3–5, 44–48. Bulloch summarizes his initial meeting in his letter to Mallory, June 30, 1863, *Official Records (Navy)*, 2, 2, pp. 444–47. The Bravay letters are quoted in Bulloch, *Secret Service*, pp. 279–80. Dire finances: Bulloch to North, December 23 and 31, 1862; Bulloch to James Mason, January 5 and 23, February 4, 1863, *Official*

Records (Navy), 2, 2, pp. 319–52. Cotton smuggling: Lebergott, "Through the Blockade," pp. 872 and n19, p. 879, Table 6. Grazebrook: "Blockade Running: The Case of Mr. J.W. Grazebrook," *New York Times*, August 22, 1863.

V–VI

Terms of contract: Lester, "Construction of Confederate Ironclad Rams in Great Britain," p. 77. *North Carolina* and *Mississippi*: Mallory to Bulloch, October 29, 1862, pp. 286–87. Erlanger Loan: Bulloch to Mallory, May 7 and 26, July 20, ibid., pp. 417–18, 428–29, 467–68. Paris: Bulloch to Mallory, June 30, pp. 444–47. Launch of the first Ram: Bulloch to Mallory, July 8, 1863, pp. 452–54. Disguise: Wilson and McKay, *James D. Bulloch*, p. 144. Wilmington: Mallory to Bulloch, August 29, and Mallory to Barron, August 30, 1863, pp. 483–87. Bulloch's ambitions: Bulloch to Mallory, July 9, 1863, pp. 455–57. Unless otherwise noted, in *Official Records (Navy)*, 2, 2. Dudley's evidence, intimidation of sources, and difficulty of acquiring intelligence: Letters to Seward, July 3 and 7, September 4, 1863, *LCD*, 25. In this period, Dudley's intelligence costs fell almost to zero (see his second-quarter invoice, July 23, *LCD*, 25). Hand: Affidavit, July 15, enclosed in Dudley to Seward, July 16, *LCD*, 25; English, "Laird Rams," pp. 154–55; "The Rebel Rams—A Fit Case for Aid," *New York Times*, October 17, 1864; "The Steam Rams Seized at Birkenhead," *Liverpool Mercury*, March 10, 1864. Dudley's payments to Hand and Brady: Maguire invoices, July 31, Dudley Papers, DU-2801, and August 7, DU-2802, and see Maguire to Dudley, March 12, 1864, asking him to give William Brady his "immediate attention" (DU-2813). Neil Black: Dudley to Seward, July 3, *LCD*, 25. Dudley's visit to London: Adams diary, July 8, at https://www.masshist.org/publications/cfa-civil-war/index.php/view?id=DCA63d189#sn=17. Affidavits: Yonge, April 6; Chapman, June 29; Dudley, July 7; Russell and Ellis, July 7, enclosed in Adams to Russell, July 11, *The Case of Great Britain as Laid Before the Tribunal of Arbitration, Convened at Geneva* (Washington, DC: Government Printing Office, 3 vols., 1872), 2, pp. 367–73. Edwards's opinion: Edwards to commissioners of customs, July 8, *Case of Great Britain*, 2, pp. 374–75. Dudley's meeting with Edwards: Letter to Seward, July 16, *LCD*, 25. Wilding's report on his conversation with the vice-consul was sent by Dudley to Adams, who forwarded it to Russell. Dudley submitted his own report to Seward on July 25 (*LCD*, 25). Russell himself followed up with Baron Gros, the French ambassador, who confirmed Lenglet's version. See Wilding to Adams, July 24, 1863, enclosed in Adams to Russell, July 25, and Gros to Russell, July 27, *Case of Great Britain*, 2, pp. 381–82. Law officers' opinion: Atherton, Palmer, and Phillimore to Russell, July 24, *Case of Great Britain*, 2, p. 380.

VII–VIII

Colquhoun's dispatch: Colquhoun to Russell, February 26, 1863, *Case of Great Britain*, 2, p. 367. Sa'id's desire to keep Constantinople out of his affairs: As Bravay put it in his December 28, 1862, letter to Adrien (quoted in Bulloch, *Secret Service*, p. 280),

"He [Sa'id] stipulates above everything that it [the deal] not be made known that they [the ships] are for the Egyptian Government, for he has political reasons for that." Colquhoun's follow-up telegram: August 31, *Case of Great Britain*, 2, p. 396. Customs officials and Lairds story: Morgan to Edwards, August 29; Laird Brothers to Russell (care of Henry Layard, undersecretary of state), September 5, *Case of Great Britain*, 2, pp. 397, 411. Rams would not be interfered with: Russell to Adams, September 1, *Case of Great Britain*, 2, pp. 398–99. That same day, Layard confirmed that Russell "thinks the vessels ought to be detained" *only* if "sufficient evidence can be obtained to lead to the belief that they are intended for the Confederate States of America." Otherwise, they were to be left alone. (Layard to lords commissioners, September 1, *Case of Great Britain*, 2, p. 398.)

IX

Stopping the vessels: Russell to Layard, September 3, quoted in D. F. Krein, "Russell's Decision to Retain the Laird Rams," *Civil War History*, 22 (1976), no. 2, pp. 162–63; Layard to lords commissioners, same date, *Case of Great Britain*, 2, p. 403. The next day, Palmerston told Russell that he agreed (English, "Laird Rams," p. 187), and the day after that, September 5, Adams angrily told Russell that if the Rams got out and raised the blockade "it would be superfluous in me to point out to your lordship that this is war" (Adams to Russell, *Case of Great Britain*, 2, pp. 408–9.) Much has been made of this letter (for example, Brooks Adams, "The Seizure of the Laird Rams," *Proceedings of the Massachusetts Historical Society*, 45 [1911], p. 297), the claim being that it frightened Russell so much he immediately detained the Rams. The problem with this theory is that Russell had *already* decided to do so *and* had received Palmerston's blessing. Explaining Adams's threatening tone is a simple matter of chronology: Only on September 4 had he received Russell's September 1 note saying he would not interfere with the Rams, the three-day difference the result of the communications lag between Scotland and London. Within a week, in any case, Russell and Adams understood that their letters had crossed. This was partly Russell's fault. On September 4, instead of directly telling Adams he'd ordered the Rams' detention, he wrote ambiguously that "the matter is under the serious and anxious consideration of Her Majesty's Government" (Russell to Adams, *Case of Great Britain*, 2, p. 406). It was only on September 8 that Russell clarified his detention order, leading to some embarrassment on Adams's part. On September 11, Russell asked Adams not to "yield to . . . hasty conclusions," while the minister, who'd been hoping Russell had forgotten the overheated "this is war" line, denied that he had ever threatened hostilities and the foreign secretary gracefully pretended that he must have misunderstood Adams's meaning. See Russell to Adams, September 11 and 25; Adams's replies of September 16 and 29, *Case of Great Britain*, 2, pp. 415–18, 420–25, 434, 438–39, 443.

Chapter Twelve: The Man with No Hands

I

Colquhoun to Russell, August 28, but received September 5, *Case of Great Britain*, 2, pp. 409–10. Russell summarized the Colquhoun findings in a note to Adams, September 11, *Case of Great Britain*, 2, p. 416. On October 17, Russell instructed Colquhoun to "inquire of the Viceroy if he remembers or can ascertain at what date he first refused to accept Bravay's alleged contracts." A week later, October 24, Colquhoun replied that Isma'il "positively refused acceptance of any of Bravay's contracts within a few days after his succession, that is to say, probably about the 30th of January." Telegrams, *Case of Great Britain*, 2, pp. 466, 479. Russell's disbelief in Bravay's story: E. Hammond to the secretary of the treasury, September 21, *Case of Great Britain*, 2, pp. 428–29.

II

W. G. Grey to Russell, September 22, enclosing Hore's report, same date, and a copy of the Deed of Release, *Case of Great Britain*, 2, pp. 431–33. Bulloch, *Secret Service*, p. 276n, describes the secret agreement with Bravay.

III

Bulloch's fury: Bulloch to Mallory, October 20, *Official Records (Navy)*, 2, 2, pp. 507–11. Dacres's visit: W. G. Romaine (secretary to the admiralty) to Hammond, September 19, and Hammond to secretary of the treasury, same date, *Case of Great Britain*, 2, pp. 425–26. Lairds' fears and reactions: Laird Brothers to Edwards, September 18, p. 431; Dacres to Romaine, September 20, pp. 429–30; Edwards to commissioners of customs, September 22, pp. 435–36, *Case of Great Britain*, 2.

IV

Edwards: W. G. Stewart to commissioners of customs, October 6, *Case of Great Britain*, 2, pp. 447–48. Bulloch defends Edwards in *Secret Service*, pp. 185–86, but Moran quotes Squarey, December 15, 1863, in Wallace and Gillespie (eds.), *Journal of Benjamin Moran*, 2, p. 1,246. Dudley's intelligence: Letter to Seward, September 16, *LCD*, 25, regarding the coal, which tip he passed on to Inglefield, who told Commodore Ryder that he enjoyed "a system of espionage" (referring anonymously to Dudley), October 6, 1863, *Case of Great Britain*, 2, p. 445. Murphy and De Costa: Maguire invoice, August 28 (Dudley Papers, DU-2805), notes large payment of £5 to Murphy; September 18 invoice (DU-2809) notes him giving £1 to "Murphy's & De Costa's men"; on the Murphys, Macilwee, *The Liverpool Underworld*, pp. 121–22. Property protection and seizure: Hamilton (treasury) to Laird Brothers, October 7; Romaine to Hammond, October 8; Hammond to secretary to the treasury, October 8; Romaine to Inglefield, October 9, *Case of Great Britain*, 2, pp. 448–49, 451, 453.

Lairds' behavior: Inglefield to Admiralty, October 23, and to Vice-Admiral Grey, October 25, *Case of Great Britain*, 2, pp. 480, 482–83. Royal Marine beaten up: Jones, *Confederate Rams at Birkenhead*, p. 95. Dudley's glee: Letter to Seward, October 10, *LCD*, 25.

V

Legal process: Moran, November 4 and December 5, 1863, in Wallace and Gillespie (eds.), *Journal of Benjamin Moran*, 2, pp. 1,232–33, 1,244. Bulloch's responses and negotiations: Bulloch to Mallory, September 1, October 20, December 6, 1863; January 6, February 17, 1864, *Official Records (Navy)*, 2, 2, pp. 487–89, 510, 565–66, 571, 583–86. The Laird Brothers complained about the postponements to Hamilton, January 25 and February 3, 1864, *Case of Great Britain*, 2, pp. 519–20. Commission to Egypt: Hammond to Hamilton, February 2, 1864, same source, p. 519. Russell's thoughts on the Koran: Jones, *Confederate Rams at Birkenhead*, pp. 101–2. Appraisals and final sale: Luke to Admiral Robinson, November 6, 1863; Messrs. Rowcliffe and Cotterill (Bravay/Lairds solicitors) to J. Greenwood (Treasury), May 20, 1864, *Case of Great Britain*, 2, pp. 509, 528–29.

Chapter Thirteen: The Great Red God

I

N. C. Delaney, "Fight or Flee: Raphael Semmes' Decision to Engage the *Kearsarge*, June 1864," *Journal of Confederate History*, 4 (1989), pp. 15–28; Summersell, CSS *Alabama*, pp. 72–90; Merli, "Raphael Semmes and the Challenge at Cherbourg," in Merli (ed. Fahey), *The* Alabama, *British Neutrality, and the American Civil War*, pp. 141–57. Winslow replied to a congratulatory letter from Dudley, June 24, 1864, DU-4456, Dudley Papers.

II

Hassler, "How the Confederates Controlled Blockade Running," pp. 47–49; Scharf, *History of the Confederate Navy*, pp. 483–85; Wise, *Lifeline of the Confederacy*, pp. 196, 198, and Appendix 22, pp. 285–328; E. C. Coddington, "The Activities and Attitudes of a Confederate Business Man: Gazaway B. Lamar," *Journal of Southern History*, 9 (1943), pp. 30–32. Bulloch's runners: Wardle, "Mersey-Built Blockade Runners," pp. 183–85; see also Dudley's detailed summary to Seward, January 17, 1865, *LCD*, 30.

III

Depositions of John Ellison, Thomas Everall, George Kelly, October 29, 1864, and John Wilson and John Hercus, no date, *Treaty of Washington* (1872), 1, pp. 375–80; Consul Grattan (in Tenerife) to Russell, October 30, 1863, pp. 374–75; W. C. Whittle

Jr. (eds. D. A. Harris and A. B. Harris), *The Voyage of the CSS* Shenandoah: *A Memorable Cruise* (Tuscaloosa: University of Alabama Press, 2005), pp. 11–13.

IV

South's expectations: A. Brettle's important article, "Confederate Imaginations with the Federals in the Postwar Order," *Civil War History*, 65 (2019), no. 1, pp. 43–72. Loan: Brown and Burdekin, "Turning Points in the Civil War," pp. 218, 224, Fig. 1. Bazaar: Prioleau's employment advertisement in the *Liverpool Mercury*, October 8, and articles, October 18, 19, 20, 22, and 24. Hotze's reporter: *The Index*, October 20, cutting enclosed with letter, Dudley to Seward, October 22, *LCD*, 29. Dudley's comment on the bazaar is in Dudley to Seward, October 24. Bazaar's proceeds and Prioleau: Hughes, "Liverpool and the Confederate States," pp. 278–301.

V

Florida capture: *Morning Chronicle*, November 2, 1864. Bulloch's outrage at the illegal "assassination" of the *Florida* is fully expressed in *Secret Service*, pp. 125–59, where he reprints the relevant military and diplomatic correspondence. Erlanger Loan: Hall, "Liverpool Cotton Market and the American Civil War," pp. 162–63; Brown and Burdekin, "Turning Points in the Civil War," Fig. 1, p. 224. Reaction to Prioleau: *Liverpool Mercury*, December 22 (Seward's refusal) and 23 (Seward to Adams), as well as Dudley to Seward, December 24, *LCD*, 29.

VI

Whittle (Harris and Harris, eds.), *Voyage of the CSS* Shenandoah, pp. 17, 21; diary, December 4, 1864, pp. 82–83; June 22, 1865, p. 166; July 4, p. 173; August 2, p. 182; Appendix, pp. 215–16; Waddell, "Abstract Log of CSS *Shenandoah*," in B. M. Thomsen (ed.), *Blue and Gray at Sea: Naval Memoirs of the Civil War* (New York: Tom Doherty Associates, 2003), p. 287. Arrival in Liverpool: "The Confederate Cruiser *Shenandoah* in the Mersey," November 7; "The *Shenandoah*—Parole of the Crew," November 9; "The *Shenandoah*," November 10; "The Vessel Handed Over to the Americans," November 11; "Departure from the Mersey of the Ex-Confederate Cruiser *Shenandoah*," November 22, *Liverpool Mercury*. See also Bulloch, *Secret Service*, p. 429, and Kinnaman, *Captain Bulloch*, p. 406.

Chapter Fourteen: Retribution

I

Settlement: Memorandum of Agreement, November 6, 1866; Morse to Seward, November 10 and 17; Morse to Dudley, November 13; Dudley to Seward, November 14; Dudley to Morse, November 15, pp. 15–16, enclosed in letter to Seward, November 16; Gibbs to Dudley, November 19; Morse to Seward, November 28, *Executive*

Documents (House of Representatives), 39th Congress, Second Session (Washington, DC: Government Printing Office, 1867), 10, pp. 5–19, 29–30, 39–40. Seward's decision: Telegram, November 29; Adams to Seward, December 1; Seward to Adams, January 4, 1867; Seward to Isaac Redfield (special consul), January 12, *Executive Documents*, pp. 19–20, 46–47, 47–49. Adams sides with Dudley: Adams to Morse, November 23, 1866, in Freeman Harlow Morse Papers, Western Reserve Historical Society. Postwar fall: Farley, "'The Manners of a Prince,'" p. 25; Wilson, *Historical Sketch of the Prioleau Family*, pp. 32–33; Anon. (ed.), *Civil War and the Confederacy: The Business Records of Fraser, Trenholm & Company of Liverpool*, listing of letters.

II

Moran-Hudson episode: Diary, October 21 and November 18, 1865, "Diary of Benjamin Moran, 1860–1868," *Proceedings of the Massachusetts Historical Society*, 48 (1914–15), pp. 481, 483; Long, *In the Shadow of the* Alabama, pp. 148, 151–54, 158–64, contains the fullest examination. Buckley's speculations were revealed in "The Rebel Loan," *New York Times*, December 9, 1865, noting that he purchased two hundred bonds. The majority of investors bought between five and twenty. Even Prioleau bought only forty.

III

T. Bingham, "The *Alabama* Claims Arbitration," *International and Comparative Law Quarterly*, 54 (2005), no. 1, pp. 1–25.

IV

Yonge: Yonge to Dudley, January 18, 1864, Dudley Papers, DU-4497; Yonge (alias "J. Edwards Davies") to Dudley, November 20, 1864, DU-4505. Regarding Yonge's move to Alabama, this is speculative. In a notice in the *Opelika Weekly Era and Whig* on March 31, 1871, he—or a completely different "Clarence R. Yonge"—advertised his services as an "Architect," by which he meant house contractor. Perhaps the business did not do so well, for seven years later in the *Opelika Times* (March 1, 1878) we find the same individual announcing that he "is now prepared to do any and all kinds of painting at prices to suit the times." Dudley's later career and death: Dyer, "Thomas H. Dudley," pp. 412–13; Potts, "Biographical Sketch," pp. 124–25.

V

Bulloch's postwar life: Wilson and McKay, *James D. Bulloch*, pp. 225–74. For Bulloch's attachment to the "Lost Cause," see the review of his book in the *New York Times*, "The Anglo-Confederate Cruisers," November 7, 1883, which noted its endless "general excursions on the Southern cause" that must be "accepted as those of a sincere adherent and admirer of the lost cause." See also T. Roosevelt, *The Naval War of 1812; or The History of the United States Navy During the Last War with Great Britain* (New York: G.P. Putnam's Sons, 1882), p. vii, for dedicatory note.

BIBLIOGRAPHY

Archives

James Dunwoody Bulloch Papers. Mariners' Museum and Park, Newport News, Virginia.

Despatches from United States Consuls in Liverpool, 1790–1906. M141, Rolls 19–31. National Archives and Records Administration, College Park, Maryland.

Thomas Haines Dudley Papers. Huntington Library, San Marino, California.

Freeman Harlow Morse Papers. Western Reserve Historical Society, Cleveland, Ohio.

Henry Shelton Sanford Papers. Sanford Museum, Sanford, Florida.

Official Sources

The Case of Great Britain as Laid Before the Tribunal of Arbitration, Convened at Geneva. Washington, DC: Government Printing Office, 3 vols., 1872.

Correspondence Concerning Claims Against Great Britain. Washington, DC: Government Printing Office, 1871.

Executive Documents (House of Representatives), 39th Congress, Second Session. Washington, DC: Government Printing Office, 1867.

Journal of the Congress of the Confederate States of America, 1861–1865. Washington, DC: Government Printing Office, 1904.

Letter of the Secretary of State, Transmitting a Report of the Commercial Relations of the United States with Foreign Nations. Washington, DC: Government Printing Office, 1862.

Moore, J. B., ed. *History and Digest of the International Arbitrations to Which the United States Has Been a Party.* Washington, DC: Government Printing Office, 6 vols., 1898.

The Official Correspondence on the Claims of the United States in Respect to the Alabama. London: Longmans, Green, and Co., 1867.

Official Records of the Union and Confederate Navies in the War of the Rebellion. Washington, DC: Government Printing Office, 30 vols., 1894–1927.

Papers Relating to Foreign Affairs, 1861–1865. Washington, DC: Government Printing Office, 1861–65.

Papers Relating to the Treaty of Washington. Washington, DC: Government Printing Office, 6 vols., 1872–74.

Report of the Trial Before the Right Honorable the Lord Chief Baron and a Special Jury in the Court of Exchequer at Westminster, Trinity Term, 26th Victoria. London: George E. Eyre and William Spottiswoode, 1863.

The War of the Rebellion: A Compilation of the Official Records of the Union and Confederate Armies. Washington, DC: Government Printing Office, 70 vols., 1880–1901.

Secondary Sources

Adams, B. "The Seizure of the Laird Rams." *Proceedings of the Massachusetts Historical Society* 45 (1911–12): 243–333.

Adams, C. F. *Charles Francis Adams, by His Son Charles Francis Adams.* Boston and New York: Houghton Mifflin and Co., 1900.

Adams, E. D. *Great Britain and the American Civil War.* London: Longmans, Green and Co., 2 vols., 1925.

Amundson, R. J. "The American Life of Henry Shelton Sanford," unpublished Ph.D. dissertation, Florida State University, 1963.

———. "Sanford and Garibaldi." *Civil War History* 14, no. 1 (1968): 40–45.

Anon. *Civil War and the Confederacy: The Business Records of Fraser, Trenholm & Company of Liverpool and Charleston, South Carolina, 1860–1877, from the Merseyside Maritime Museum, Liverpool.* Marlborough, Wiltshire (U.K.): Adam Matthew Publications, 1999.

Anon., ed. *Crossfire: A Civil War Anthology [American Civil War Round Table].* Milton Keynes (U.K.): Military Press, 2003.

Anon. "In Memoriam [Benjamin Moran]." *Trübner's American, European & Oriental Literary Record* 5 (1884): 48.

Anon. "A Visit to Birkenhead." *Littell's Living Age* 6, no. 60 (1845): 25–26.

Arielli, N., G. A. Frei, and I. Van Hulle. "The Foreign Enlistment Act, International Law, and British Politics, 1819–2014." *International History Review,* 38, no. 4 (2016): 636–56.

Barry, P. *Dockyard Economy and Naval Power.* London: Sampson Low, Son & Co., 1863.

Beaman, C. C., Jr. *The National and Private "Alabama Claims" and Their "Final and Amicable Settlement."* Washington, DC: W. H. Moore, 1871.

Beckert, S. *Empire of Cotton: A Global History.* New York: Vintage, 2014.

Bell, F. *Midnight Scenes in the Slums of New York: Or, Lights and Shadows.* London: W. Kent and Co., 1881.

Bennett, F. M. *The Steam Navy of the United States: A History of the Growth of the Steam Vessel of War in the U.S. Navy and of the Naval Engineer Corps.* Pittsburgh: Warren & Co., 1896.

Bennett, J. D. *The London Confederates: The Officials, Clergy, Businessmen, and Journalists Who Backed the American South During the Civil War.* Jefferson, NC: McFarland & Co., 2008.

Bernard, M. *A Historical Account of the Neutrality of Great Britain During the American Civil War.* London: Longmans, Green, Reader, and Dyer, 1870.

Bingham, T. "The *Alabama* Claims Arbitration." *The International and Comparative Law Quarterly* 54, no. 1 (2005): 1–25.

Blackett, R. J. M. *Divided Hearts: Britain and the American Civil War.* Baton Rouge: Louisiana State University Press, 2001.

Bleser, C., ed. *Secret and Sacred: The Diaries of James Henry Hammond, a Southern Slaveholder.* New York: Oxford University Press, 1989.

Brettle, A. "Confederate Imaginations with the Federals in the Postwar Order." *Civil War History* 65, no. 1 (2019): 43–72.

Brown, L., and I. Colby. "The *Sonora* and the *Alabama.*" *Civil War Times Illustrated* 10, no. 6 (1971): 32–39.

Brown, W. O., Jr., and R. C. K. Burdekin. "Turning Points in the U.S. Civil War: A British Perspective." *Journal of Economic History* 60, no. 1 (2000): 216–31.

Bulloch, J. D. *The Secret Service of the Confederate States in Europe; or, How the Confederate Cruisers Were Equipped.* New York: Modern Library, 2001 ed. (1883 orig.).

Bulloch, J. G. B. *A Biographical Sketch of Hon. Archibald Bulloch, President of Georgia, 1776–77.* Privately printed, 1907.

Bullock-Willis, V. "James Dunwoody Bulloch." *The Sewanee Review* 34, no. 4 (1926): 386–401.

Burnett, L. A., ed. *Henry Hotze, Confederate Propagandist: Selected Writings on Revolution, Recognition, and Race.* Tuscaloosa: University of Alabama Press, 2008.

Burt, D. *Major Caleb Huse C.S.A. & S. Isaac Campbell & Co.: The Arms, Clothing and Equipment Supplied to the Confederate States of America, 1861–64.* Milton Keynes (U.K.): AuthorHouse, 2009.

Campbell, D. A. *English Public Opinion and the American Civil War.* Woodbridge, Suffolk (U.K.): Boydell Press, 2003.

Clark, A. H. *The Clipper Ship Era: An Epitome of Famous American and British Clipper Ships, Their Owners, Builders, Commanders, and Crews, 1843–1869.* New York: G.P. Putnam's Sons, 1911.

Coddington, E. C. "The Activities and Attitudes of a Confederate Business Man: Gazaway B. Lamar." *Journal of Southern History* 9 (1943): 3–36.

Cooper, E. K. "Printing Presses Financed the Southern War Effort," *Civil War Times Illustrated*, 2, no. 5 (1963): 14–16.

Cross, C. F. *Lincoln's Man in Liverpool: Consul Dudley and the Legal Battle to Stop Confederate Warships*. DeKalb: Northern Illinois University Press, 2007.

Dana, J. C., ed. *Letters of Hawthorne to William D. Ticknor, 1851–1864*. Newark, NJ: Carteret Book Club, 2 vols., 1910.

Dana, R. H. *To Cuba and Back: A Vacation Voyage*. Boston: Ticknor and Fields, 1859.

Delaney, N. C. "Fight or Flee: Raphael Semmes' Decision to Engage the *Kearsarge*, June 1864." *Journal of Confederate History* 4 (1989): 15–28.

De Leon, E. (ed. W. C. Davis). *Secret History of Confederate Diplomacy Abroad*. Lawrence: University Press of Kansas, 2005.

Dickens, C. *The Uncommercial Traveller and A Child's History of England*. London: Macmillan & Co., 1922.

Doyle, D. H. *The Cause of All Nations: An International History of the American Civil War*. New York: Basic Books, 2015.

Dudley, T. H. "The Inside Facts of Lincoln's Nomination." *The Century* 40 (1890): 477–79.

———. "Three Critical Periods in Our Diplomatic Relations with England During the Late War." *Pennsylvania Magazine of History and Biography* 17, no. 1 (1893): 34–54.

Dyer, B. "Thomas H. Dudley." *Civil War History* 1, no. 4 (1955): 401–13.

English, A. "The Laird Rams: Warships in Transition, 1862–1885," unpublished Ph.D. dissertation, University of Exeter, 2016.

Ewan, C. "The Emancipation Proclamation and British Public Opinion." *The Historian* 67, no. 1 (2005): 1–19.

Farley, M. F. "'The Manners of a Prince': Confederate Financier George Trenholm." *Civil War Times Illustrated* 21, no. 8 (1982): 18–25.

Ferris, N. B. "Tempestuous Mission, 1861–1862: The Early Diplomatic Career of Charles Francis Adams," unpublished Ph.D. dissertation, Emory University, 1962.

———. *The* Trent *Affair: A Diplomatic Crisis*. Knoxville: University of Tennessee Press, 1977.

Ford, E. A. "The Bullochs of Georgia." *The Georgia Review* 6, no. 3 (1952): 318–31.

Foreman, A. *A World on Fire: Britain's Crucial Role in the American Civil War*. New York: Random House, 2010.

Foster, K. J. "Builders vs. Blockaders: The Evolution of the Blockade-Running Steamship," in *Global Crossroads and the American Seas*, edited by C. G. Reynolds, 85–90. Missoula, MT: Pictorial Histories Publishing Co., 1988.

Fry, J. A. *Henry S. Sanford: Diplomacy and Business in Nineteenth-Century America*. Reno: University of Nevada Press, 1982.

Fulton, R. "The *Spectator* in Alien Hands." *Victorian Periodicals Review* 24, no. 4 (1991): 187–96.

Gentry, J. F. "A Confederate Success in Europe: The Erlanger Loan." *Journal of Southern History* 36, no. 2 (1970–75): 157.

George, D. M. "John Baxter Langley: Radicalism, Espionage and the Confederate Navy in Mid-Victorian Britain." *Journal for Maritime Research* 19, no. 2 (2017): 121–42.

Gooch, G. P., ed. *The Later Correspondence of Lord John Russell, 1840–1878.* London: Longmans, Green, and Co., 2 vols., 1925.

Gore's Directory for Liverpool and Its Environs. Liverpool: J. Mawdsley & Son, 1860.

Hall, N. "The Liverpool Cotton Market and the American Civil War." *Northern History* 34, no. 1 (1998): 149–69.

———. "The Liverpool Cotton Market and Cotton Re-exports, c. 1815–1914." *Northern History* 43 (2006): 257–71.

———. "The Liverpool Cotton Market: Britain's First Futures Market." *Transactions of the Historic Society of Lancashire and Cheshire* 149 (1999): 99–117.

Hancock, H. B., and N. B. Wilkinson. "'The Devil to Pay!': Saltpeter and the Trent Affair." *Civil War History* 10, no. 1 (1964): 20–32.

Harris, D. A., and A. B. Harris, eds. *The Voyage of the CSS Shenandoah: A Memorable Cruise.* Tuscaloosa: University of Alabama Press, 2005.

Harris, T. L. *The Trent Affair: Including a Review of English and American Relations at the Beginning of the Civil War.* Indianapolis, IN: Bobbs-Merrill Company, 1896.

Hassler, W. W. "How the Confederates Controlled Blockade Running." *Civil War Times Illustrated* 2, no. 6 (1963): 43–49.

Hawthorne, J. *Hawthorne and His Circle.* New York: Harper & Brothers, 1903.

Hawthorne, N. *Our Old Home: A Series of English Sketches.* Edinburgh: William Paterson, 1884.

———. *Passages from the English Note-Books.* Boston: James R. Osgood and Co., 1875.

Henderson, W. O. "The American Chamber of Commerce for the Port of Liverpool, 1801–1908." *Transactions of the Historic Society of Lancashire and Cheshire* 85 (1933): 1–61.

Hernon, J. M., Jr. "British Sympathies in the American Civil War: A Reconsideration." *Journal of Southern History* 33, no. 3 (1967): 356–67.

Hertslet, E., ed. *The Foreign Office List, Forming a Complete British Diplomatic and Consular Handbook.* London: Harrison, 1865.

Hobart-Hampden, A. C. *Never Caught: Personal Adventures Connected with Twelve Successful Trips in Blockade-Running During the American Civil War, 1863–64.* London: John Camden Hotten, 1867.

———. *Sketches from My Life.* New York: D. Appleton & Co., 1887.

Hollett, D. *Men of Iron: The Story of Cammell Laird Shipbuilders, 1828–1991.* Birkenhead, Merseyside (U.K.): Countyvise Ltd., 1992.

Hoole, W. S., ed. *Confederate Foreign Agent: The European Diary of Major Edward C. Anderson.* University, AL: Confederate Publishing Company, 1976.

————, ed. *Four Years in the Confederate Navy: The Career of Captain John Low on the CSS* Fingal, Florida, Alabama, Tuscaloosa, *and* Ajax. Athens: University of Georgia Press, 1964.

————. "Letters from a Georgia Midshipman on the CSS *Alabama*." *Georgia Historical Quarterly* 59, no. 4 (1975): 416–32.

Hourani, F. *Manchester and Abraham Lincoln: A Side-Light on an Earlier Fight for Freedom.* Manchester: R. Aikman & Sons, 1900.

Hughes, F. "Liverpool and the Confederate States: Fraser, Trenholm and Company Operations During the American Civil War," unpublished Ph.D. dissertation, University of Keele, 1996.

Hume, A. *Condition of Liverpool, Religious and Social; Including Notices of the State of Education, Morals, Pauperism, and Crime.* Liverpool: T. Brakell, 1888.

Huse, C. *The Supplies for the Confederate Army: How They Were Obtained in Europe and How Paid For.* Boston: T. R. Marvin & Son, 1904.

Hussey, J. *Cruisers, Cotton and Confederates: Liverpool Waterfront in the Days of the Confederacy.* Merseyside (U.K.): Countyvise Ltd., 2009 ed.

Jameson, J. F. "The London Expenditures of the Confederate Secret Service." *American Historical Review* 35, no. 4 (1930): 811–24.

Jones, W. D. *The Confederate Rams at Birkenhead: A Chapter in Anglo-American Relations.* Tuscaloosa, AL: Confederate Publishing Co., 1961.

Kesselman, B. *"Paddington" Pollaky, Private Detective: The Mysterious Life and Times of the Real Sherlock Holmes.* Stroud, Gloucestershire (U.K.): History Press, 2015.

King, W. "Victor Buckley (1838–1882)," unpublished essay.

Kinnaman, S. C. *Captain Bulloch: The Life of James Dunwoody Bulloch, Naval Agent of the Confederacy.* Indianapolis, IN: Dog Ear Publishing, 2013.

Krein, D. F. "Russell's Decision to Retain the Laird Rams." *Civil War History* 22, no. 2 (1976): 158–63.

Laas, V. J. "'Sleepless Sentinels': The North Atlantic Blocking Squadron, 1862–1864." *Civil War History* 31, no. 1 (1985): 24–38.

Lane, T. *Liverpool: Gateway of Empire.* London: Lawrence and Wishart, 1987.

Lebergott, S. "Through the Blockade: The Profitability and Extent of Cotton Smuggling, 1861–1865." *Journal of Economic History* 41, no. 4 (1981): 867–88.

Lester, R. *Confederate Finance and Purchasing in Great Britain.* Charlottesville: University Press of Virginia, 1975.

————. "Construction of Confederate Ironclad Rams in Great Britain." *Military Collector & Historian* 26 (1974): 73–80.

Long, R. E. *In the Shadow of the* Alabama: *The British Foreign Office and the American Civil War.* Annapolis, MD: Naval Institute Press, 2015.

Lorimer, D. A. "The Role of Anti-Slavery Sentiment in English Reactions to the American Civil War." *Historical Journal* 19, no. 2 (1976): 405–20.

Loy, W. "10 Rumford Place: Doing Confederate Business in Liverpool." *South Carolina Historical Magazine* 98, no. 4 (1997): 349–74.

Lynn, M. "Liverpool and Africa in the Nineteenth Century: The Continuing Connection." *Transactions of the Historic Society of Lancashire and Cheshire* 147 (1997): 27–54.

Macilwee, M. *The Liverpool Underworld: Crime in the City, 1750–1900.* Liverpool: Liverpool University Press, 2011.

Maffitt, E. M. *The Life and Services of John Newland Maffitt.* New York and Washington: Neale Publishing Company, 1906.

Maynard, D. H. "Dudley of New Jersey and the Nomination of Lincoln." *Pennsylvania Magazine of History and Biography* 82, no. 1 (1958): 100–108.

———. "Plotting the Escape of the *Alabama*." *Journal of Southern History* 20, no. 2 (1954): 197–209.

———. "Union Efforts to Prevent the Escape of the *Alabama*." *Mississippi Valley Historical Review* 41, no. 1 (1954): 41–60.

McPherson, J. M. *War on the Waters: The Union and Confederate Navies, 1861–1865.* Chapel Hill: University of North Carolina Press, 2012.

Melvin, P. "Stephen Russell Mallory, Southern Naval Statesman." *The Journal of Southern History* 10, no. 2 (1944): 137–60.

Merli, F. J. *The* Alabama, *British Neutrality, and the American Civil War.* Edited by D. M. Fahey. Bloomington: Indiana University Press, 2004.

———. "Crown Versus Cruiser: The Curious Case of the *Alexandra*." *Civil War History* 9, no. 2 (1963): 167–77.

———. *Great Britain and the Confederate Navy, 1861–1865.* Bloomington: Indiana University Press, 1970.

———. "A Missing Chapter in American Civil War Diplomacy: The Confederacy's Chinese Fleet, 1861–1867," in *Global Crossroads and the American Seas*, edited by C. G. Reynolds, 181–96. Missoula, MT: Pictorial Histories Publishing Co., 1988.

Mestyan, A. *Arab Patriotism: The Ideology and Culture of Power in Late Ottoman Egypt.* Princeton, NJ: Princeton University Press, 2017.

Milton, D. H. *Lincoln's Spymaster: Thomas Haines Dudley and the Liverpool Network.* Lanham, MD: Stackpole Books, 2003.

Moran, B. "Diary of Benjamin Moran, 1860–1868." *Proceedings of the Massachusetts Historical Society* 48 (1914–15): 431–92.

Muir, R. *A History of Liverpool.* Liverpool: University Press of Liverpool, 1907.

Neal, F. "Shipbuilding in the Northwest of England in the Nineteenth Century," in *Shipbuilding in the United Kingdom in the Nineteenth Century: A Regional Approach*, edited by S. Ville, 111–45. St. John's, Newfoundland: International Maritime Economic History Association/Trustees of the National Museums and Galleries on Merseyside, 1993.

Negus, S. "A Notorious Nest of Offence: Neutrals, Belligerents, and Union Jails in Civil War Blockade Running." *Civil War History* 56, no. 4 (2010): 350–85.

Nepveux, E. S. *George Alfred Trenholm and the Company That Went to War, 1861–1865.* Charleston, SC: Ethel S. Nepveux, 1973.

Newell, R. R. "Capture and Burning of the Ship *Anna F. Schmidt* by *Alabama.*" *American Neptune* 25 (1965): 18–28.

Newton, T. *Lord Lyons: A Record of British Diplomacy.* London: Edward Arnold, 2 vols., 1913.

Oates, S. B. "Henry Hotze: Confederate Agent Abroad." *The Historian* 27, no. 2 (1965): 131–54.

Owsley, F. L., Sr. *King Cotton Diplomacy: Foreign Relations of the Confederate States of America.* Tuscaloosa: University of Alabama Press, 2nd ed., 1959.

Owsley, H. C. "Henry Shelton Sanford and Federal Surveillance Abroad, 1861–1865." *Mississippi Valley Historical Review* 48, no. 2 (1961): 211–28.

Palmer, R. *Memoirs.* New York: Macmillan & Co., 2 vols., 1896.

Pease, T. C., and J. G. Randall (eds.). *The Diary of Orville Hickman Browning.* Springfield: Trustees of the Illinois State Historical Library, 2 vols., 1925–33.

Porter, R. *Plots and Paranoia: A History of Political Espionage in Britain 1790–1988.* London: Unwin Hyman, 1989.

Potts, W. J. "Biographical Sketch of the Hon. Thomas H. Dudley, of Camden, N.J., Who Died April 15, 1893." *Proceedings of the American Philosophical Society* 35 (1895): 102–28.

Price, M. W. "Blockade Running as a Business in South Carolina During the War Between the States, 1861–1865." *American Neptune* 9 (1949): 31–62.

Richardson, D. "Liverpool and the English Slave Trade," in *Transatlantic Slavery: Against Human Dignity,* edited by A. Tibbles, 67–72. Liverpool: Liverpool University Press, 2005.

Rogers, A. C., ed. *Our Representatives Abroad: Biographical Sketches of Ambassadors, Ministers, Consuls-General, and Consuls of the United States in Foreign Countries.* New York: Atlantic Publishing Company, 1874.

Roosevelt, T. *The Naval War of 1812; or, The History of the United States Navy During the Last War with Great Britain.* New York: G.P. Putnam's Sons, 1882.

Rose, A. *American Rifle: A Biography.* New York: Delacorte, 2008.

Russell, W. H. *My Diary North and South.* Boston: T.O.H.P. Burnham, 1863.

Sanders, N. F. "Henry Shelton Sanford in England, April–November 1861: A Reappraisal." *Lincoln Herald* 77 (1975): 87–95.

———. "Lincoln's Consuls in the British Isles, 1861–1865," unpublished Ph.D. dissertation, University of Missouri, 1971.

Scharf, J. T. *History of the Confederate States Navy from Its Organization to the Surrender of Its Last Vessel.* New York: Rogers and Sherwood, 1887.

Sebrell, T. E. *Persuading John Bull: Union and Confederate Propaganda in Britain, 1860–1865.* Lanham, MD: Lexington Books, 2014.

Semmes, R. *My Adventures Afloat: A Personal Memoir of My Cruises and Services on the* Sumter *and* Alabama. London: Richard Bentley, 1869.

Shimmin, H. *Liverpool Sketches, Chiefly Reprinted from the* Porcupine. London: W. Tweedie, 1863.

Shine, G. P. "'A Gallant Little Schooner': The U.S. Schooner *Shark* and the Oregon Country, 1846." *Oregon Historical Quarterly* 109, no. 4 (2008): 536–65.

Sinclair, A. *Two Years on the* Alabama. Boston: Lee and Shepard, 1896.

Skelton, L. W. "The Importing and Exporting Company of South Carolina (1862–1876)." *South Carolina Historical Magazine* 75, no. 1 (1974): 24–32.

Smith, E. C. *A Short History of Naval and Marine Engineering.* Cambridge (U.K.): Cambridge University Press, 1938.

Soley, J. R. *The Blockade and the Cruisers.* New York: Charles Scribner's Sons, 1883.

Spencer, W. F. *The Confederate Navy in Europe.* Tuscaloosa: University of Alabama Press, 1997.

Still, W. N., Jr. "Facilities for the Construction of War Vessels in the Confederacy." *Journal of Southern History* 31, no. 3 (1965): 285–304.

———. "A Naval Sieve: The Union Blockade in the Civil War." *Naval War College Review* 36, no. 3 (1983): 38–45.

Summersell, C. G. *CSS* Alabama: *Builder, Captain, and Plans.* Tuscaloosa: University of Alabama Press, 1985.

Surdam, D. G. "The Confederate Naval Buildup: Could More Have Been Accomplished?" *Naval War College Review* 54, no. 1 (2001): 107–27.

———. "King Cotton: Monarch or Pretender? The State of the Market for Raw Cotton on the Eve of the American Civil War." *Economic History Review* 51, no. 1 (1998): 113–32.

———. "The Union Navy's Blockade Reconsidered." *Naval War College Review* 51, no. 4 (1998): 85–107.

Sweeney, M. F. "An Annotated Edition of Nathaniel Hawthorne's Official Dispatches to the State Department, 1853–1857," unpublished Ph.D. dissertation, Bowling Green State University, 1975.

Symonds, C. L., ed. *Charleston Blockade: The Journals of John B. Marchand, U.S. Navy, 1861–1862.* Newport, RI: U.S. Naval War College, 1976.

———. *The U.S. Navy: A Concise History.* Oxford (U.K.): Oxford University Press, 2016.

Tanselle, G. T., ed. *Redburn, White-Jacket, Moby-Dick.* New York: Library of America, 1983.

Taylor, J. M. "Shark Hunt." *Civil War Times Illustrated* 38, no. 6 (1999): 66–74, 91.

Taylor, T. E. *Running the Blockade: A Personal Narrative of Adventure, Risks, and Escapes During the American Civil War.* New York: Charles Scribner's Sons, 1896.

Thiesen, W. H. *Industrializing American Shipbuilding: The Transformation of Ship Design and Construction, 1820–1920*. Gainesville: University Press of Florida, 2006.

Thompson, S. B. *Confederate Purchasing Operations Abroad*. Chapel Hill: University of North Carolina Press, 1935.

Thorp, R. *Mersey Built: The Role of Merseyside in the American Civil War*. Wilmington, DE: Vernon Press, 2018.

Tibbles, A. *Liverpool and the Slave Trade*. Liverpool: Liverpool University Press, 2018.

———. "Oil Not Slaves: Liverpool and West Africa After 1807," in *Transatlantic Slavery: Against Human Dignity*, edited by A. Tibbles, 73–77. Liverpool: Liverpool University Press, 2005.

Trahan, J. V., III. "Henry Hotze: Propaganda Voice of the Confederacy," in *Knights of the Quill: Confederate Correspondents and the Civil War Reporting*, edited by P. G. McNeely, D. R. Van Tuyll, and H. H. Schulte, 216–37. West Lafayette, IN: Purdue University Press, 2010.

Wallace, S. A., and F. E. Gillespie, eds. *The Journal of Benjamin Moran, 1857–1865*. Chicago: University of Chicago Press, 2 vols., 1948–49.

Wardle, A. C. "Mersey-Built Blockade Runners of the American Civil War." *Mariner's Mirror* 28 (1942): 179–88.

Warren, K. *Steel, Ships and Men: Cammell Laird, 1824–1993*. Liverpool: Liverpool University Press, 1998.

Watts, G. P. "Phantoms of Anglo-Confederate Commerce: An Historical and Archaeological Investigation of American Civil War Blockade Running," unpublished Ph.D. dissertation, University of St. Andrews, 1997.

Weddle, K. J. "The Blockade Board of 1861 and Union Naval Strategy." *Civil War History* 48, no. 2 (2002): 123–42.

Weidenmier, M. D. "The Market for Confederate Cotton Bonds." *Explorations in Economic History* 37, no. 1 (2000): 76–97.

Welles, G. *Diary of Gideon Welles, Secretary of the Navy Under Lincoln and Johnson*. Boston and New York: Houghton Mifflin, 3 vols., 1911.

White, H. *Fossets: A Record of Two Centuries of Engineering*. Bromborough, Cheshire (U.K.): Fawcett Preston & Co., 1958.

Williams, C., J. Powell, and J. Kelly. "Liverpool's Abercromby Square and the Confederacy During the U.S. Civil War." (2015).

Wilson, R. "Historical Sketch of the Prioleau Family in Europe and America." *Transactions of the Huguenot Society of South Carolina* 6 (1899): 5–37.

Wilson, W. E., and G. L. McKay. *James D. Bulloch: Secret Agent and Mastermind of the Confederate Navy*. Jefferson, NC: McFarland & Co., 2012.

Wise, S. R. *Lifeline of the Confederacy: Blockade Running During the Civil War*. Columbia: University of South Carolina Press, 1988.

ILLUSTRATION CREDITS

INDEX

ABOUT

MARINER BOOKS

MARINER BOOKS traces its beginnings to 1832 when William Ticknor cofounded the Old Corner Bookstore in Boston, from which he would run the legendary firm Ticknor and Fields, publisher of Ralph Waldo Emerson, Harriet Beecher Stowe, Nathaniel Hawthorne, and Henry David Thoreau. Following Ticknor's death, Henry Oscar Houghton acquired Ticknor and Fields and, in 1880, formed Houghton Mifflin, which later merged with venerable Harcourt Publishing to form Houghton Mifflin Harcourt. HarperCollins purchased HMH's trade publishing business in 2021 and reestablished their storied lists and editorial team under the name Mariner Books.

Uniting the legacies of Houghton Mifflin, Harcourt Brace, and Ticknor and Fields, Mariner Books continues one of the great traditions in American bookselling. Our imprints have introduced an incomparable roster of enduring classics, including Hawthorne's *The Scarlet Letter*, Thoreau's *Walden*, Willa Cather's *O Pioneers!*, Virginia Woolf's *To the Lighthouse*, W.E.B. Du Bois's *Black Reconstruction*, J.R.R. Tolkien's *The Lord of the Rings*, Carson McCullers's *The Heart Is a Lonely Hunter*, Ann Petry's *The Narrows*, George Orwell's *Animal Farm* and *Nineteen Eighty-Four*, Rachel Carson's *Silent Spring*, Margaret Walker's *Jubilee*, Italo Calvino's *Invisible Cities*, Alice Walker's *The Color Purple*, Margaret Atwood's *The Handmaid's Tale*, Tim O'Brien's *The Things They Carried*, Philip Roth's *The Plot Against America*, Jhumpa Lahiri's *Interpreter of Maladies*, and many others. Today Mariner Books remains proudly committed to the craft of fine publishing established nearly two centuries ago at the Old Corner Bookstore.